IMAGES
of America

AROUND MONTGOMERY BOROUGH 1940–1990

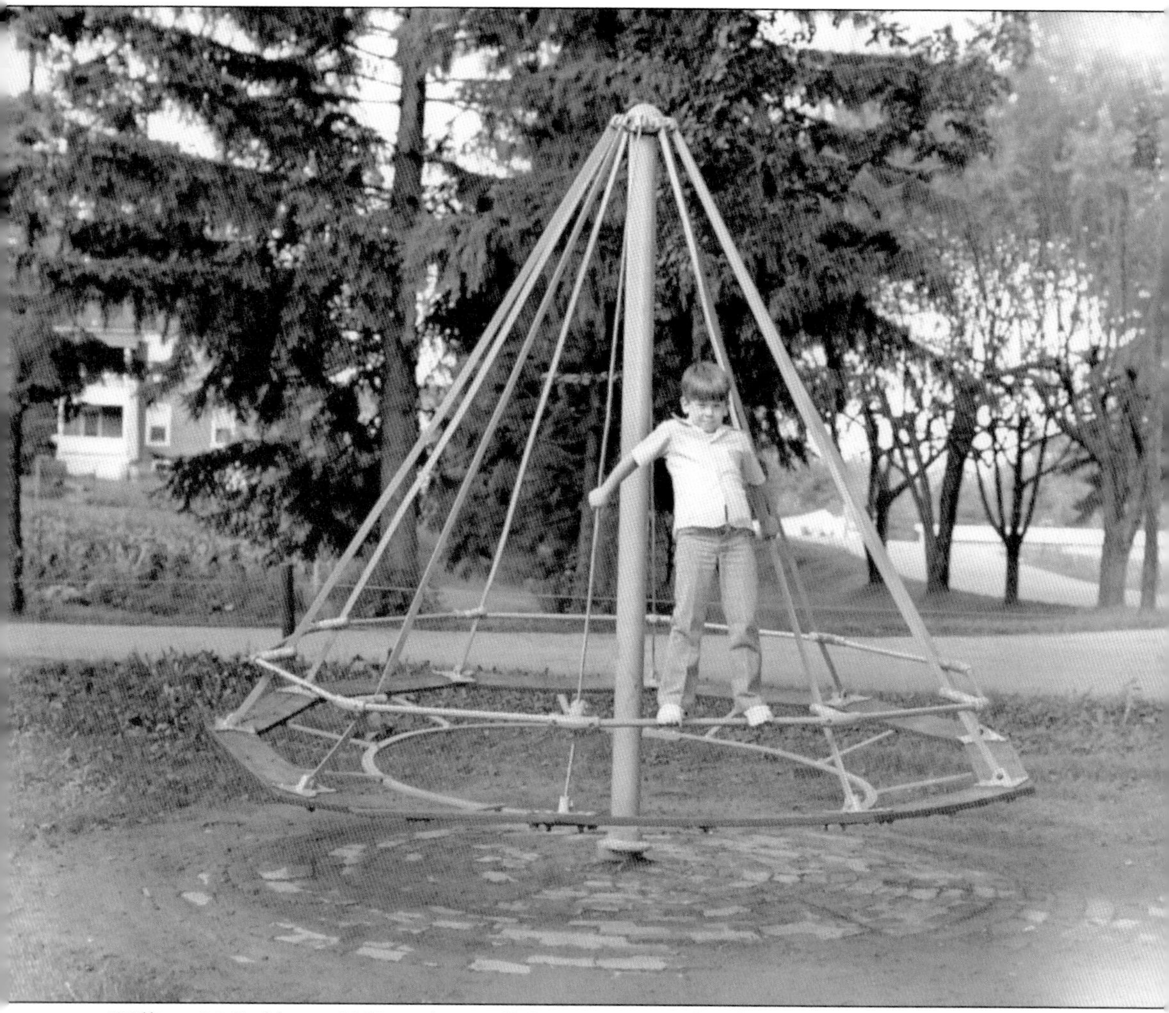

William McFadden, a 1963 graduate of Montgomery High School, returned to his hometown in the fall of 1974 to take a series of photographs with a Speed Graphic 4x5 camera for a graduate school photography assignment. As he walked around town looking for interesting subjects, he found eight-year-old James Bennett Jr. on the merry-go-round at the Montgomery Park playground. (Courtesy MAPL; photographed by William McFadden Jr.)

On the Cover: This scene of the Memorial Day Parade in 1956 features Montgomery business-sponsored Little League teams riding in a fleet of convertibles provided by Delroy Schneck, the owner of Hulsizer's Chevrolet. Leading the way in the toy car is Schneck's young son Bill. Additional information about this photograph is found on pages 52 and 53. (Courtesy Hulsizer's Chevrolet.)

IMAGES
of America

AROUND MONTGOMERY BOROUGH 1940–1990

Joan Wheal Blank

ARCADIA
PUBLISHING

ISBN 978-0-7385-7521-6

Published by Arcadia Publishing
Charleston, South Carolina

Printed in the United States of America

Library of Congress Control Number: 2010940525

For all general information, please contact Arcadia Publishing:
Telephone 843-853-2070
Fax 843-853-0044
E-mail sales@arcadiapublishing.com
For customer service and orders:
Toll-Free 1-888-313-2665

Visit us on the Internet at www.arcadiapublishing.com

To Steve, whose love brought me back home

Contents

ACKNOWLEDGMENTS

My sincere thanks go to Sue Thomas and Cindy Bryan, the guardians of the historical archives in the Montgomery Area Public Library. Without your assistance and the granting of liberal borrowing privileges, this book would not exist.

The following people have contributed to the completion of this book in ways large and small—please accept my thanks: Rev. Gunther Bernhart, Jackie Clinard, Leona Dewalt, Paula Fenstermacher, Andy and Dee Follmer, Carol Grady, Dennis and Nancy Gruver, Michael Hill, Steve Huddy, David Johnson, Norm and Elaine Kobbe, Larry LeFeber, John Lynch, Montgomery Police chief Terry Lynn, Paul Metzger, Mayor Andy Onufrak, Clyde Peeling, Cindy Roberts, Becky Sanguedolce, Howard and June Snyder, Ron Winder, Todd Winder, Gary Yocum, and members of the Montgomery Area Historical Society.

Also, my sincere thanks to everyone who allowed me to borrow personal photos that appear in this book. During the past five years, as I located historical photos and information about Montgomery, I have met some of the most generous and kind people—thank you for allowing me to document the history of the town you love.

Finally, I want to thank my husband, Steve. You have been my greatest supporter as I researched and wrote about the past. I look forward to the future with you as our adventure continues.

INTRODUCTION

If you are reading this, you were either born in Montgomery, grew up in Montgomery, got married to someone from Montgomery, or thought the little guy driving the toy car on the front cover was pretty cute. Whatever the reason, I invite you to browse through these chapters, which I hope will bring back a memory or two, encourage a question, or arouse your curiosity.

Although many topics are covered in the following pages, it was impossible to locate a photographic image from every event or activity both natural and man-made—that occurred in Montgomery and in the surrounding townships of Clinton, Brady, and Washington over the past 70 years. Anyone with photographs of these missing events is encouraged to pull them out, identify the people in them, and write the names and date on the back. Or better yet, donate copies of them to the library or historical society for future generations to enjoy.

For some, Montgomery was one of those small towns that made you feel like you had to leave the minute you graduated from high school. You feel like there is a whole, wide world waiting for you to explore. It's true—there is—and for most of us, our hometown will wait patiently until the day comes—and it will come—when you feel the need to return. Usually, our hometown will still be there.

Unfortunately, that has not always been the case. When American writer Conrad Richter attempted to return to the home near Alvira where he spent his teenage years during a visit with his brothers in the early 1940s, he discovered that some of their favorite places were off-limits, surrounded by a tall fence and guards. According to his biographer, David R. Johnson, this experience inspired Richter to write *The Waters of Kronos*. The novel, which was dedicated to his brothers Joe and Fred, tells the story of a man and his quest to return home only to find it submerged underwater—off-limits to the main character. But soon, he finds himself going back in time and interacting with family and friends of his youth, who do not recognize him. Even if our childhood home may be gone, or if old neighbors no longer recognize us, it is still possible to return home through memories and photographs.

During the 1940s, World War II was certainly paramount on everyone's minds. To help deal with the uncertainty of the situation, many mothers assisted in collecting and mailing letters and packages to local soldiers stationed overseas. Neighbors helped each other as friends in Alvira were asked to sacrifice their homes and farms to benefit the war effort. In spite of all this, it was evident that life in Montgomery revolved primarily around school, church, family, and friends. Entertainment could be found at the pool down by the river, on the baseball fields at the park, at the Eagle movie theater on Main Street, and at stage shows presented by the Rotary Club and the alumni association. When Jim and Jane Claar started to invite country singers and comedy performers to an outdoor stage near the borough, fans came in droves to spend the day with friends and listen to music. Businesses were established: Rochelle Furniture Manufacturing and Adam Print Shop opened, Murray Snyder established a funeral home on East Houston Avenue, and Memorial Park Plan Cemetery (now Green Lawn Cemetery) was started at the corner of Routes 54 and 15.

The 1950s in Montgomery were filled with dedications, renovations, and celebrations, and also expectations of a brighter future. D&M Tool & Machine Company and J.A. Habig Veneer Company established their businesses in the borough, as did Myco Manufacturing, Montgomery Sylvania, Plasti-Vac, and S&S Screw Machine Products Company. A new Evangelical Lutheran church building was constructed on East Houston Avenue as well as the new elementary school building in Elimsport. A drive-in theater built on the Montgomery Pike was appropriately named Pike Drive-In. Children were involved in the local Girl and Boy Scout troops and the Juvenile Eagle Grange. Other organizations founded in Montgomery during the 1950s included the Montgomery Chapter of the Muncy Valley Hospital Auxiliary, the Montgomery Lions Club, and Theta Iota, a local chapter of Beta Sigma Phi. Tragedy occurred when Michael Guido, a beloved coach and teacher at Montgomery High School, suffered a heart attack and died unexpectedly.

Montgomery's Diamond Jubilee celebration in 1962 was a weeklong affair honoring the borough's 75th birthday. The festivities highlighted many of the borough's best attributes. After a day of welcome and a day for worship, the remainder of the week was devoted to recognition of the Montgomery community, including Little League, schools, and firefighters, and ending with an apron and beard judging and the grand-finale parade of marching units and floats. Following the Jubilee, residents recognized the importance of local history and organized the Montgomery Historical Society. During the 1960s, the Lions Club sold brooms and doormats, White Deer Golf Course opened for business, and the new post office was built on what was then Park Street. Before Christmas, the children would go see Santa (was it George Amos Smith or Tom Holtzapple?) in his workshop and feed the so-called reindeer in the pen outside. The swimming beach along the river was opened, and Construction Specialties was established in Clinton Township.

In 1972, Hurricane Agnes caused flooding in Montgomery, resulting in loss of property unseen since the last flood more than 30 years earlier. Recovery was quick, however, as the borough prepared for the bicentennial celebration in 1976. The Hotel Bash in the spring of that year paid homage to the Montgomery Hotel before it was demolished. The Montgomery Senior Citizens group was formed during the 1970s, the municipal garage was built next to the post office, and the first female member of the Montgomery Borough Council was elected.

Entering the 1980s, the Montgomery Lioness Club was formed, and Time Markets and Med-Plus opened in the plaza at the intersection of Routes 54 and 15. Old church buildings were renovated and new churches established, the library moved down the street, and Grumman celebrated a milestone. The area was subjected to terrible forces of nature in the form of a devastating tornado in 1985, and once again, the community rebounded to celebrate its centennial two years later.

Has this list brought back a memory or two? Well, this is just the beginning. Turn the page and you will find over 230 photographs that are meant to bring you back to a time when life was simpler, women wore aprons, and men wore hats—at least up until the 1970s. Names that appear in this book are the historic names used at the time the photograph was taken. Photographs that are currently archived in the Montgomery Area Public Library historical room are credited as MAPL.

I hope you enjoy the journey as much as I have.

One

THE 1940s

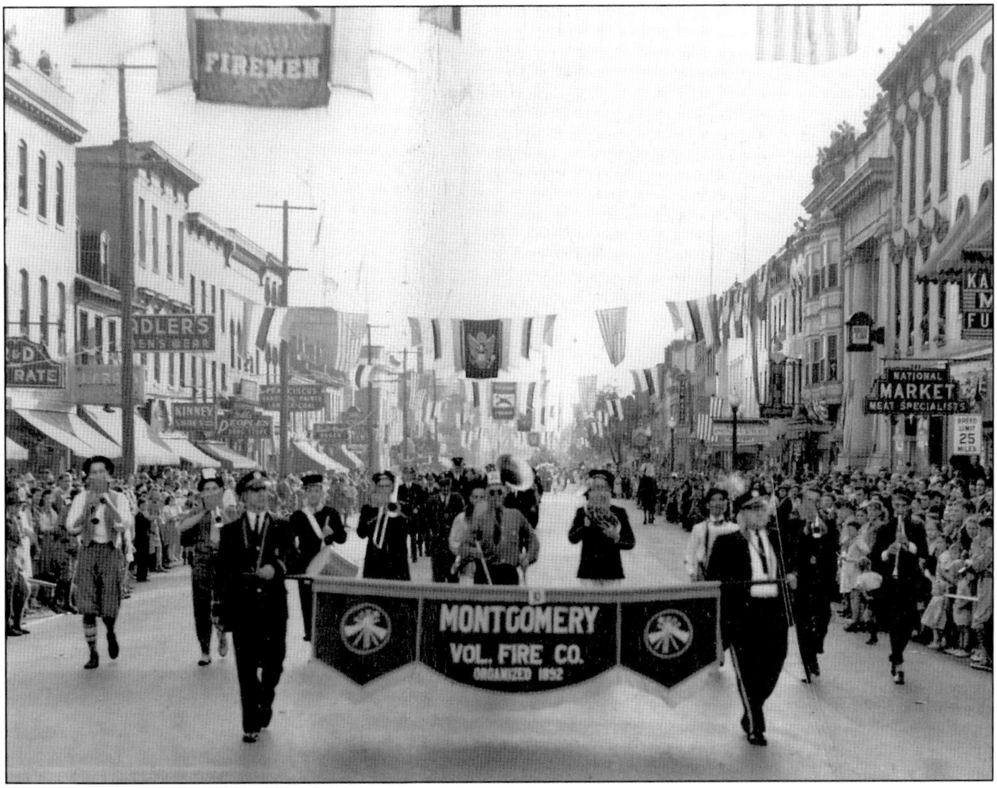

At the 1940 Pennsylvania State Firemen Convention in Lewistown, Montgomery was represented by the borough's volunteer firemen, who were also talented musicians. They included Carl O'Conner and Clair Felix (banner carriers), Claude Miller and Eugene Decker (clarinet), Joe Barlett and Charles Berger (trumpet), Joe Krimm (snare drum), Richard Buck (trombone), Franklin Hall (bass horn), Arthur Hughes (drum major), Harold Strouse (baritone), and Allen Horn (bass drum). (Courtesy Montgomery Volunteer Fire Company.)

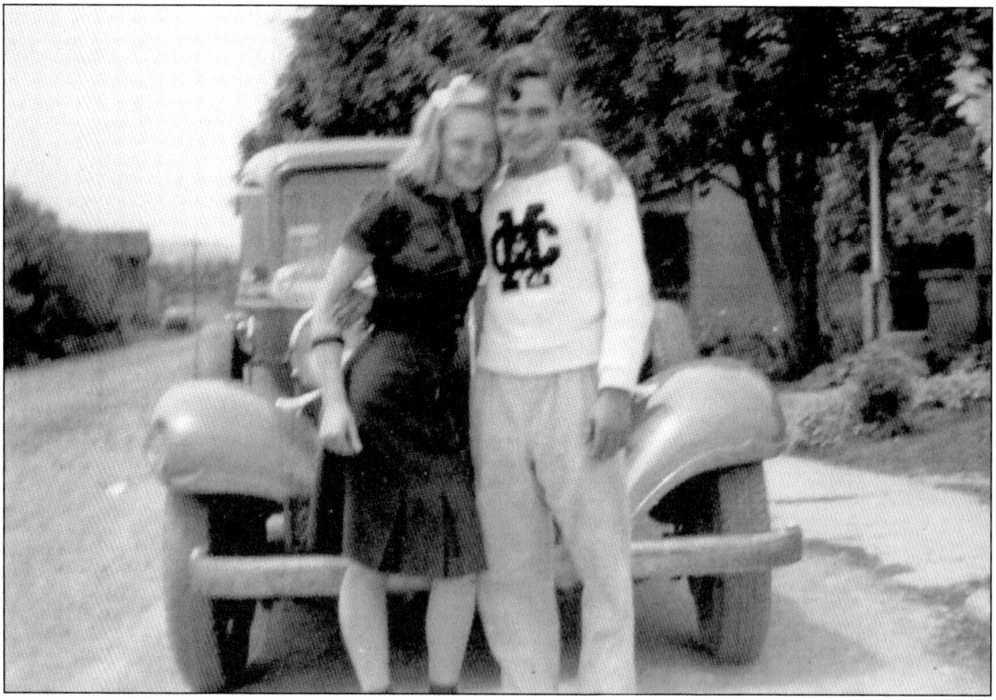

Leroy Pentz, wearing his varsity football letter sweater from Montgomery-Clinton High School, poses with friend Betty Canada (above). A graduate of the class of 1942, Pentz was also a member of the boxing team during his junior year. The high school building on Penn Street (below), which was constructed in 1930, received an addition of eight rooms—six classrooms and rooms for a dental hygienist and a nurse—in the late 1930s. Workers from the Works Progress Administration (WPA) built the addition, which became known as the annex. The WPA also demolished the original school building on East Houston Avenue in 1936. (Both courtesy MAPL.)

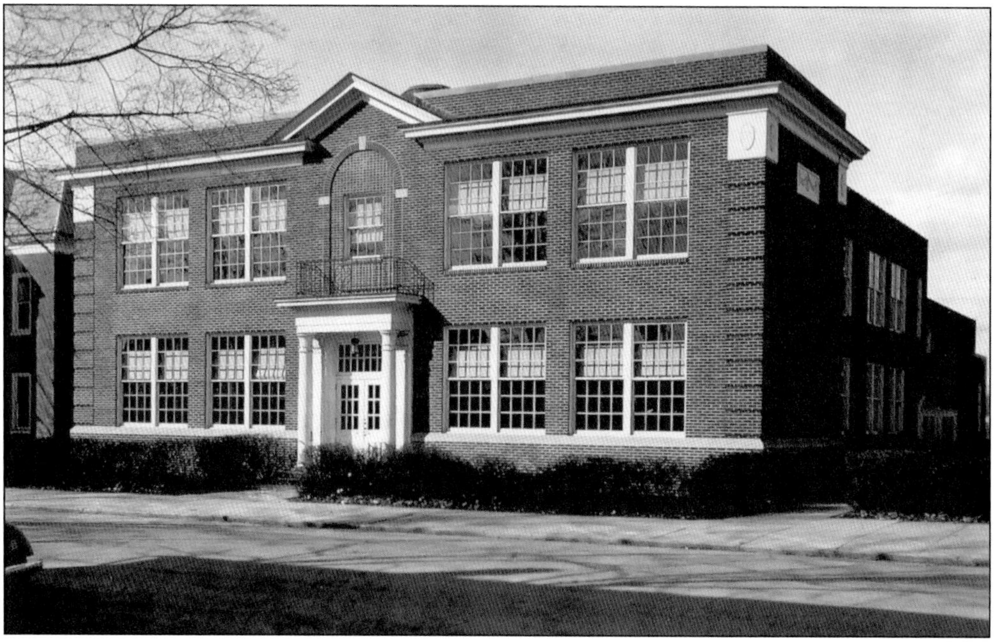

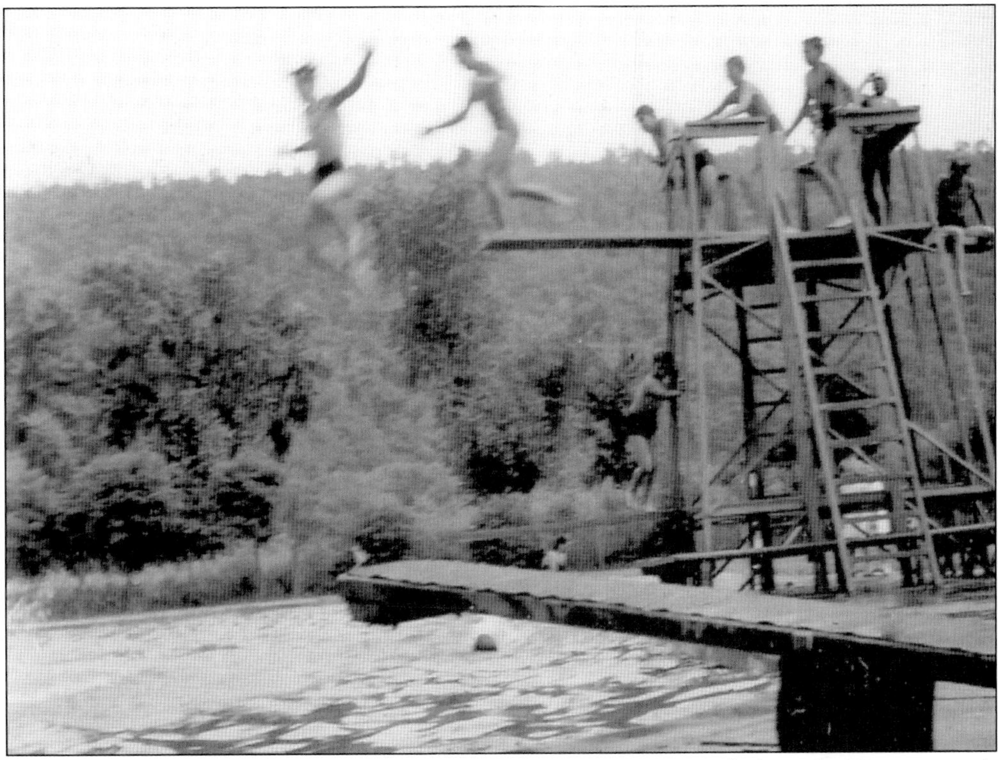

In addition to building the school's annex and constructing a stone wall along the Narrows north of the borough, the WPA also built this swimming pool. Located across from the park near the river, it was opened, along with the playground at the park, in 1937. The pool was the source of many hours of entertainment for the youth of Montgomery. Chemicals were not used, however, and the pool had to be drained and cleaned regularly. In the 1950s, it was closed and filled in to make the Little League field. (Above, courtesy MAPL; below, courtesy Glenda and Jade Heasley.)

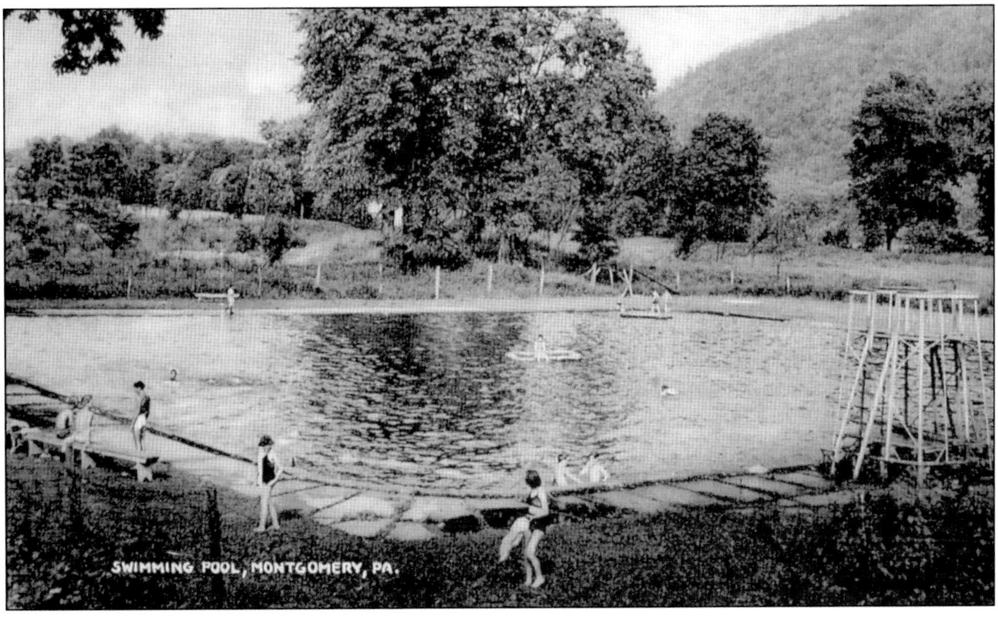

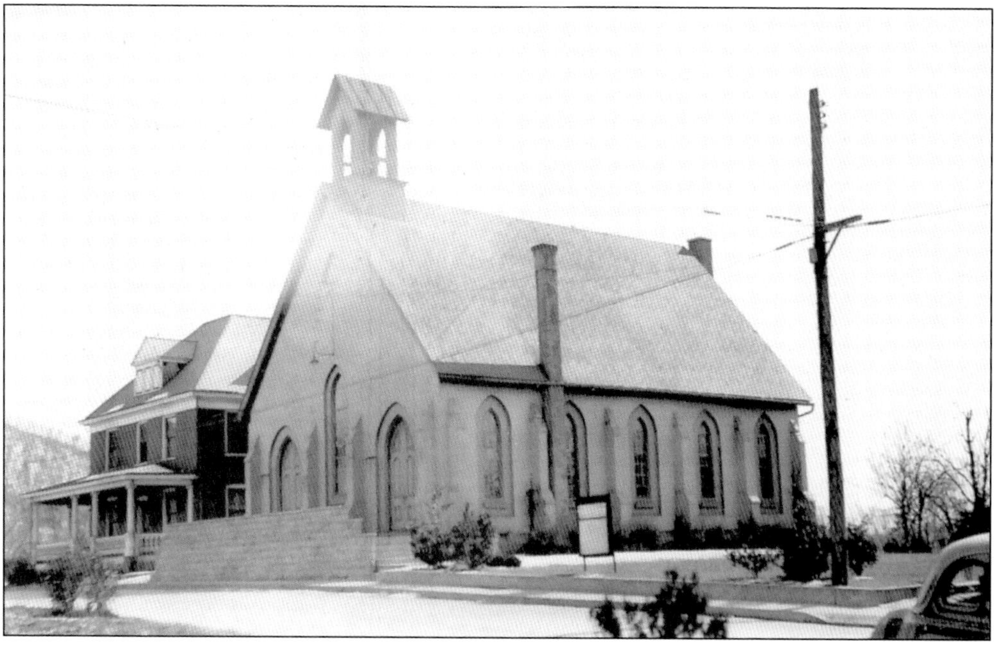

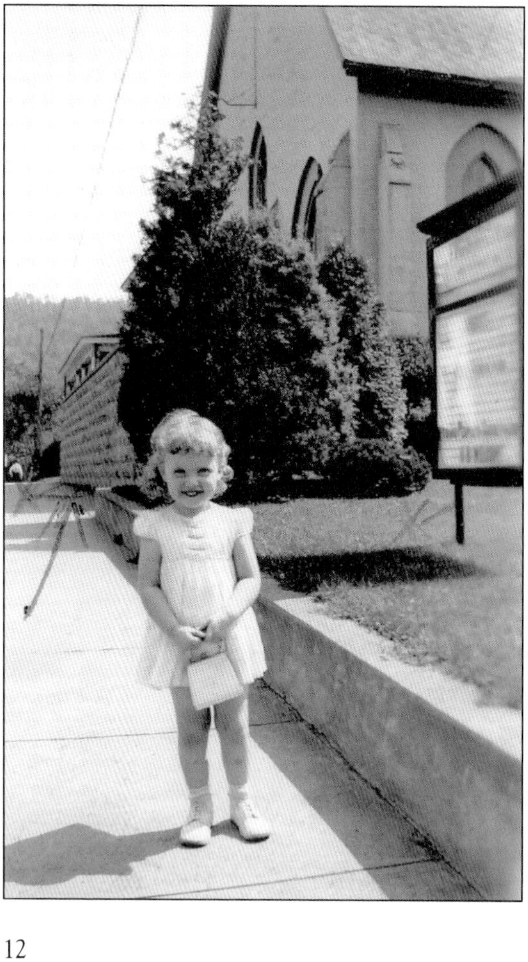

Presbyterian worshipers first organized in Montgomery in 1869 and, by 1872, the church building shown above was erected on Second Street (formerly known as Ferry Road). Improvements were made over the years, including excavation under the sanctuary in 1914 to build Sunday school rooms. Members of the church Men's Club completed this work by hand over a period of almost a year. In 1931, members of the First Presbyterian and Grace Reformed Churches merged to form the Grace Presbyterian Church. Also that year, the road in front of the church was widened, and a new wall and steps were built, as seen in the photograph above. At left, two-year-old Nona Tilburg poses in front of the church building on August 30, 1941. (Above, courtesy MAPL; left, courtesy Grace Presbyterian Church.)

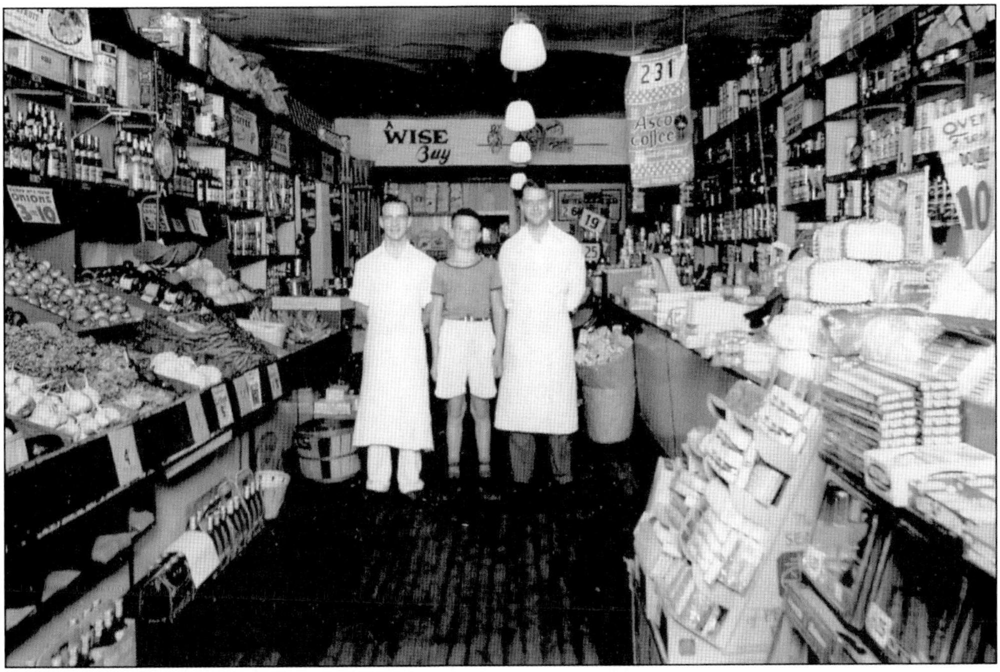

In 1942, the American Store Company was advertised as "Montgomery's Headquarters for Fresh Green Produce," as well as local favorites such as Asco coffee and Wise potato chips. Other local grocers during the early 1940s included the A&P, DeHotman's Grocer, Cole's Meat Market, Weis Market, and O'Dell's Grocery. Pictured in the American Store Company, from left to right, are Alem LaForme, Paul Smith, and Eugene Wolf. (Courtesy MAPL.)

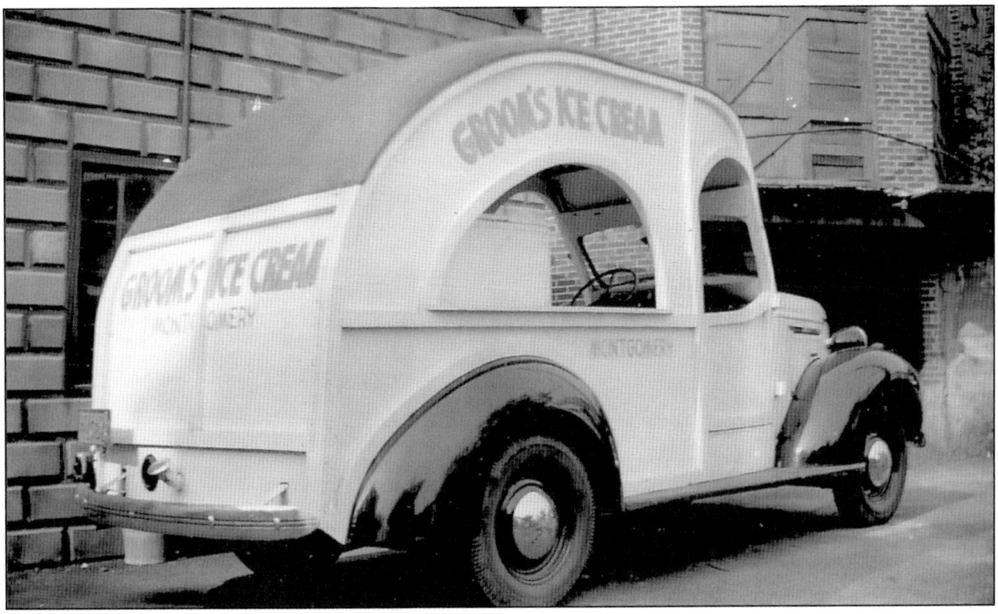

Ivan Groom owned and operated a diner on the Montgomery Pike, a store in Williamsport at the corner of Fourth and Walnut Streets, and a small ice cream shop on Brook Street in Montgomery. Located behind the Eagle Theatre, the Groom Dairy Store was a favorite place to gather after the movies. (Courtesy June Grube.)

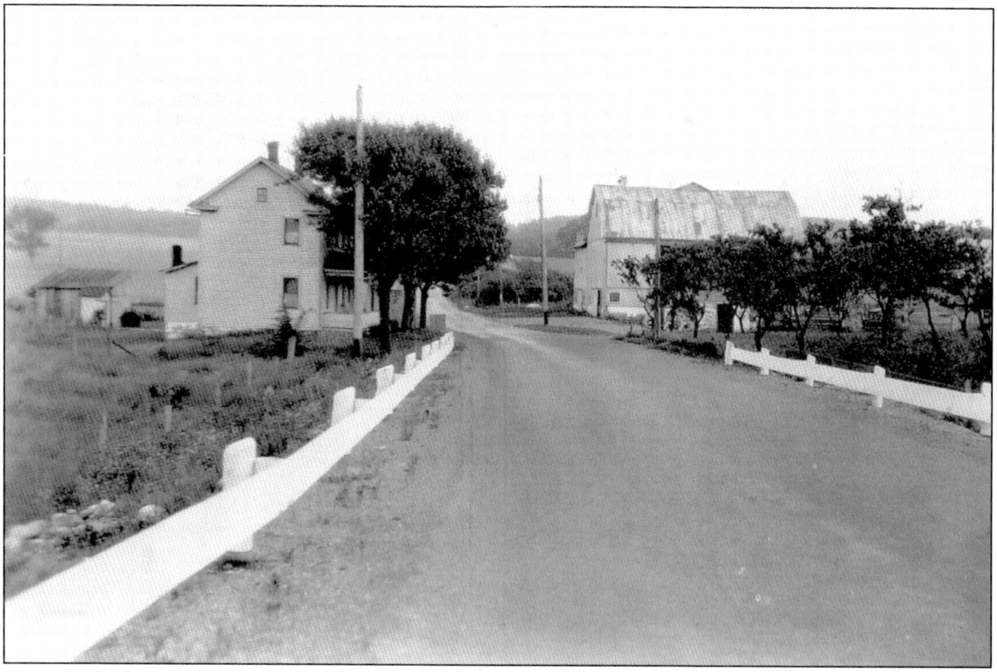

In 1939, the Pennsylvania State Highway Department announced plans to reconstruct and widen Montgomery Pike, the road extending from Allenwood over the mountain north to Williamsport. Above is a view of the Albert Baker farm along the Montgomery Pike before the road was widened. This improvement project involved moving the historic hall of the Eagle Grange No. 1, which was built in 1887, as well as the demolition of the one-room Pine Street School nearby. Below is the Grange hall before it was moved and Pine Street School before it was razed. The Lycoming County commissioners agreed to pay $1,600 to the Grange to cover the cost of moving the hall and for damages. The hall was moved at a cost of $390. (Above, courtesy Ralph Baker; below, courtesy Carl Jarrett.)

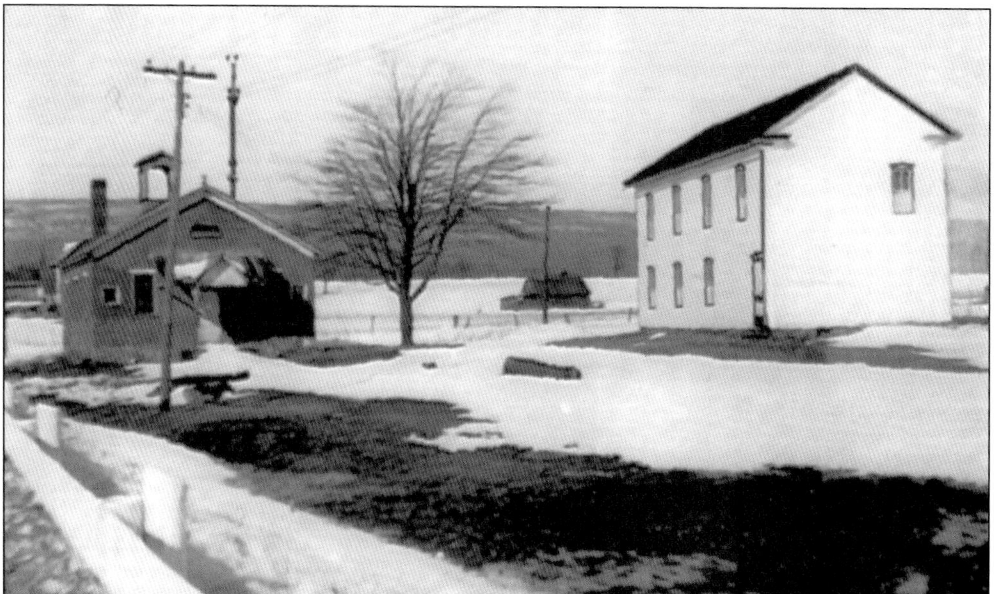

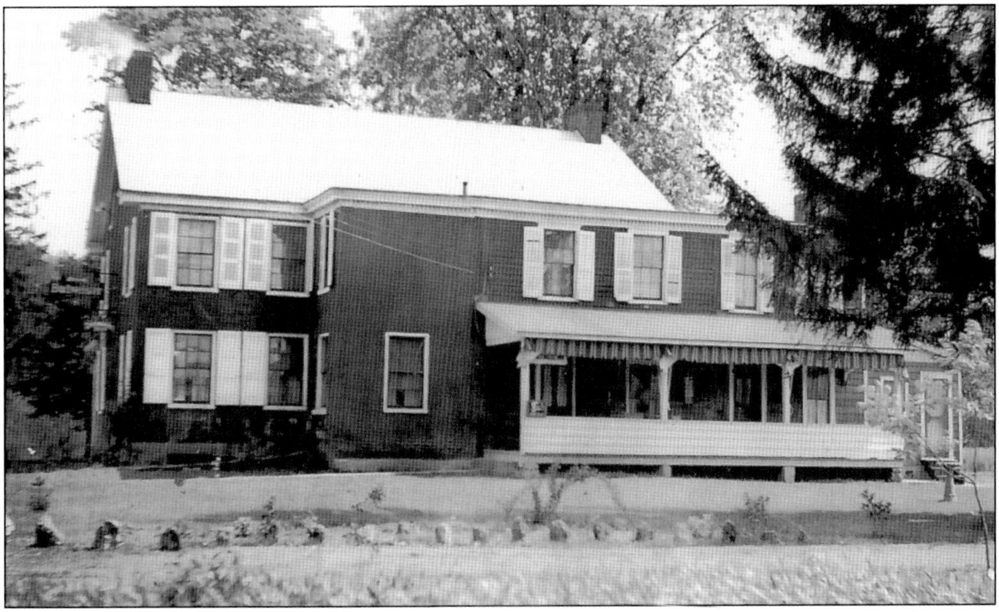

Formerly a private residence, the Martinique Inn (above) offered a peaceful riverside location for local groups to gather. Below, the workers from Penn Garment pose for a photograph on the Martinique's front lawn. They include, from left to right, (first row) Bertha Dorman, Kathryn Smith, Lena Keiss, Ida Moyer, Bud Smith, Emma Fessler, and Frank Dietz; (second row) Mrs. Saxton, Nell Slattery, Frances Minnier, Bertha Hazen, Ben Smith, Larry Skehan, Cora Ruth, Ruth Travlett, Fleta Walizer, and George Koons Jr.; (third row) Anna Fischer, Bess Gramley, Carrie Vogel, Margaret Huffman, A.C. Burch, Gertie Beemer, Ida Sander, George Koons Sr., Mamie White, Myrtle Flory, Stella Myers, Ronald Reid, Jane Fessler, F.E. Plankenhorn, and Elmer Frendberg. (Both courtesy Becky Sanguedolce.)

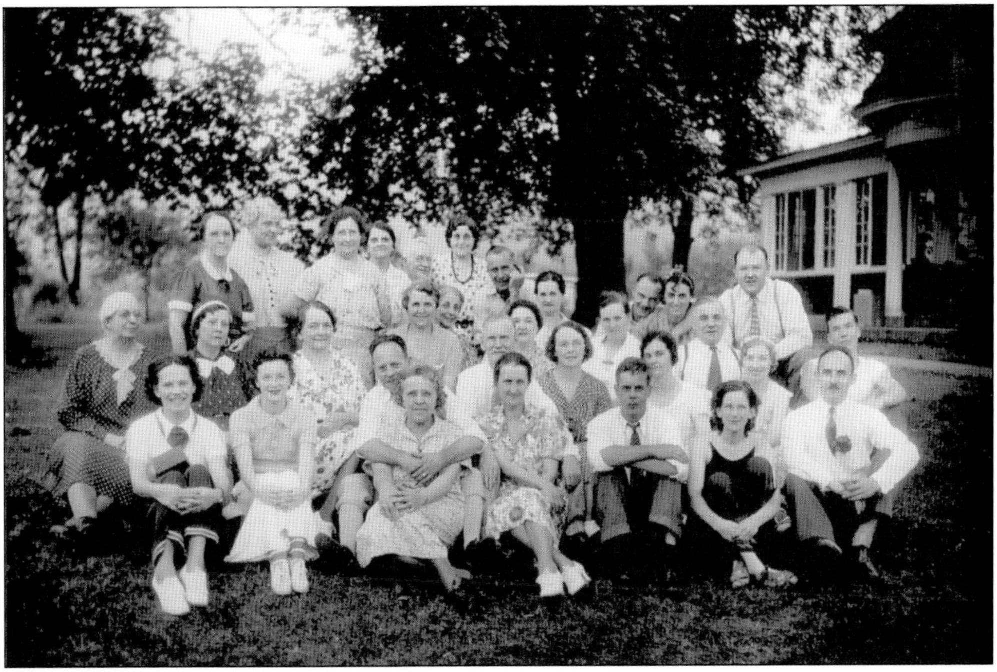

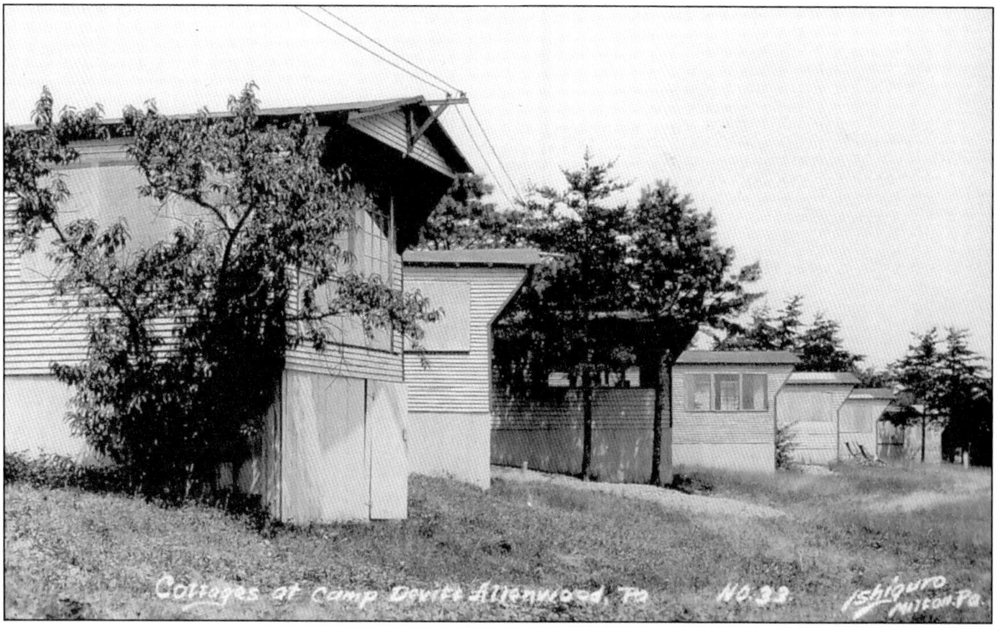

Philadelphia physician William Devitt founded Devitt's Camp, a facility to treat tuberculosis patients, in 1912 on 60 wooded acres on the side of White Deer Mountain near Montgomery. He set up a treatment camp with his first 10 patients housed in an old barn that was on the property. Eventually, cottages were built to house the patients and their families. News of this rural treatment facility spread and generous benefactors began to contribute to Devitt's endeavor. Donations financed the construction of a nurse's residence, staff bungalows, an infirmary, and homes for the families of Dr. Devitt and Dr. Herbert Norton, who was the camp's superintendent. (Both courtesy Bill and Jack Devitt.)

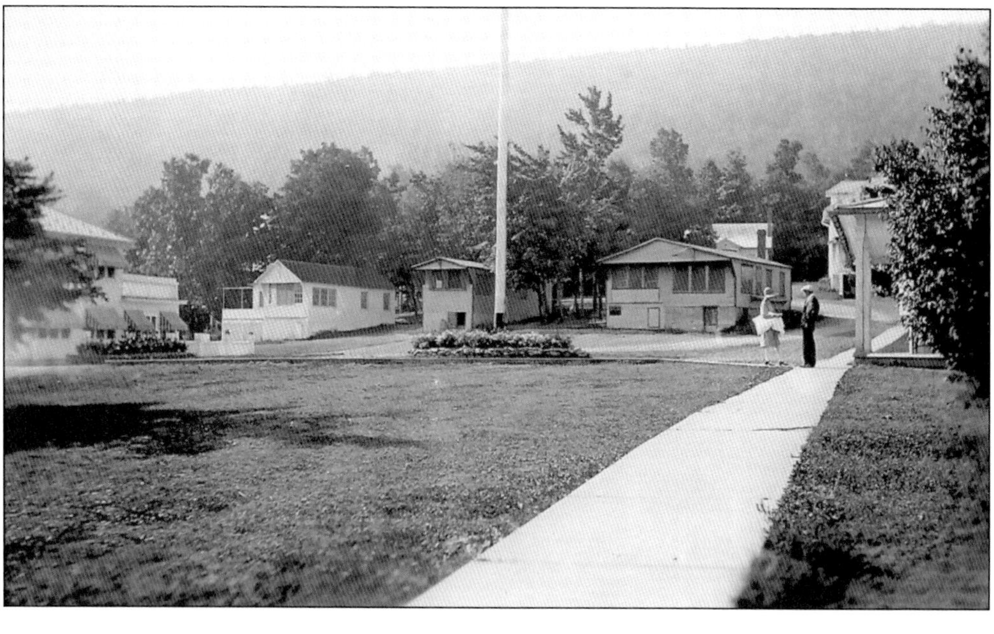

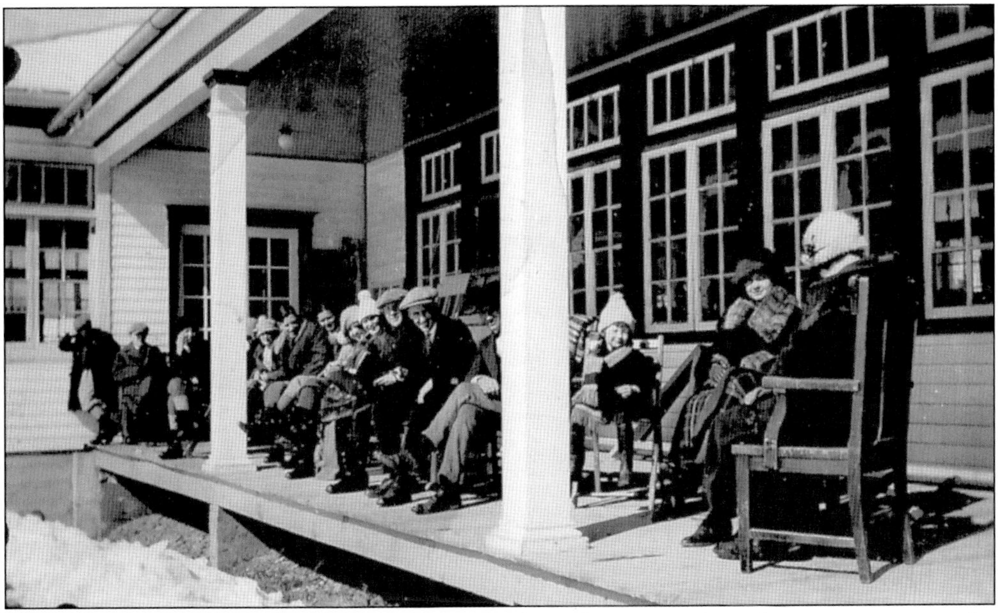

Dr. Devitt believed that an effective treatment for pulmonary tuberculosis was exposing the patient to a regular routine of clean, fresh air. In a promotional brochure for the camp, there were promises of "supervised rest, good food, and refreshing climate," as well as a trained resident staff equipped to "render the most advanced treatment of chest conditions." Patients were assured that they would receive physical and mental relaxation in addition to having access to "only the best food obtainable," "laboratory tested milk," and "clean, stimulating air far from industrial plants." A regimen of sunbaths year-round was encouraged, as evidenced by these photographs of patients of Devitt's Camp. (Both courtesy Bill and Jack Devitt.)

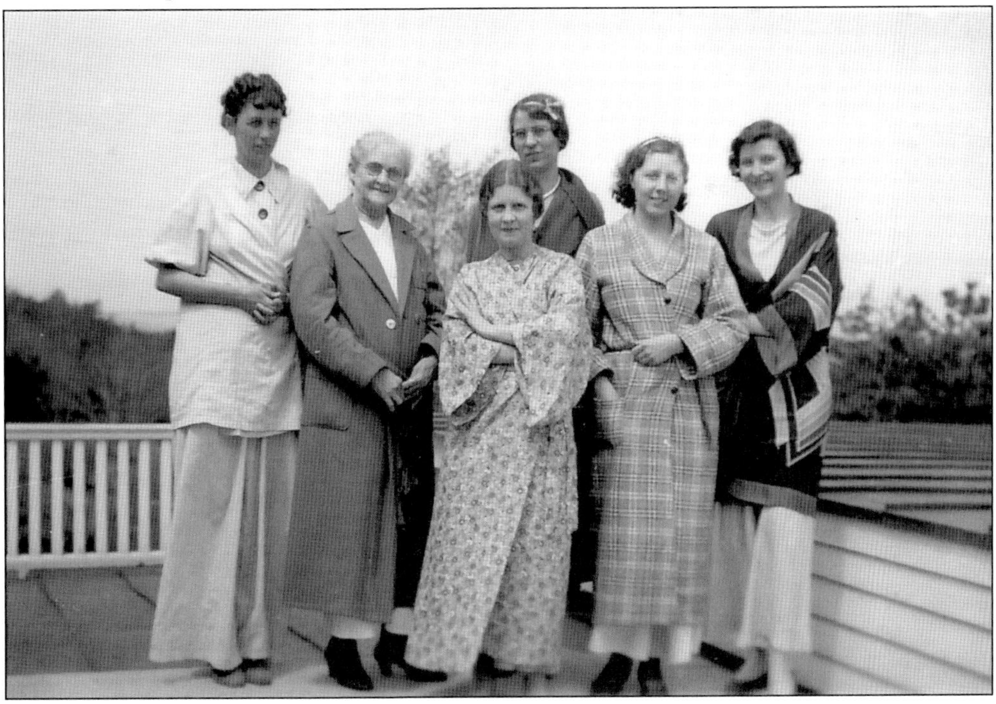

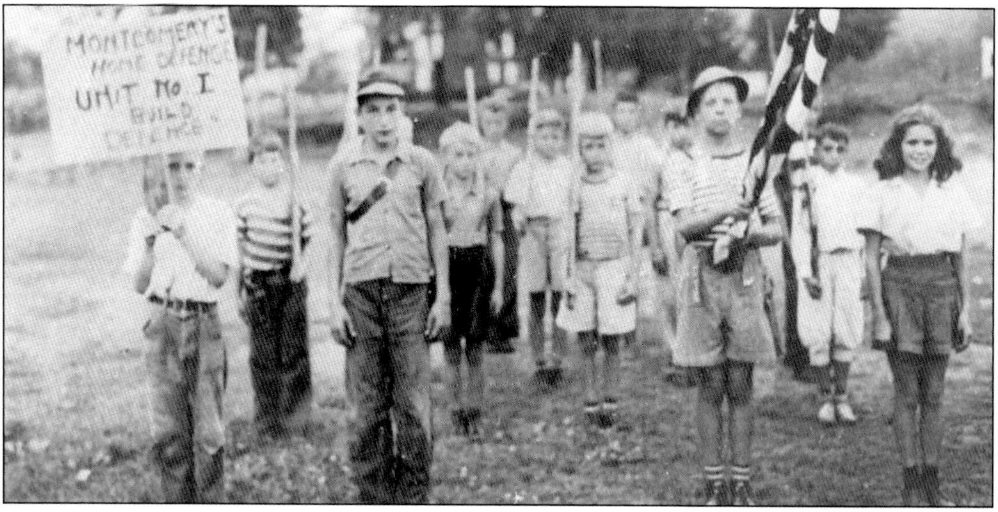

As the war escalated in Europe in the early 1940s, Montgomery youngsters formed the "Montgomery Home Defence [sic] Unit No. I" to express their patriotism. Identified in the photograph above are Joe Ragno (strap across chest), Eugene Dewalt (with flag), Marion Decker (long dark hair), and Tom Yeagle (white knickers). Shortly after the Japanese attack on Pearl Harbor in December 1941 and the subsequent US declaration of war against Japan, Germany, and Italy, rumors began circulating throughout White Deer Valley. In the spring of 1942, representatives from the War Department announced at Christ's Lutheran Church near Alvira (known as the Stone Church and shown below) that about 8,000 acres of land would be used to erect the Pennsylvania Ordnance Works, a TNT plant. Residents of Alvira would be forced to sell their farms and homesteads or eminent domain would be imposed. (Both courtesy MAPL.)

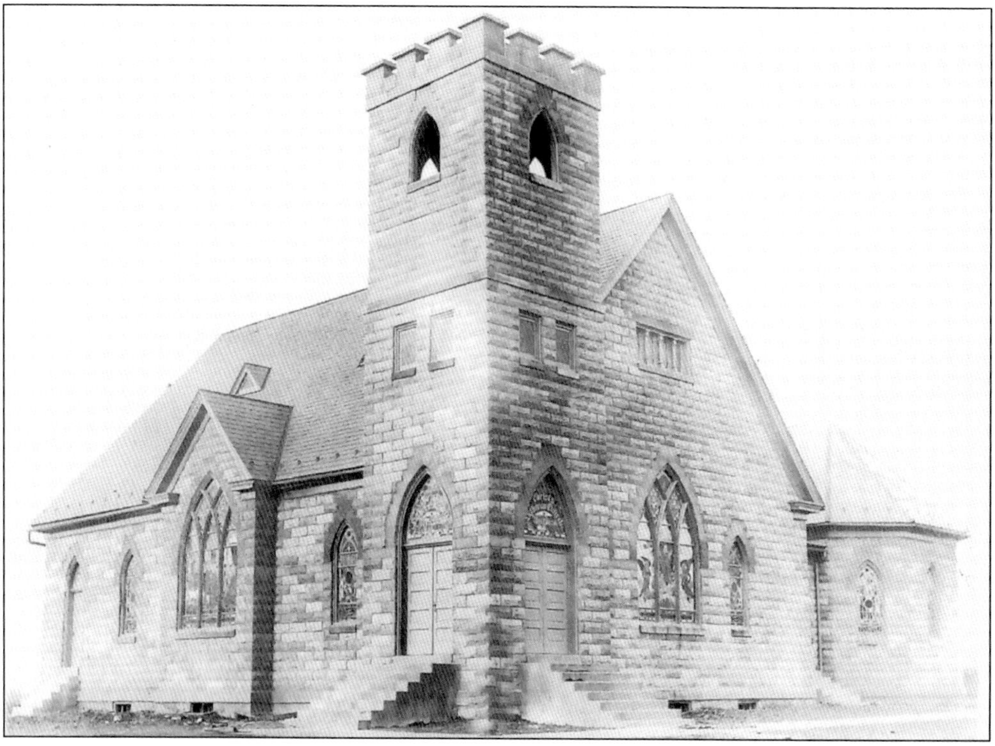

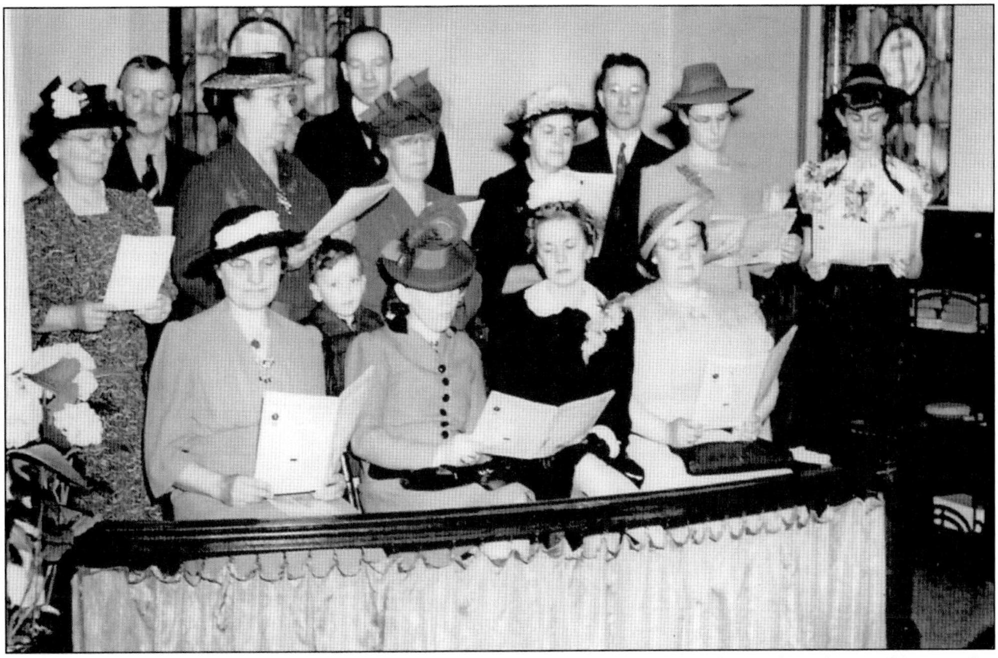

After being told that they must move out of their homes and that their church would soon be closed, members of the Stone Church gathered for a final worship service on Sunday, April 5. Members of the choir pictured above, from left to right, are: (first row) Marian Rump, Catharine Harman's young grandson, Mrs. Strauser, Dorothy Searles, and Inez Persun; (second row) Emmie Hively, Pauline Pysher, Catharine Harman, Jennie Waltman, Marvene Waltman, and Frances Baker; (third row) William Shrader, Wilson Harman, and Robert Searles. Following the service, group photographs were taken of the congregation that included the following families: Searles, Kahle, Persun, Albright, Hulsizer, Tallman, Shrader, Waltman, Decker, Shindel, Myers, Bush, Murray, Page, Pysher, Harman, McQuay, Baker, McCewen, Watson, Hively, Tallman, Bennett, Reamsnyder, Rump, Faust, Bensinger, Reynolds, Bastian, Swartz, Shrey, Jarrett, Kline, Best, Sealy, Horner, and Hoffman. (Both courtesy MAPL.)

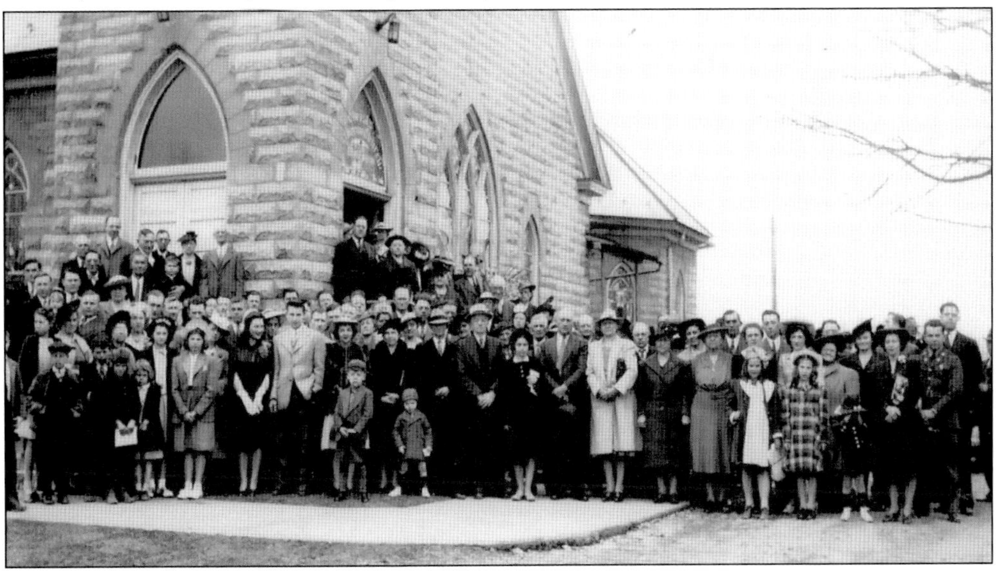

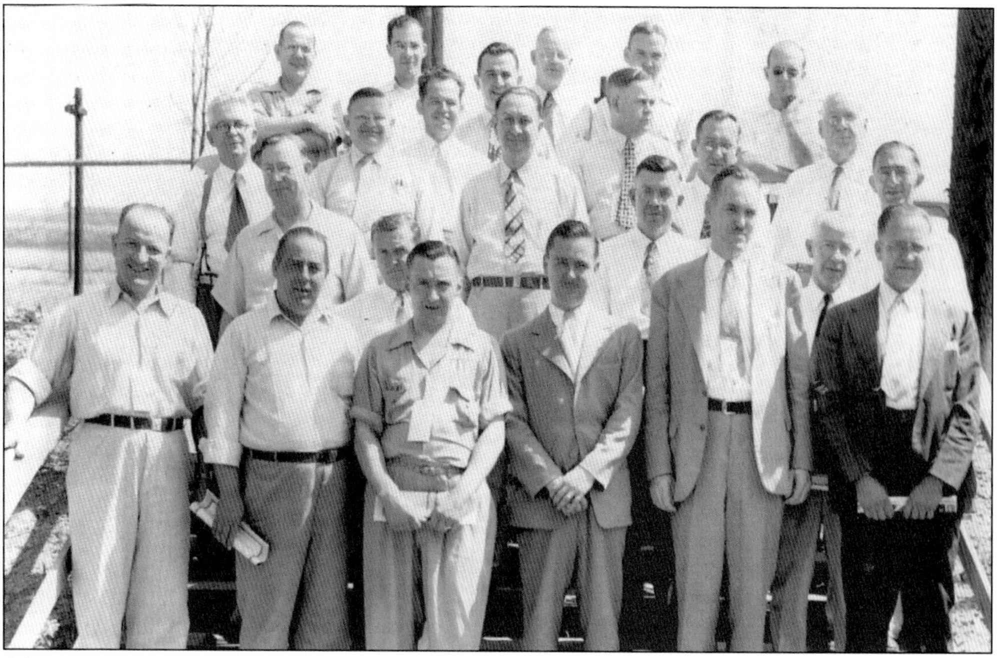

Above are Montgomery businessmen at the Pennsylvania Ordnance Works. From left to right are (first row) Don Hutchinson, Forrest "Ham" Bardo, Max Cole, two unidentified men, and Wilbur Decker; (second row) William Burchfield, Tommy Hill, and Ed Shollenberger; (third row) Steven Wells, Paul Miller, Marlin Spaid, Paul Decker, Dr. Clarence Oniel, and Isaac Decker; (fourth row) Robert Pysher, Sol Ginsberg, Ed Ginsberg, Lawrence Henderson, Bill Young, and Frank Thomas. Below, workers at the POW, from left to right, included (front row) Bernice Englert (second from left) and Ruth Stugart (fourth from left); (second row) all unidentified; (third row) Mary Ellis, Helen Hall, and ? Hughes; (fourth row) Jim Kemery, four unidentified workers, Roxanna Hively, two more unidentified workers, Stella Decker, unidentified, Phyllis Kuntz, two more unidentified workers, Walborn Mitchell, Peg Kemery, Catherine McCormick, four more unidentified workers, Carl Berger, and Wilden McCormick. (Both courtesy MAPL.)

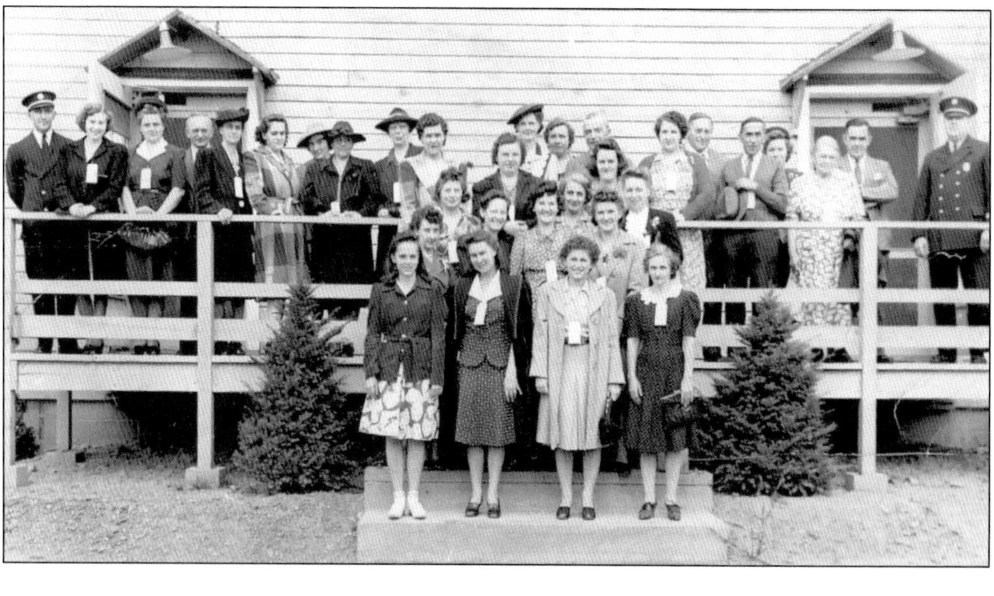

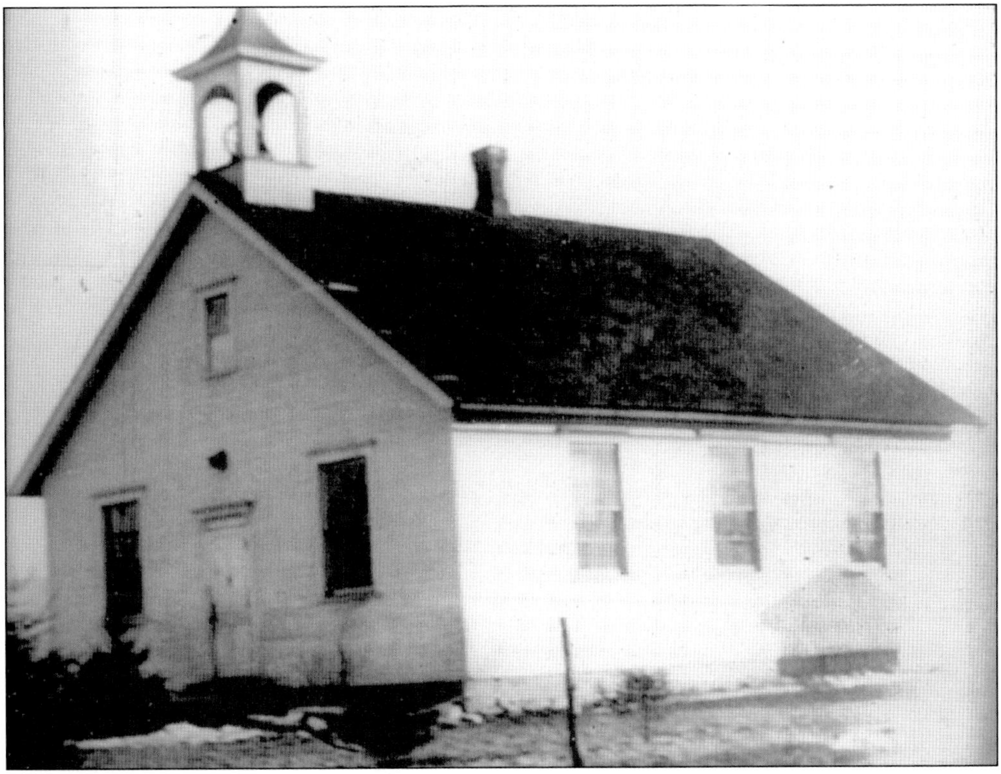

After the final church service was held in early April 1942 at the Stone Church, the church building was utilized as a storage facility and surrounded by a fence, which made it inaccessible, even to the families of those buried in the adjoining cemetery. The Alvira School, pictured above, was razed in 1942, along with the other school in the area known as the Stone School. Members of the Washington Presbyterian Church (pictured below) and the Messiah Lutheran Church, also known as the Pine Knot Church, held their final worship services before POW workers boarded up the buildings. Although these two churches were not torn down, they were abandoned, fell into disrepair, and were finally dismantled in the 1960s. (Both courtesy MAPL.)

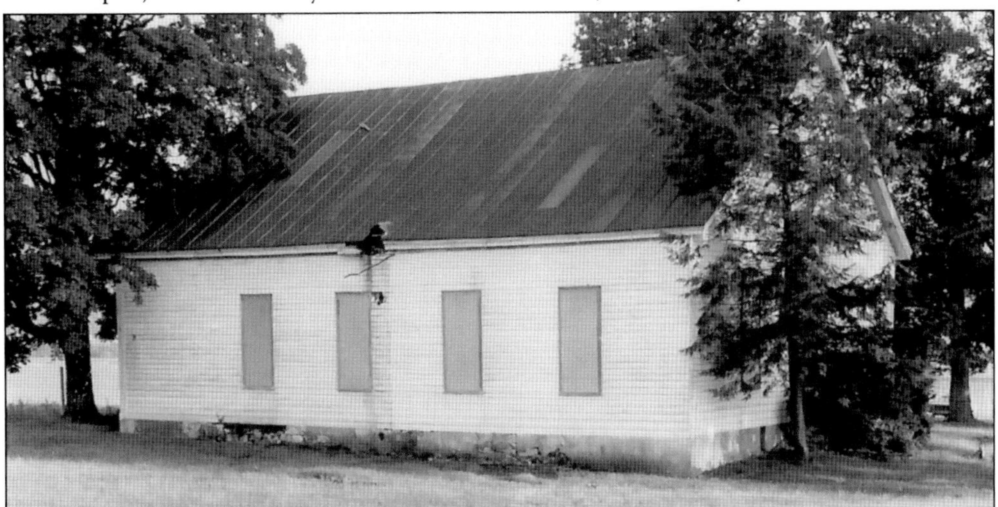

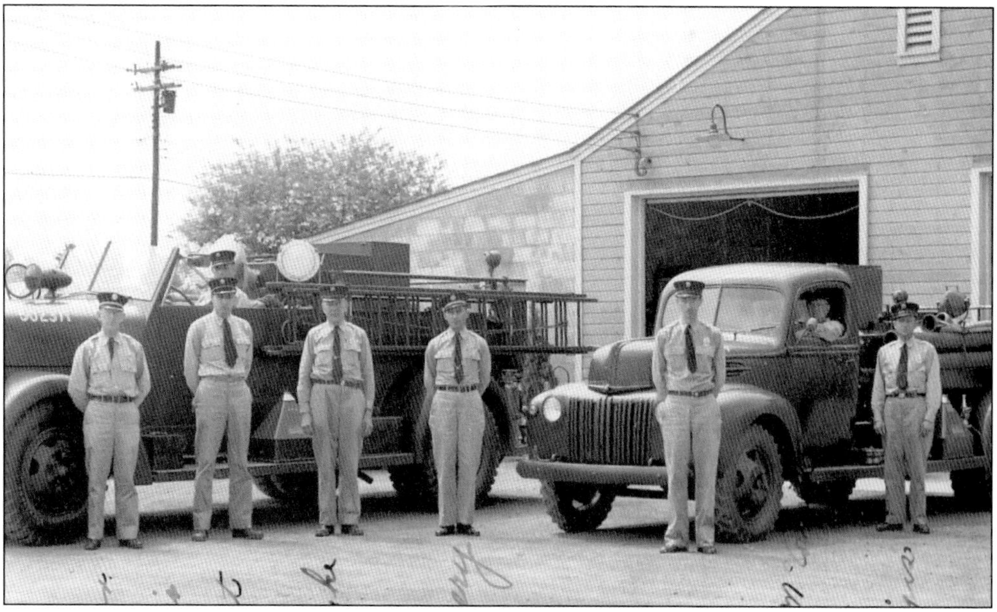

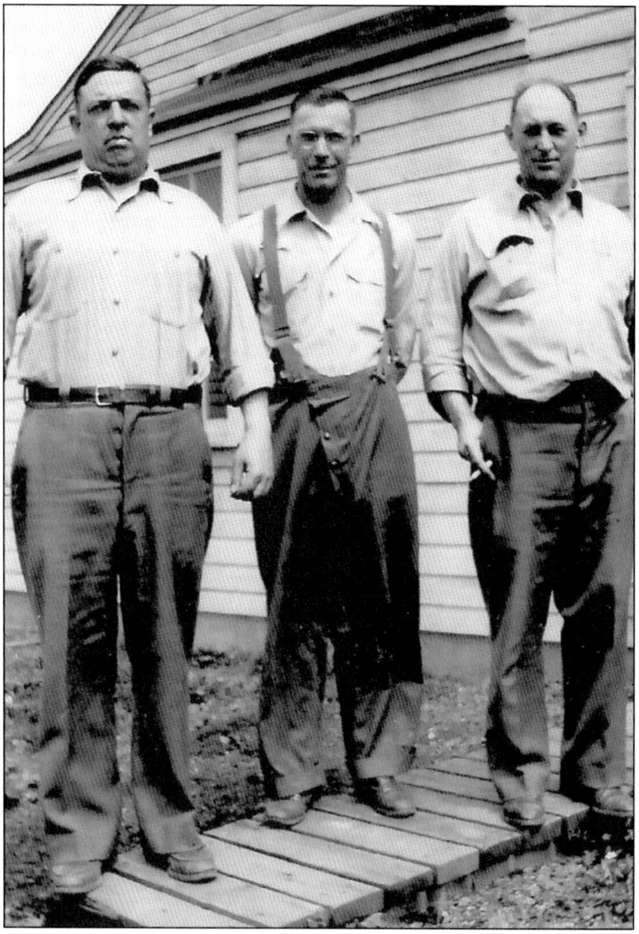

Although residents of Alvira were not alone in their sacrifice of property and homes—similar displacements were occurring across the country in the spring of 1942—their anger and feelings of mistrust were difficult to temper. When the TNT production facility was closed after only 11 months of operation, the government retained it to store and maintain munitions; the property became the Susquehanna Ordnance Depot. In the above photograph of Depot firefighters in front of the fire station in May 1944, several are identified as Montgomery residents. From left to right are the following: Captain Derr, Charles "Spook" Ellis, M.L. Foust, R.J. Franke, Chief Kemery, Louis Cox Jr., Wilden McCormick, and A.C. Phillips. At left, firemen Wilden McCormick (left) and Charles "Spook" Ellis pose with an unidentified man (center). (Both courtesy MAPL.)

After the Susquehanna Ordnance Depot became a munitions storage and transfer depot in 1944, the secrecy surrounding the facility dispersed somewhat and, on occasion, area dignitaries and local journalists were invited in for tours. The photographs on this page were taken in 1948 during one of those media events, during which visitors were allowed to examine the storage igloos (right). The gentleman in this photograph is identified as Leo C. Williamson, who served as Williamsport's mayor between 1940 and 1952. The nurses pictured with him at Bunker 98 may have been employed at the Susquehanna Ordnance Depot during that time. Below, the three men standing on the bomb—one of two dozen stored at the Depot—are identified, from left to right, as Major Lundhal (commanding officer of the Depot), Captain Severaid, and Lieutenant Elaiss. (Both courtesy MAPL.)

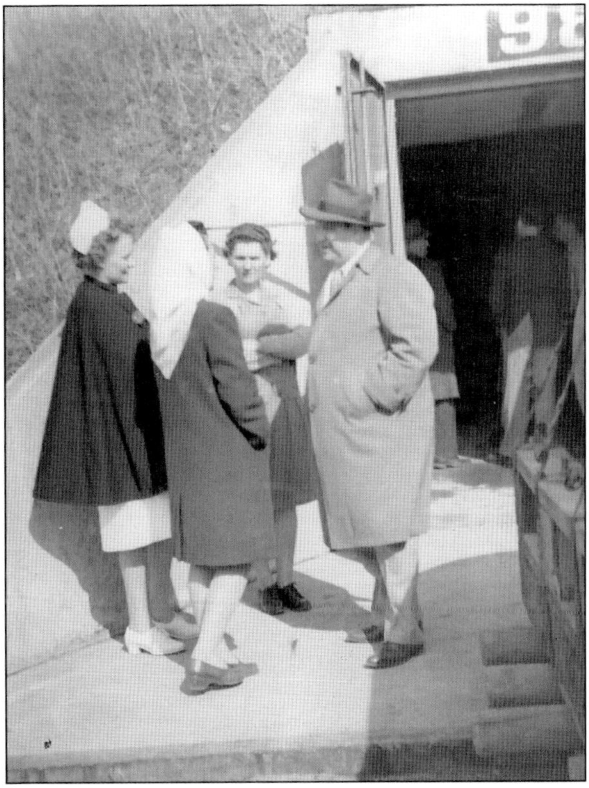

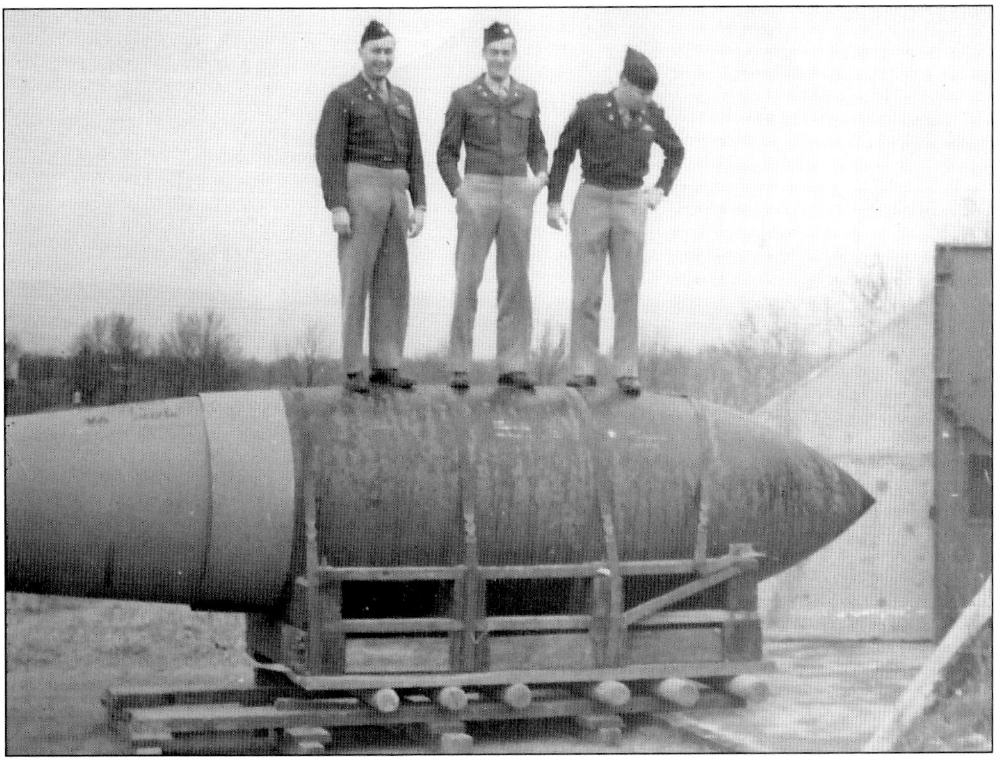

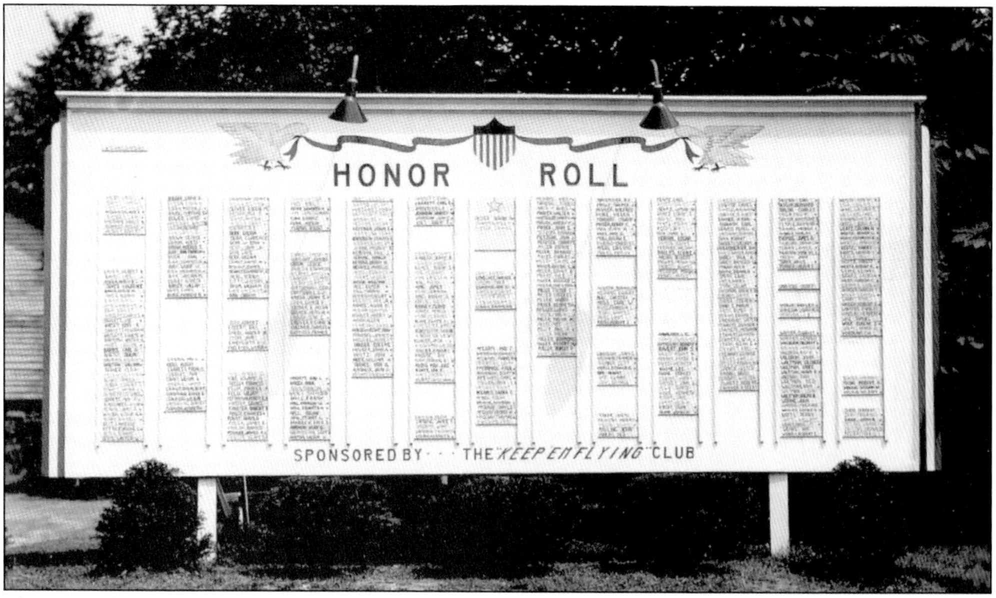

Photographed in August 1944, this Honor Roll board displayed the names of all Montgomery-area servicemen and women. The billboard was sponsored by the Keep 'Em Flying Club, which originated with Ruth Decker, the mother of Aaron and Delmar Decker (see next page), and Mrs. Harry Golder. The purpose of the club was to regularly send gifts, letters, and copies of local newspapers to the soldiers in service. (Courtesy Marion McCormick.)

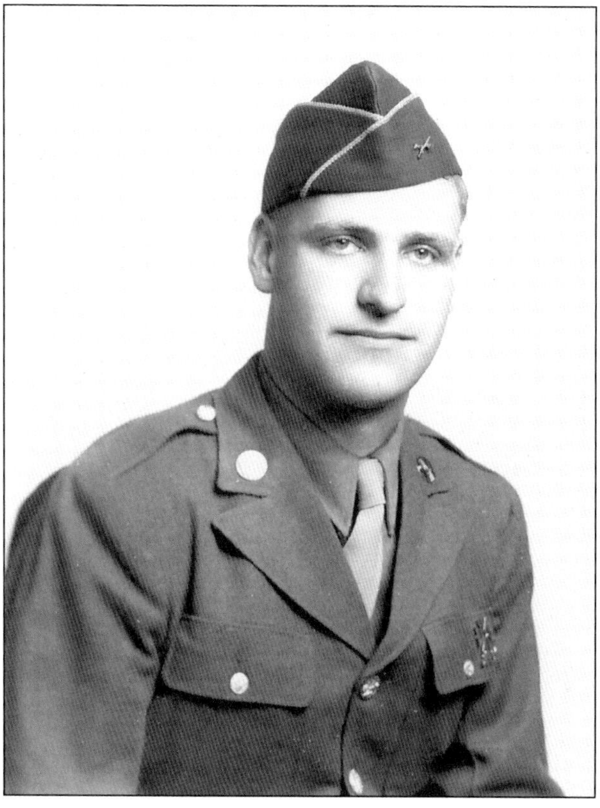

While serving in the military during World War II, five men from the Montgomery area perished. S.Sgt. B. Allen Gruver, pictured here, was one of the five; he graduated from the Montgomery-Clinton High School in 1939. Gruver enlisted in the army, was wounded in Germany, and died December 1, 1944. In 1948, Gruver's body was returned to the area and interred at the cemetery of St. John Lutheran Church, known locally as the Brick Church. (Courtesy MAPL.)

Of the five Montgomery servicemen killed in action, two were brothers. Lt. Delmar Decker, a navigator for the Air Force, was shot down over Holland on February 21, 1944, and Lt. Aaron Decker, US infantry, was killed in North Africa on March 20, 1943 (both pictured at right). A third brother, Paul Jr., also volunteered for service and returned home safely. The Montgomery High School senior class of 1946 installed a plaque in the school in memory of the five men from the borough who died in service to their country during World War II: Aaron Decker, Delmar Decker, Maurice Felix, Allen Gruver, and Fred Kennedy. Pictured below looking at the plaque are Paul and Ruth Decker, parents of Aaron and Delmar. (Both courtesy Marion McCormick.)

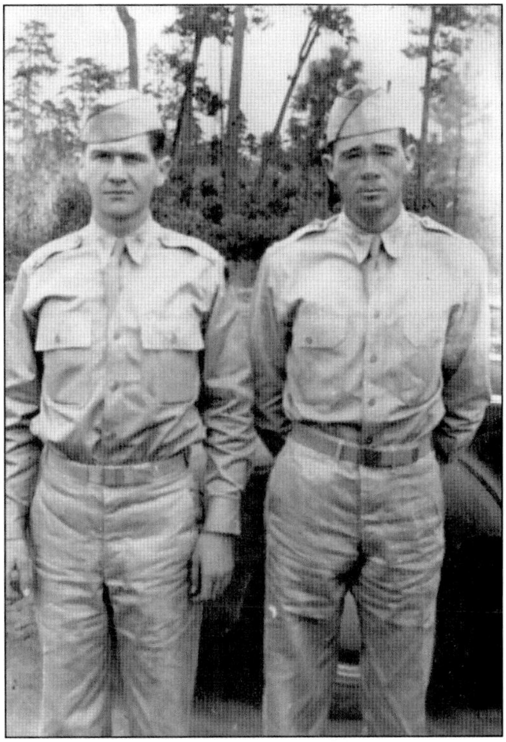

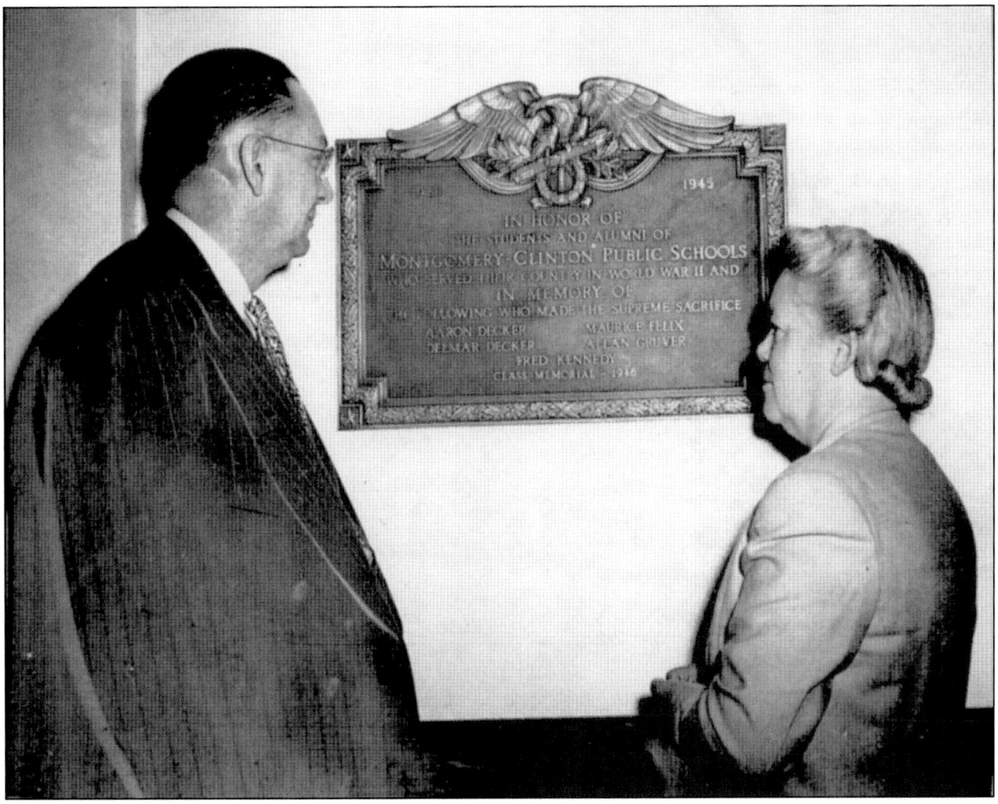

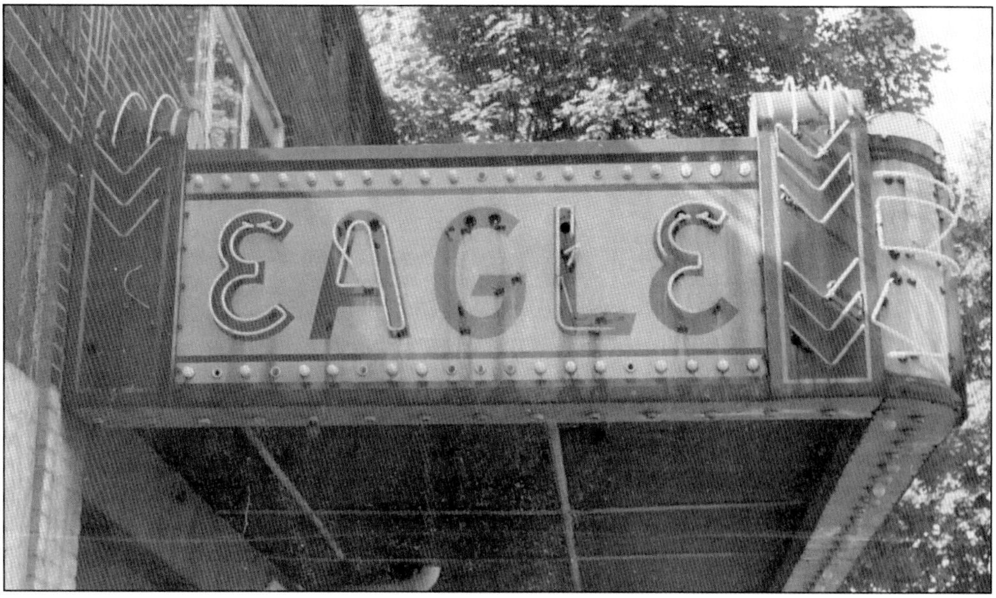

The Eagle Theatre opened in May 1942 with William Sherkel and his wife, Jane, managing the Main Street attraction. The theater showed four films per week at a cost of 10¢ a show, which included a 1¢ war tax. Before the opening of the Eagle Theatre, movies were sponsored by the Parent Teacher Association (PTA) and shown at the high school auditorium. Below is a view of South Main Street with the Farmer's and Citizen's Bank on the left next to the former post office building, which was also used by the Lions Club and Boy and Girl Scout troops for meeting space. (Both courtesy MAPL.)

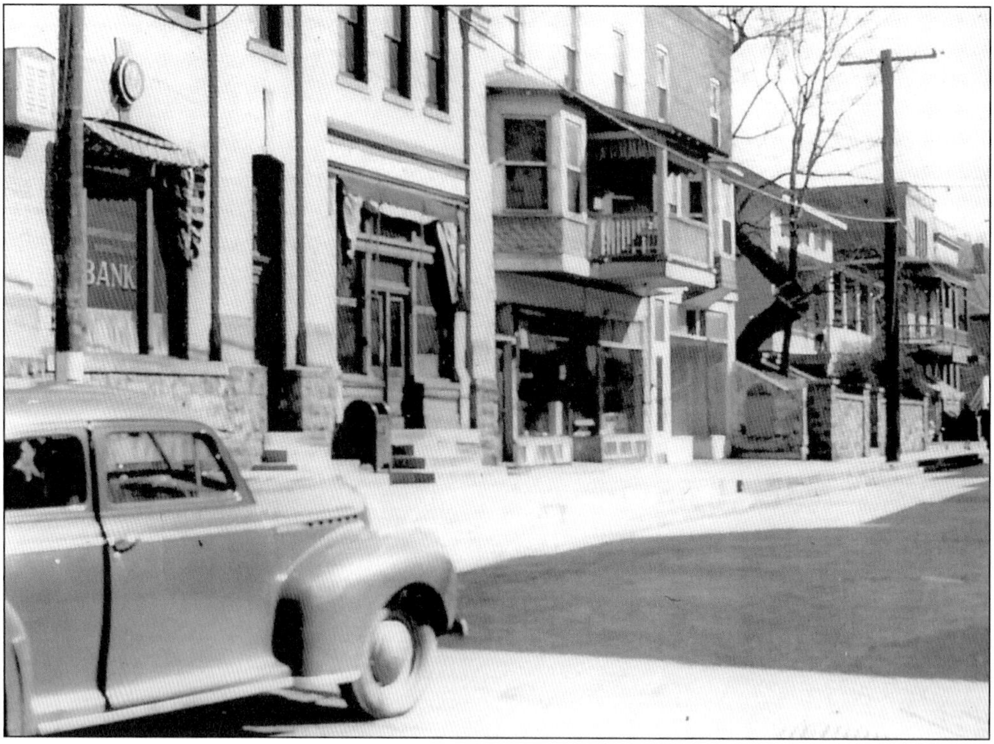

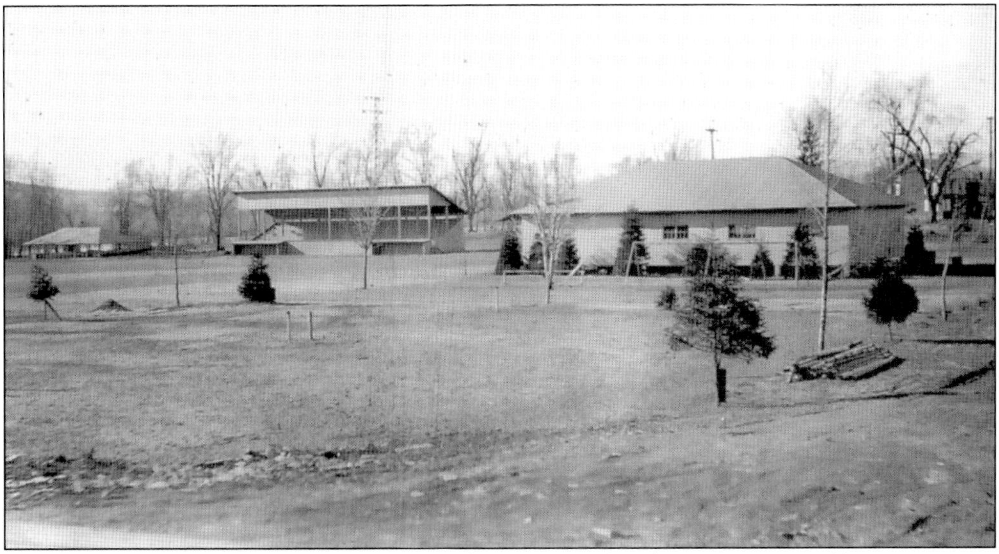

The Montgomery Park area near the Susquehanna River has been the scene of horse racing in the 1920s; a historic pageant, *Wings of Time*, commemorating Montgomery's semi-centennial in 1937; the beginning of Little League baseball in the late 1940s; and innumerable festivals and celebrations in the 1950s, 1960s, 1970s and 1980s. It survived disastrous flooding to be revived and restored. (Courtesy MAPL.)

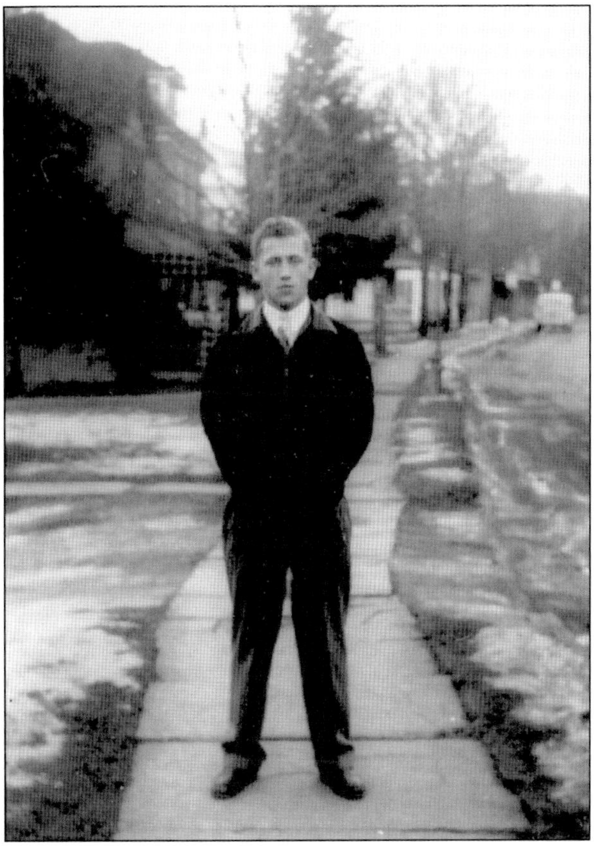

Standing in front of his childhood home at 75 North Main Street, 17-year-old Glenn Harman poses for a photograph on January 12, 1947, the day before he was scheduled to leave for induction into the Marine Corps. Harman served from January 1947 to January 1950 and again from September 1950 to January 1951, during the Korean Conflict. (Courtesy Glenda and Jade Heasley.)

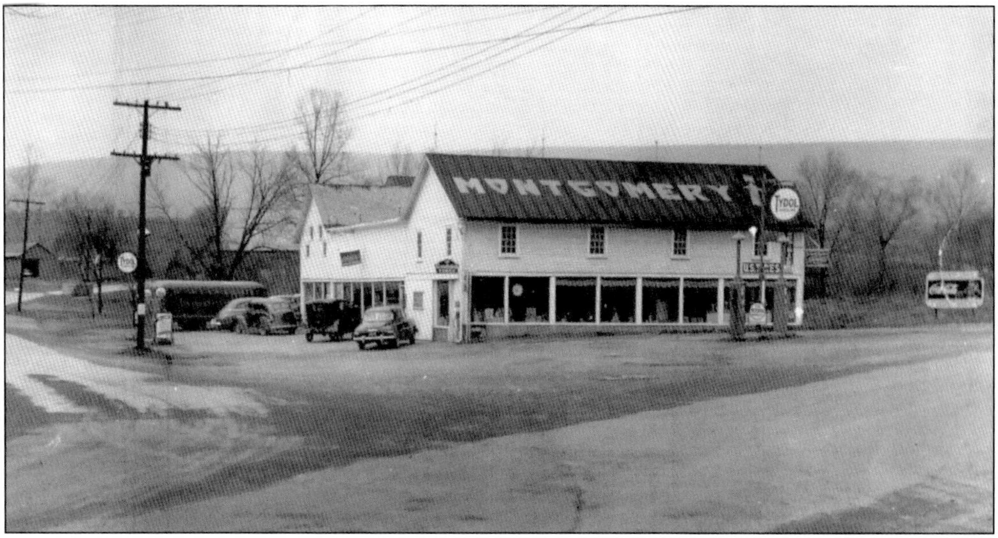

From its inception in 1946, the Clinton Township Volunteer Fire Company has benefitted from the generosity of C.L. Hulsizer, the owner of the auto dealership located just north of the borough in Clinton Township (above). When the fire company was organized that year, Hulsizer was elected treasurer. He donated cinderblocks for a new building, and when a Howe pumper was purchased, Hulsizer donated the Chevrolet chassis for it. In 1976, the fire company dedicated its social building in memory of Hulsizer with the placement of a plaque that read "In memory of C.L. Hulsizer for his guidance and many contributions, which made the Clinton Township Fire Company possible—1946." (Both courtesy Clinton Township Volunteer Fire Company.)

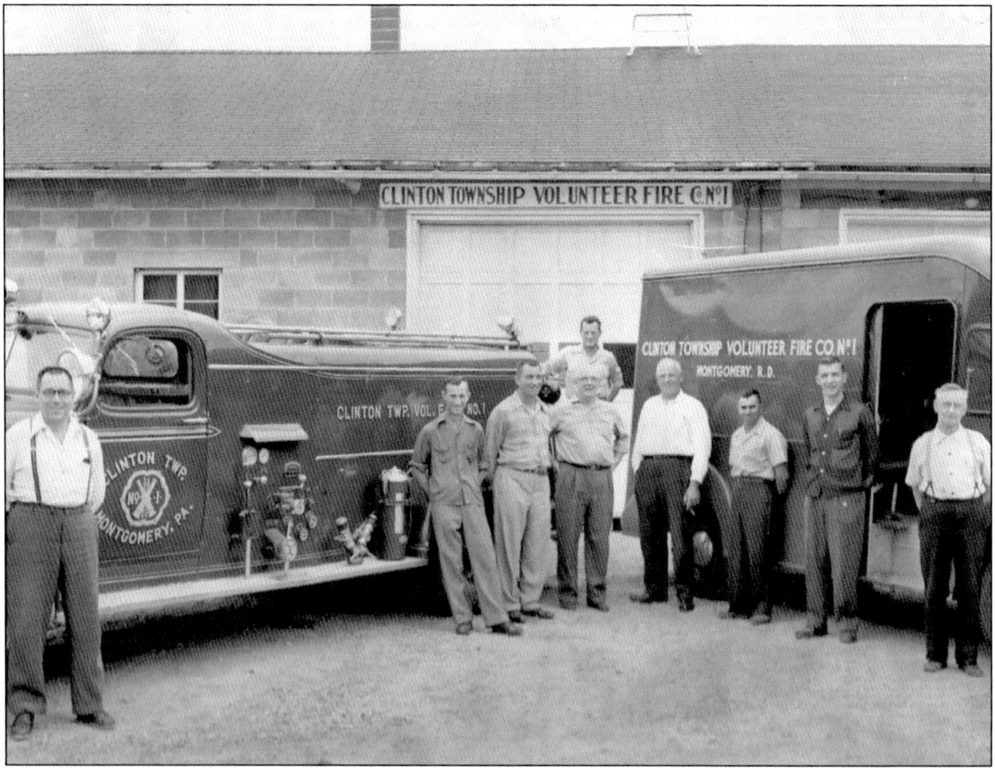

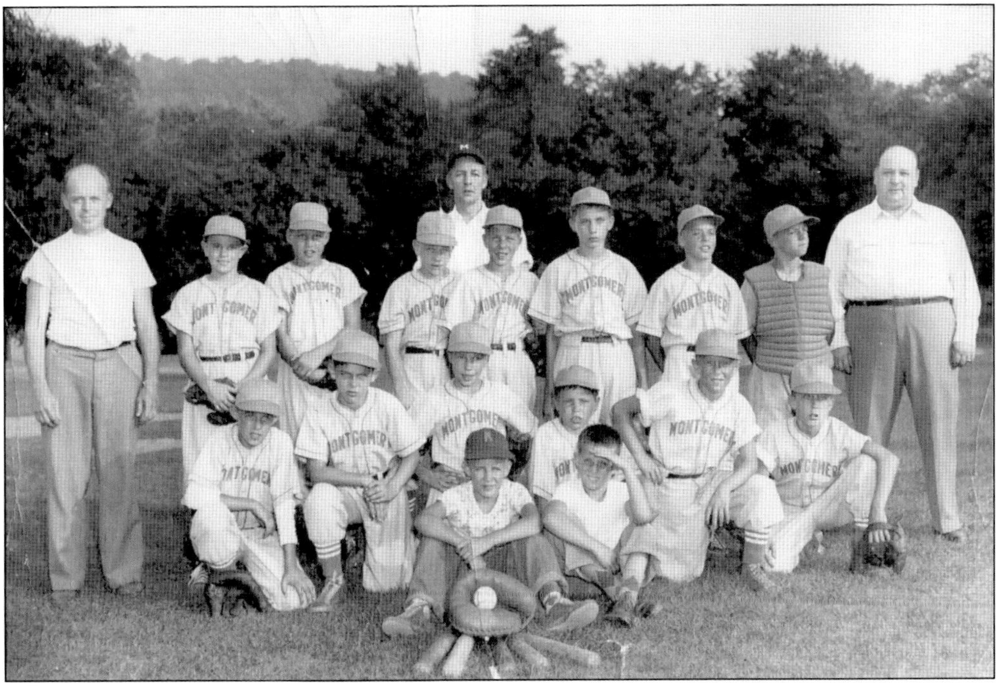

The All-Stars were boys selected from sports teams sponsored by area businesses. From left to right, they are (first row) Richard Tobias and Neil McCormick; (second row) Gene Foust, Max Burrows, Bill Wertz, "Buggs" Bennett, Jack Heiges, and Mike Grady; (third row) Dick Stahl, Al Young, Bob Farley, Dick Flick, Bob Young, Bob Lagrand, Topper Stahl, Don Yohn, and Ray Koons; (fourth row) Harold Tobias. (Courtesy MAPL.)

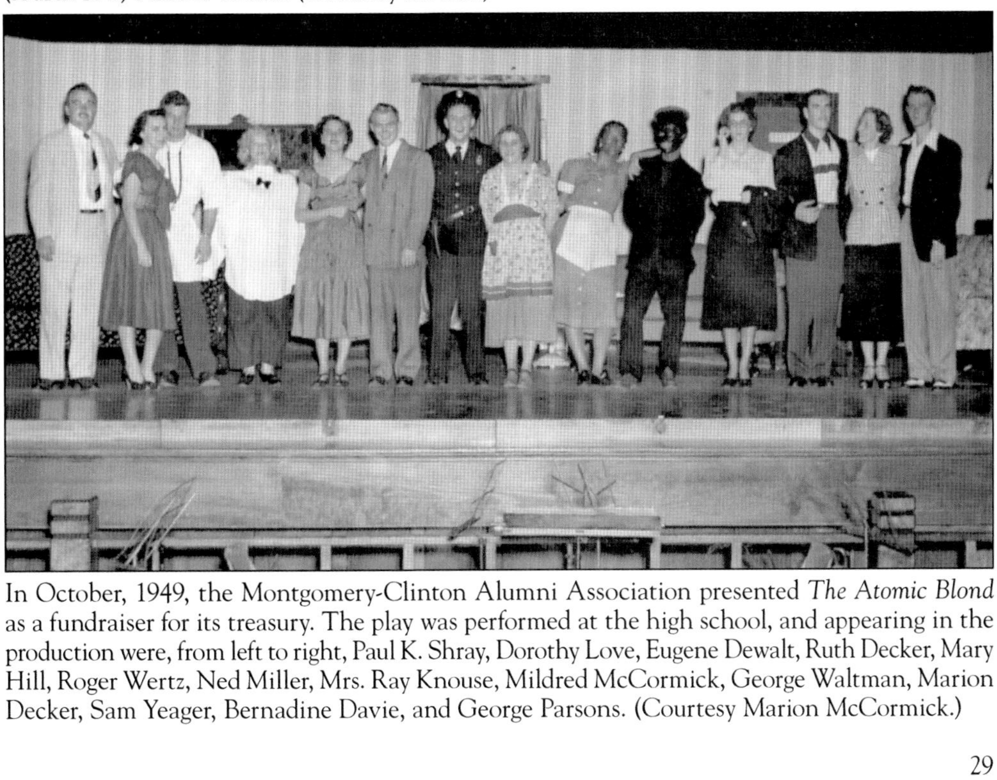

In October, 1949, the Montgomery-Clinton Alumni Association presented *The Atomic Blond* as a fundraiser for its treasury. The play was performed at the high school, and appearing in the production were, from left to right, Paul K. Shray, Dorothy Love, Eugene Dewalt, Ruth Decker, Mary Hill, Roger Wertz, Ned Miller, Mrs. Ray Knouse, Mildred McCormick, George Waltman, Marion Decker, Sam Yeager, Bernadine Davie, and George Parsons. (Courtesy Marion McCormick.)

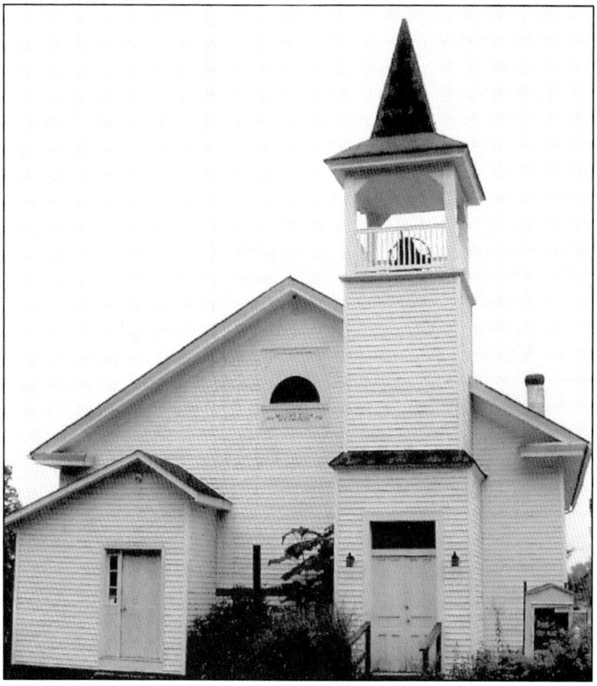

The Mt. Zion Methodist Church at Maple Hill was built in 1852 on a plot of land purchased from Enoch and Susannah Fritz for $50. Church membership gradually declined until the church was closed in 1930. By 1943, however, it was reopened to accommodate parishioners searching for a home after several churches were closed in Alvira. Fire closed Mt. Zion's doors in 1948, but within a few years, church services resumed.

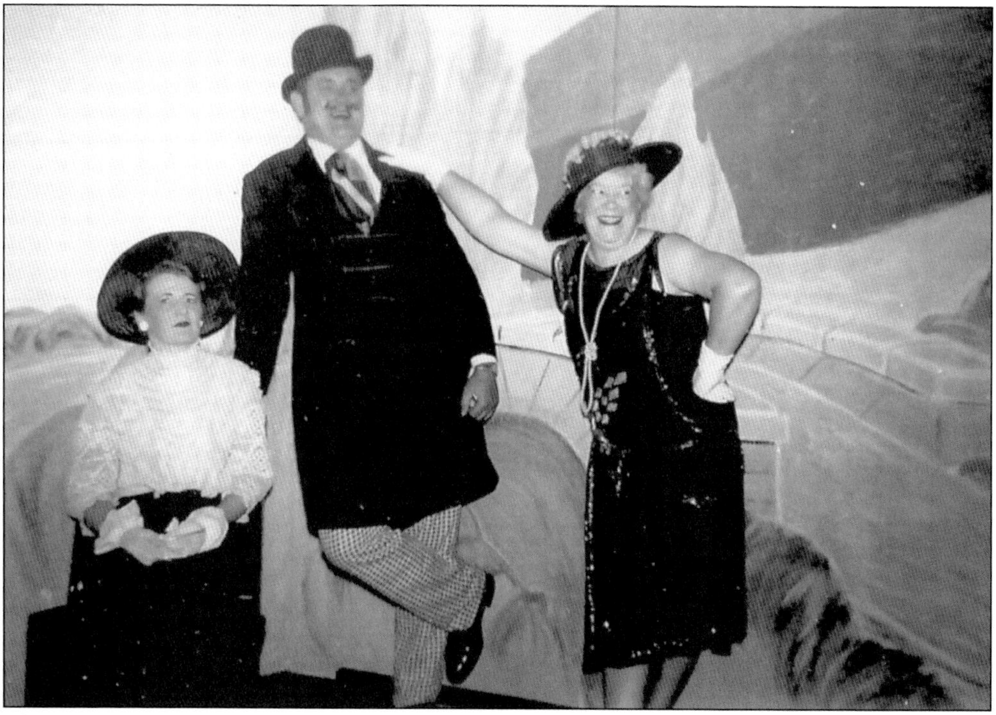

The Montgomery Rotary Club was granted its charter in 1936 and immediately began to raise funds to benefit the community. One of its more popular events was its minstrel shows. Their fourth show was held November 1949 as a benefit for the Muncy Valley Hospital Fund. Appearing in this production were, from left to right, Alma Wagner, Rev. Adam Bingaman, and Ruth Decker. (Courtesy Marion McCormick.)

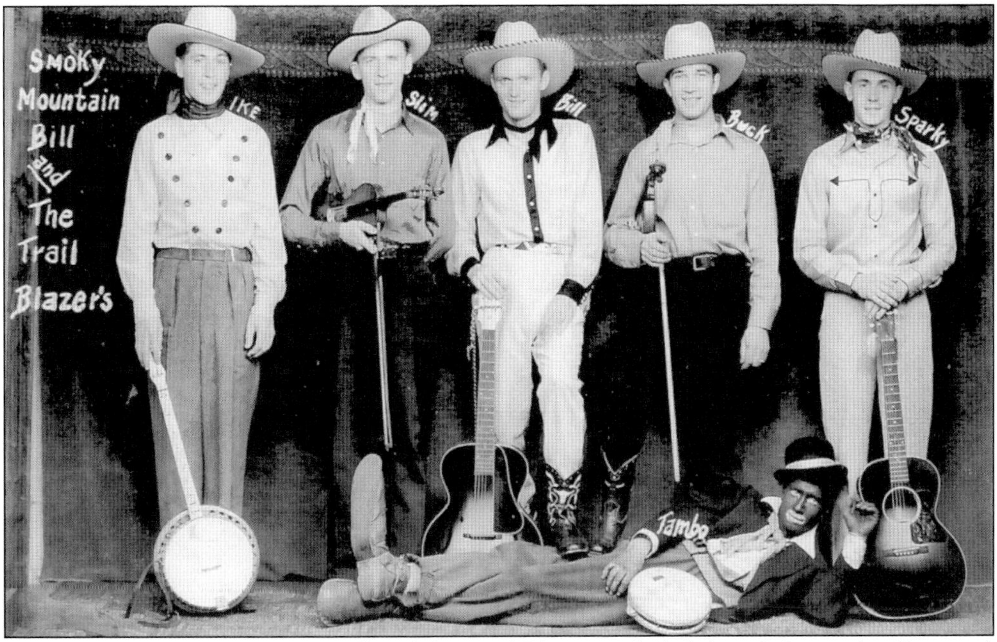

Members of Smokey Mountain Bill and the Trail Blazers included, from left to right, (first row) Jim Bumbourg (Tambo) in blackface; (second row) Herman Wertz (Ike), Harold West (Slim), cousin William West (Bill), Elmer Buck (Buck), and Herman's brother Bill Wertz (Sparky). Some members also performed as Hap Herman and his Playboys. Pictured below, from left to right, are Herman Wertz, Graydon Crawford, Dottie Wertz, sister Ruth Wertz, Harold West, and William Wertz. The pictured Wertz sisters and a third sister, Doris, sang with The Green Valley Band at the Radio Corral, an outdoor park near Montgomery. During the early 1950s, Dottie and Doris had a weekly radio show, *Tiny and Dot*, broadcast on WLYC in Williamsport. The show's announcer, Fred Kahle—known as "your old pal, Slim"—was from Montgomery, as were the Wertz sisters. (Both courtesy Glenda Heasley.)

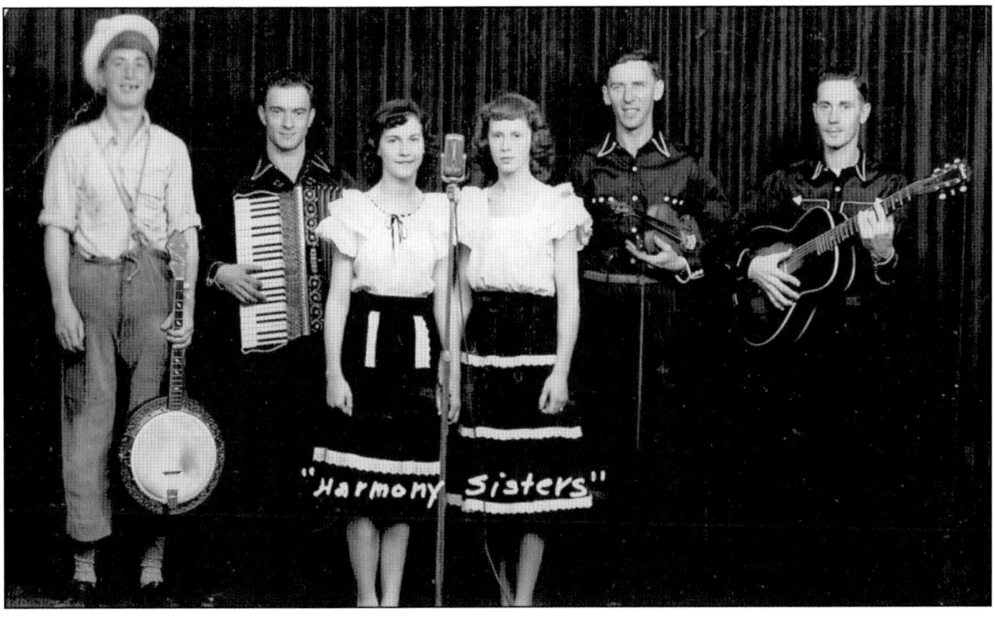

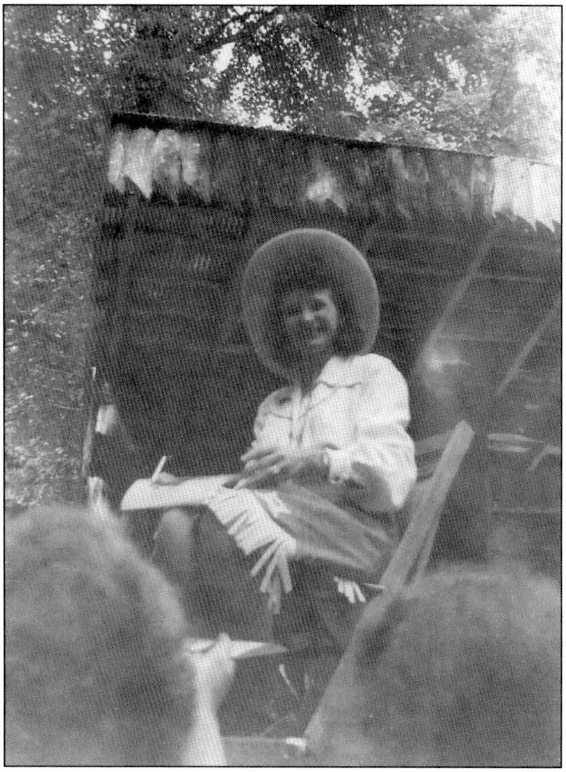

Country music singer and songwriter Patsy Montana was born Ruby Blevins in rural Arkansas, and by the time she was a teenager, she knew how to yodel and play the guitar. She appeared on *National Barn Dance* on Chicago radio station WLS, starred in a number of western films, and was the first female country singer to sell over a million copies; she recorded the hit "I Want to Be a Cowboy's Sweetheart" in 1935. She is pictured at left signing autographs after her performance in 1948 at Jim and Jane's Radio Corral, an outdoor stage near Montgomery. Below, singer Dean McNett poses with fans Lena Gray (left) and Millie Champlin in 1949 at the Radio Corral photograph booth. (Left, courtesy Lewis and Ruth Jones; below, courtesy Kathi Wertman.)

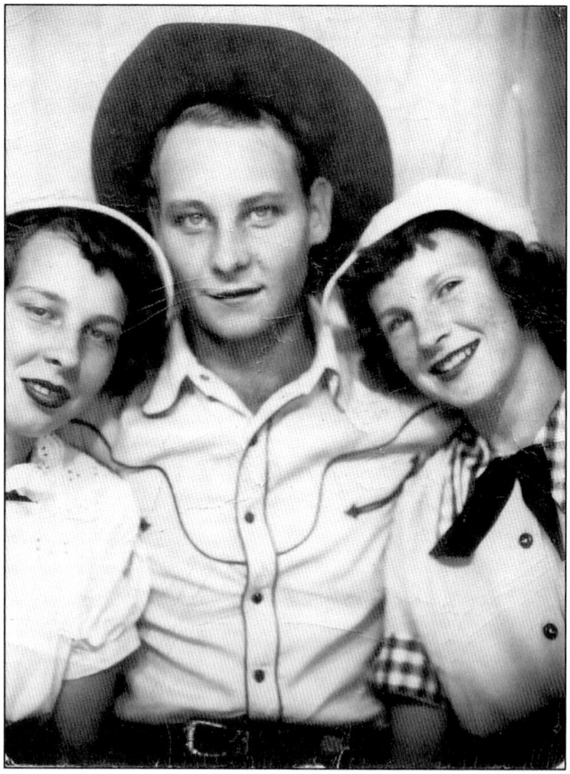

Two

The 1950s

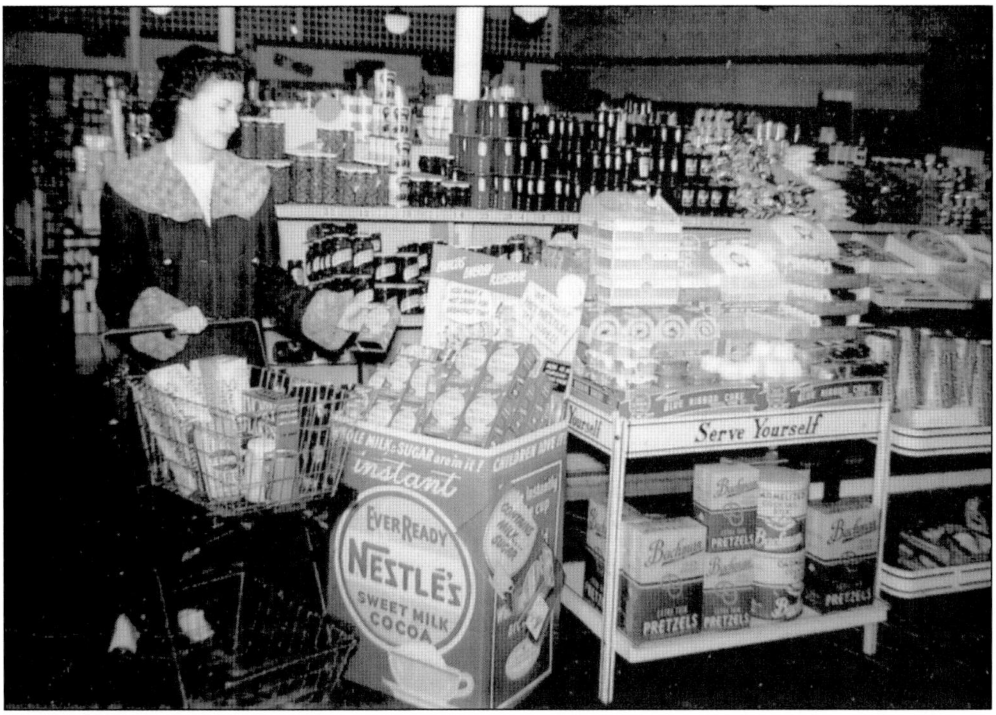

Dottie Wertz worked in the Weis Pure Foods store on Houston Avenue from 1949 to 1954. Here, she is posing in the early 1950s for a photograph, which was submitted for a contest run by Nestlé's Sweet Milk Cocoa—a "swell" drink with whole milk and sugar to build "energy reserves." (Courtesy Glenda Heasley.)

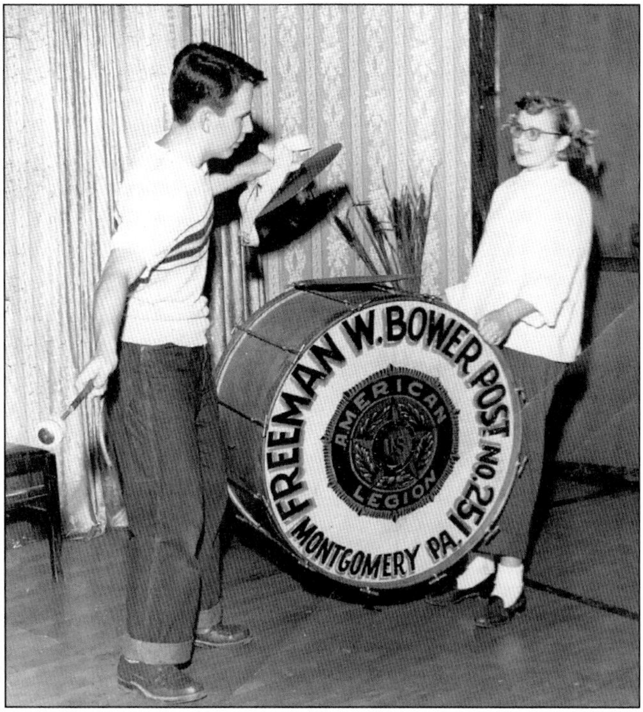

Thomas Winder (left) was a member of the Montgomery-Clinton High School band and the band's student director in 1952 and 1953, during his senior year. He is pictured with sister Dolly, who graduated in 1955. Later, as an army veteran of the Korean Conflict, Thomas Winder joined the Bower-Decker American Legion Post No. 251 and served as its board director. (Courtesy MAPL.)

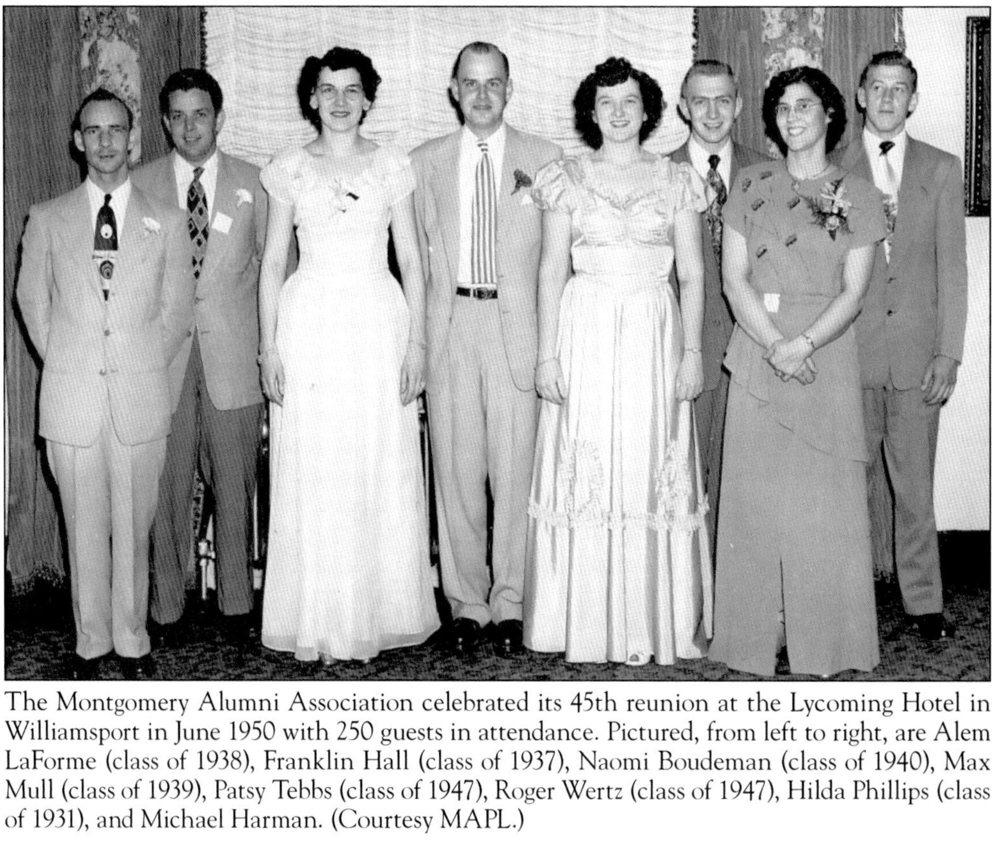

The Montgomery Alumni Association celebrated its 45th reunion at the Lycoming Hotel in Williamsport in June 1950 with 250 guests in attendance. Pictured, from left to right, are Alem LaForme (class of 1938), Franklin Hall (class of 1937), Naomi Boudeman (class of 1940), Max Mull (class of 1939), Patsy Tebbs (class of 1947), Roger Wertz (class of 1947), Hilda Phillips (class of 1931), and Michael Harman. (Courtesy MAPL.)

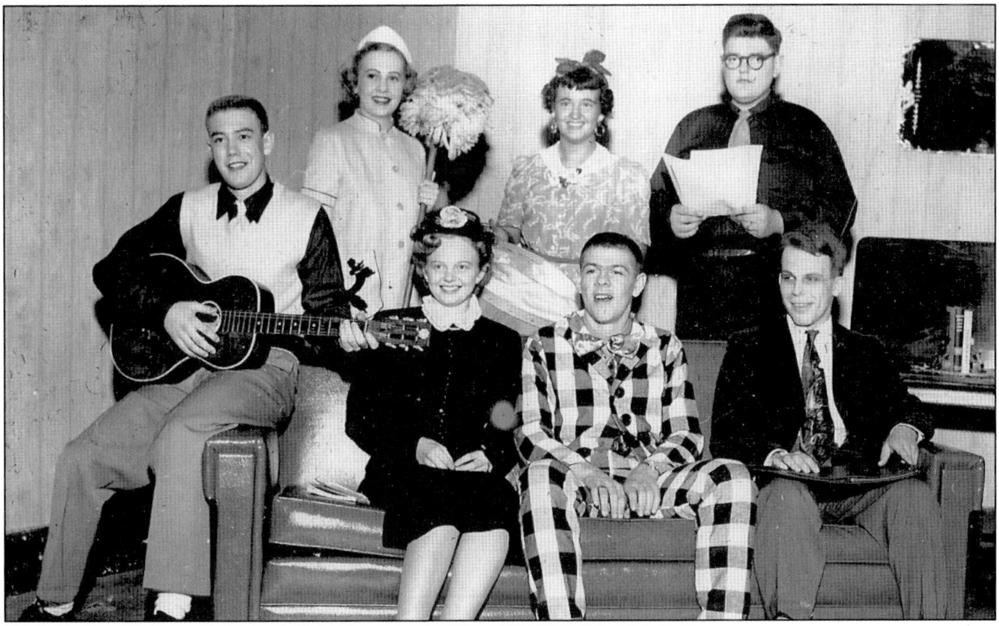

The Montgomery High School graduating class of 1953 presented a stage production entitled *Girl Shy* for their junior class play. This comedy featured a bashful college boy whose life was complicated by two women, his father, and circumstances beyond his control. Pictured, from left to right, are (seated) William Holmes, Beverly Jane Faust, John Watson, and Thomas Winder; (standing) Clarabelle Decker, Marilyn Pysher, and Leroy Adams. (Courtesy MAPL.)

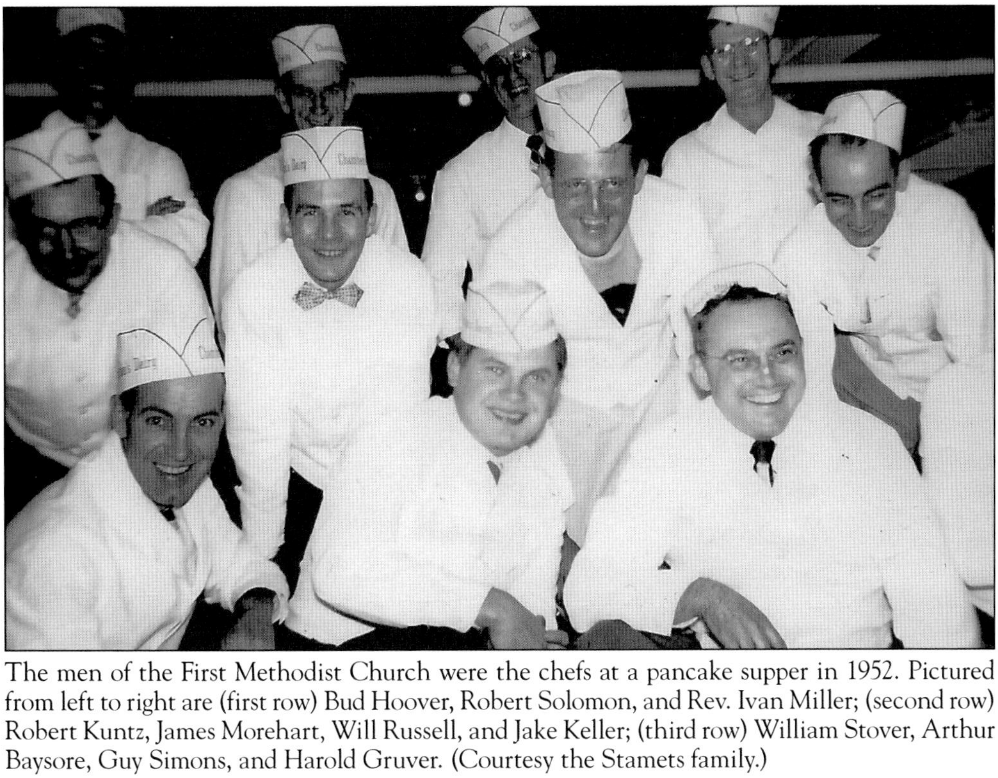

The men of the First Methodist Church were the chefs at a pancake supper in 1952. Pictured from left to right are (first row) Bud Hoover, Robert Solomon, and Rev. Ivan Miller; (second row) Robert Kuntz, James Morehart, Will Russell, and Jake Keller; (third row) William Stover, Arthur Baysore, Guy Simons, and Harold Gruver. (Courtesy the Stamets family.)

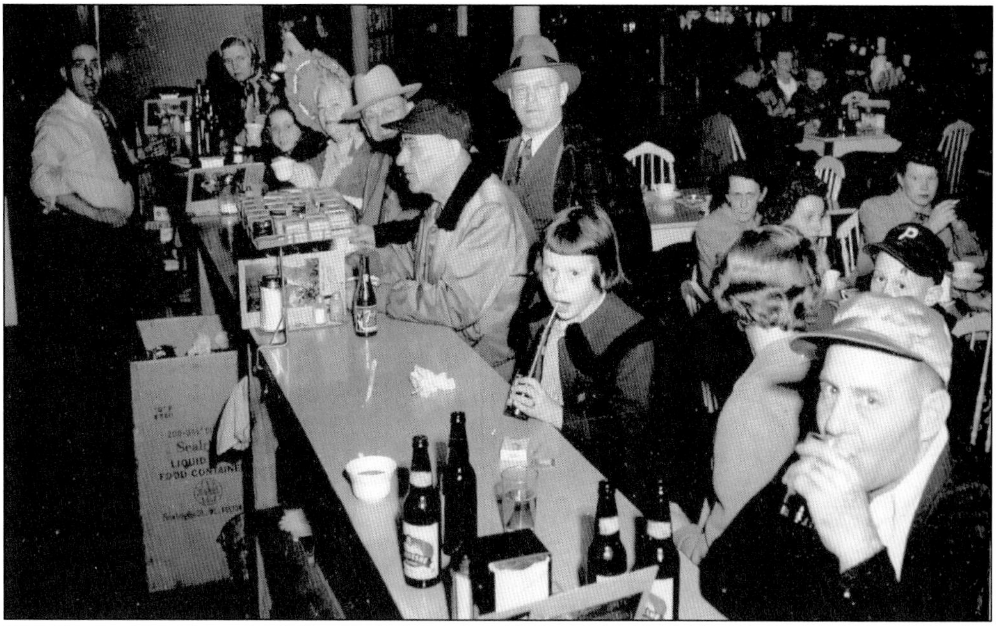

The Forrest Tea Room had been in operation since 1932 when Forrest "Ham" Bardo opened the restaurant on Main Street. In this scene inside the Tea Room in 1951, Bardo is seen serving drinks behind the bar. Ruth Decker (with bonnet) sits across from Bardo, and her husband, Paul Decker, is to her left. Dutch Reighly is on Mr. Decker's left, and Paul Shrey is standing behind Reighly. (Courtesy Marion McCormick.)

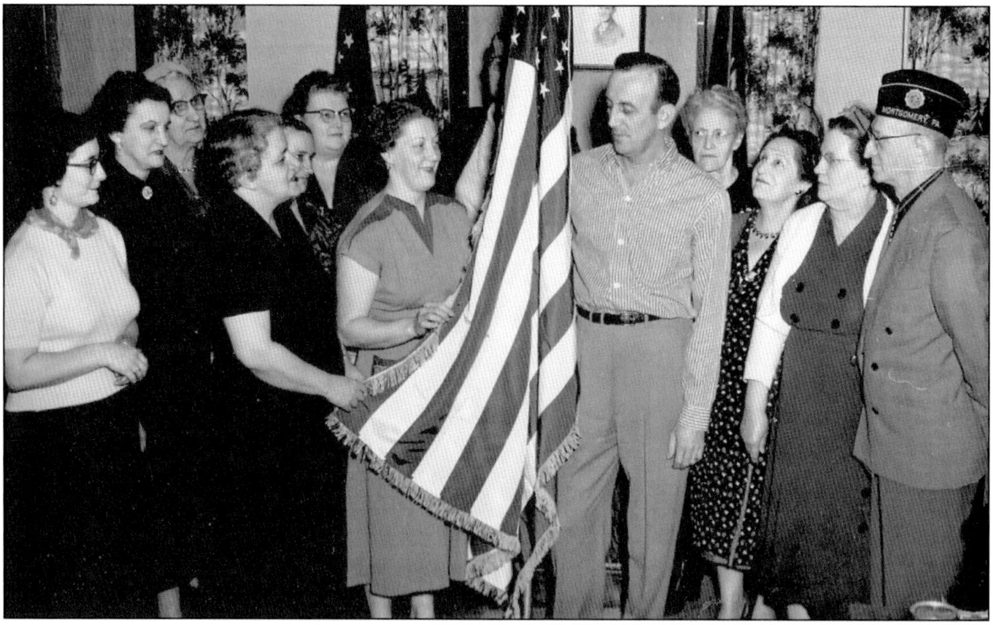

Founded in 1919, the American Legion Post in Montgomery was named Bower-Decker Post No. 251 in memory of the borough's first casualties in World Wars I and II. Pictured attending a flag presentation at the Legion Hall are, from left to right, Thelma Lindenmuth Peck, ? King, unidentified, Martha Belle Knouse, Emma Hill, ? Giltner, Nancy Flick, three unidentified, Betty Springer, Josephine Harman, and Joe Goldstein. (Courtesy Marion McCormick.)

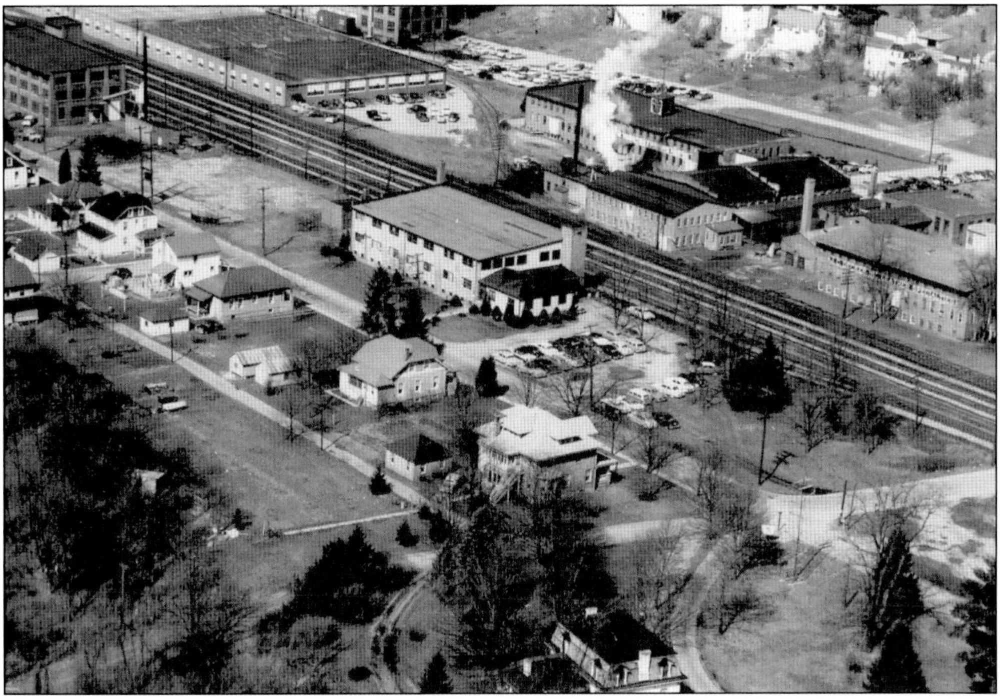

Above is an aerial view of the manufacturing facilities along Broad Street and the former home of the American Legion Post No. 251. In 1968, the Legion started construction on a new building at the end of Broad Street. In 1944, the Eastern Furniture Manufacturing Company was established in a facility on Thomas Street (below). The name of the business was eventually changed to Rochelle Furniture Manufacturing Company. The assembly-line operation produced juvenile furniture for distribution to all 50 states, Canada, and South America. (Both courtesy MAPL.)

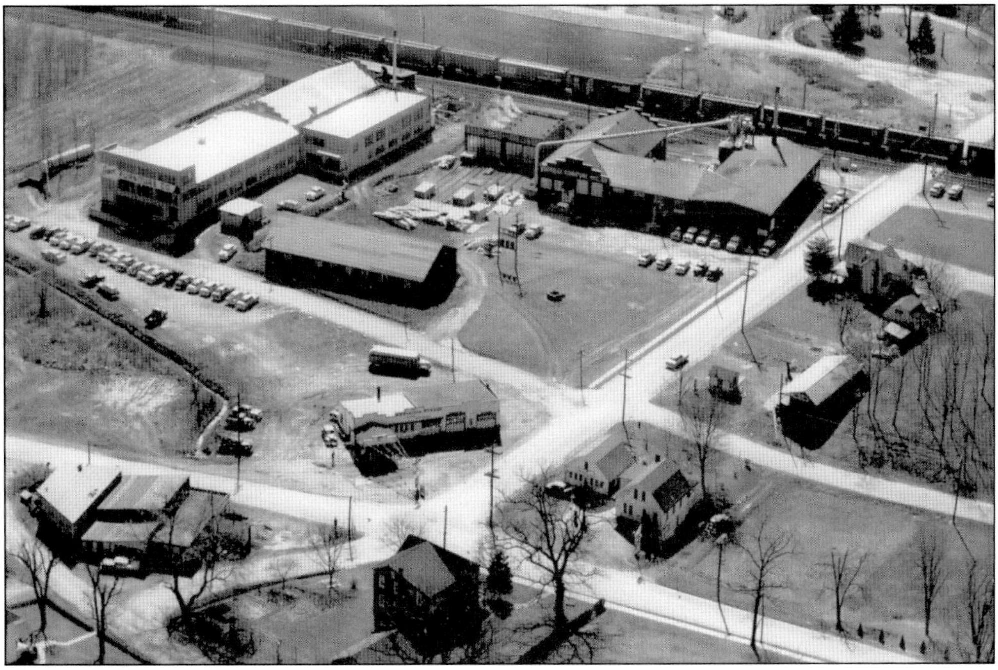

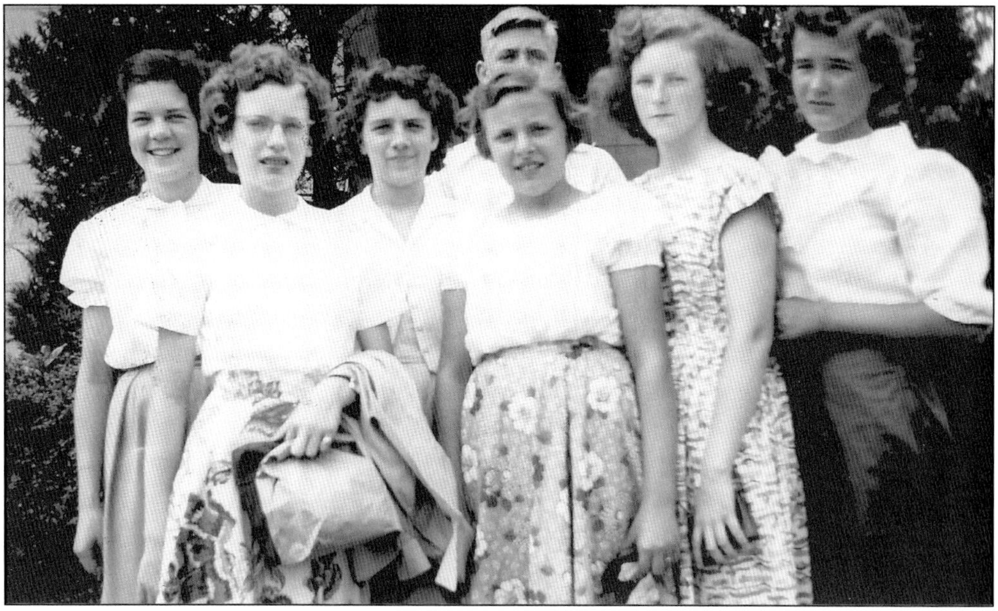

Pictured above is a group of youth from Grace Presbyterian Church on their way to Church Camp in 1951. From left to right are (first row) Anita Vetter, Cora Dawn Stamets, Alice Jane Durham, Silvia McCormick, Phyllis Brown, and Martha Jane Stahl; (second row) Gary Yocum. In 1946, C.E. Fitzgerald of Williamsport was contracted to paint the exterior and interior of the Grace Presbyterian Church. Fitzgerald chose Heilnecker Sign Studio, also of Williamsport, to paint the wall (at a cost of $67) depicting the Rock of Ages (below). The cost of the interior and exterior painting project was $1,500. In 1959, the side entrance was enclosed, and the exterior of the church was painted brick-red with white trim (at a cost of $628). (Both courtesy Grace Presbyterian Church.)

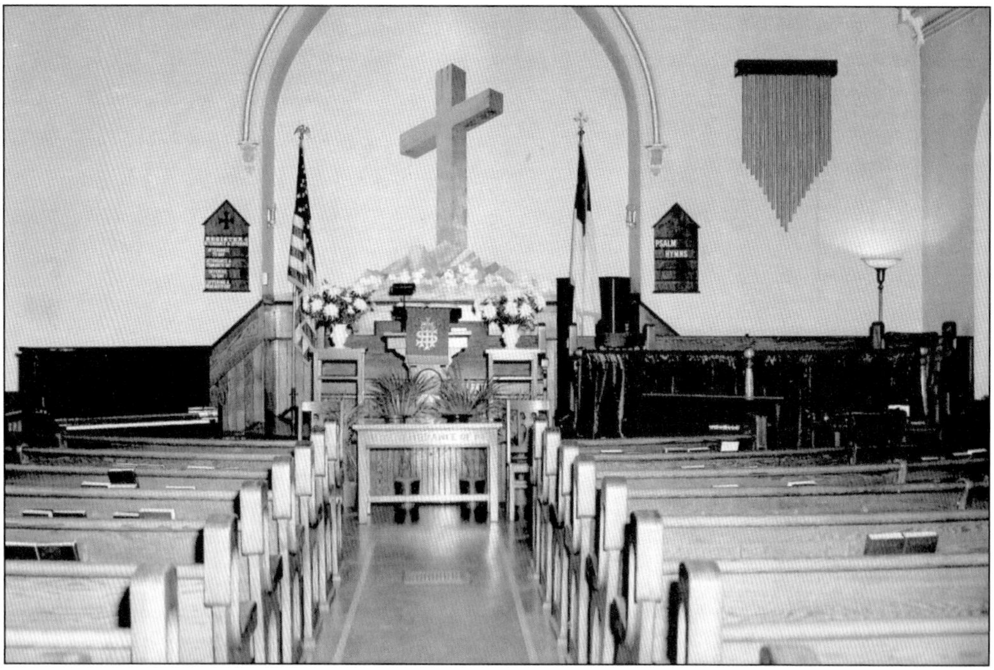

In addition to the Grace Presbyterian Church Valentine Socials, the Parcel Post Sale was also a popular fundraiser. Letters were sent to local and national celebrities requesting a package in return, which would then be auctioned off, unopened. Jean Miller (left) and Marion Decker are pictured with the packages for the 1951 auction, including those mailed from CBS Broadcasting, Inc. and the White House. Below are members of Lloyd Miller's Bible class from Grace Presbyterian Church. From left to right are (first row) Jean Miller, Ursula Martin, Helen Ryan, Ruth Kilmer, Bea Englert, Maxine Reeser, and Barb Shaffer; (second row) Neal Ryan, Max Mull, Blair Shaffer, Lloyd Miller, and Breckie Englert. (Both courtesy Grace Presbyterian Church.)

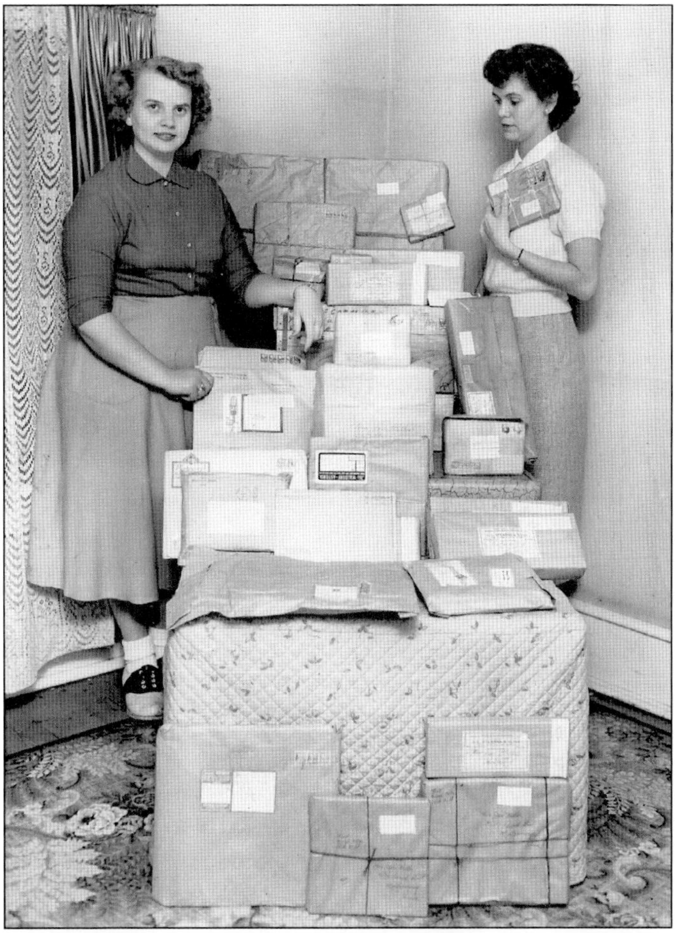

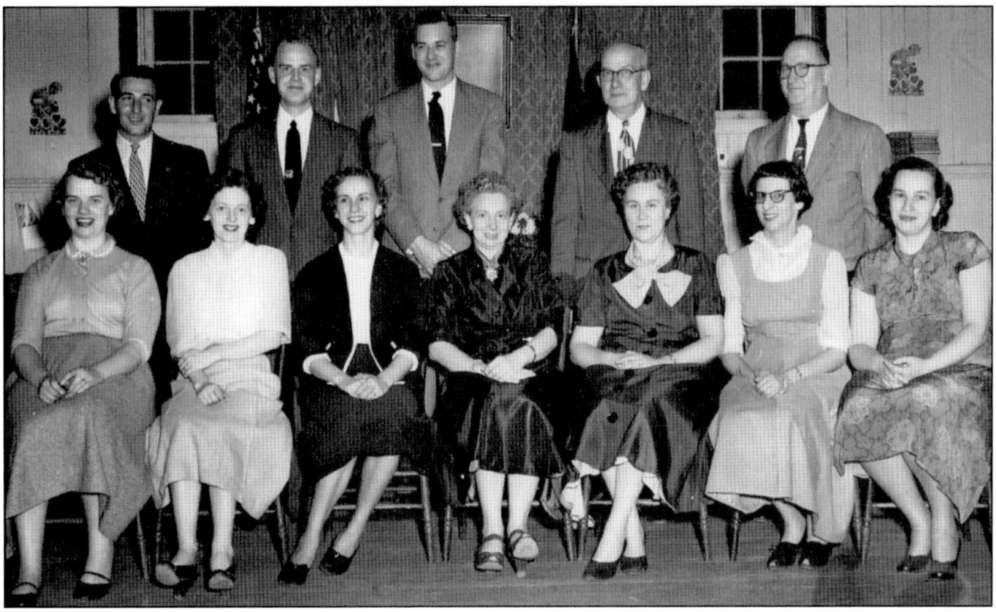

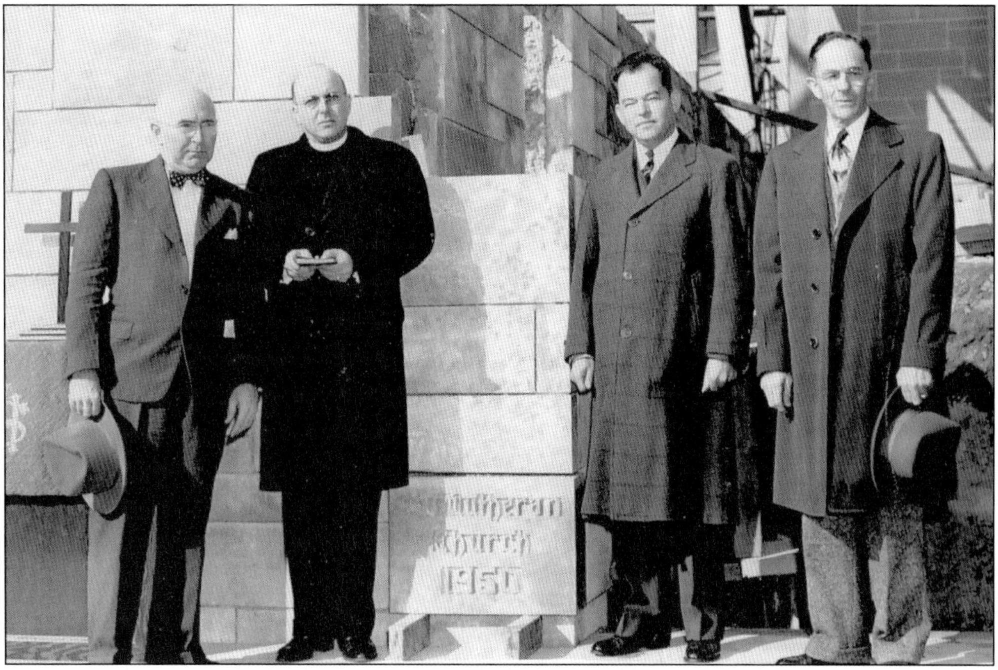

In the spring of 1950, the Evangelical Lutheran congregation authorized the construction of a new church building to replace the one destroyed in a fire in 1928. After the fire, services had been held in the Sunday school building adjacent to the church. Groundbreaking ceremonies were held May 7, 1950, and a cornerstone-laying ceremony was held that November. Pictured above are the church's pastor and members of the building committee. From left to right, they are Herbert Harman, Rev. John R. Knaul, G. Marlin Spaid, and Ralph Decker. Below, members of the congregation gather for the cornerstone ceremony. (Both courtesy Christ Lutheran Church.)

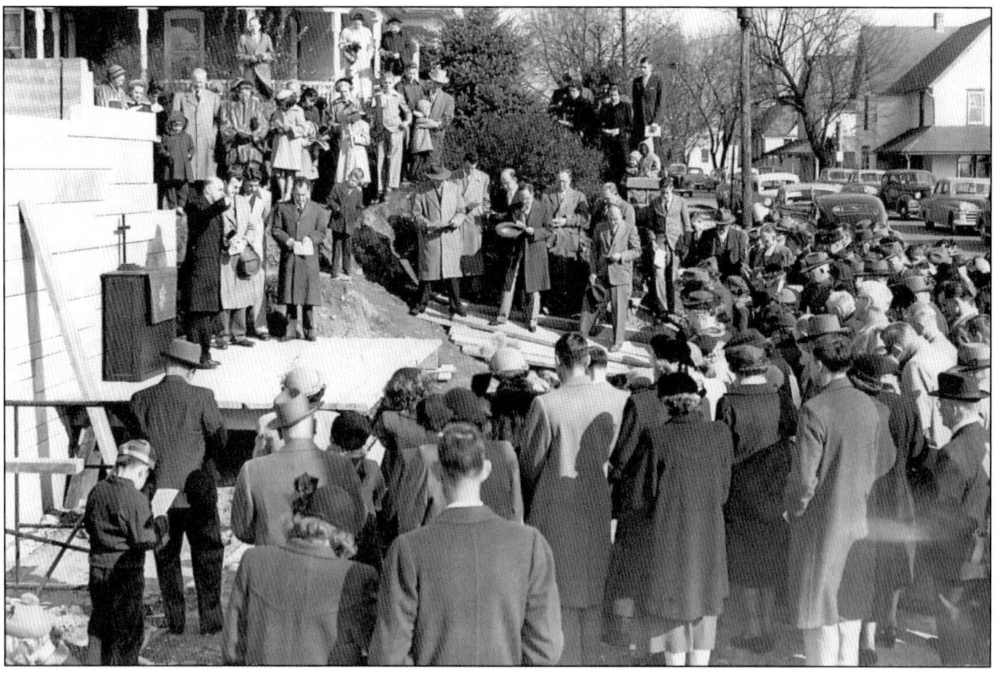

The "modern church edifice" of the Evangelical Lutheran Church began to take shape as the new building was erected in 1951 at a cost of $101,000. A member of the congregation, Russell Davie of Montgomery, was awarded the project's general contract. By the spring of 1952, the church was completed and dedicated. Pictured below is the church's senior choir on the day of dedication. From left to right are (first row) Roberta Buck, Dorothy Shelley, Ella Strickland, Elsie Best, and Janette Shollenberger; (second row) Leslie Cox, Virginia Decker, Ruth Huff, Mrs. Ray Miller, and Bernadine Davie; (third row) Bertrim Strickland, ? Buck, Frank Strickland, Clarence Strouse, and Gene Dewalt. (Both courtesy Christ Lutheran Church.)

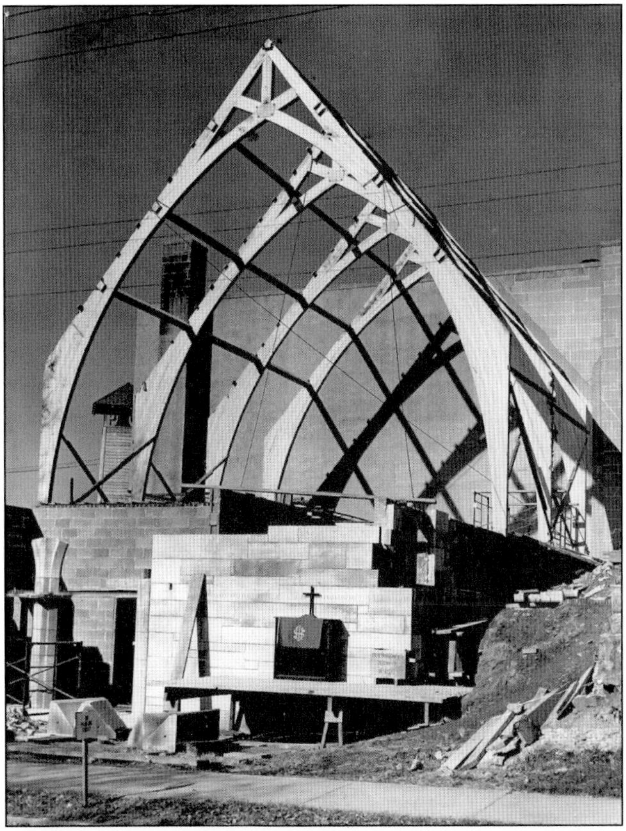

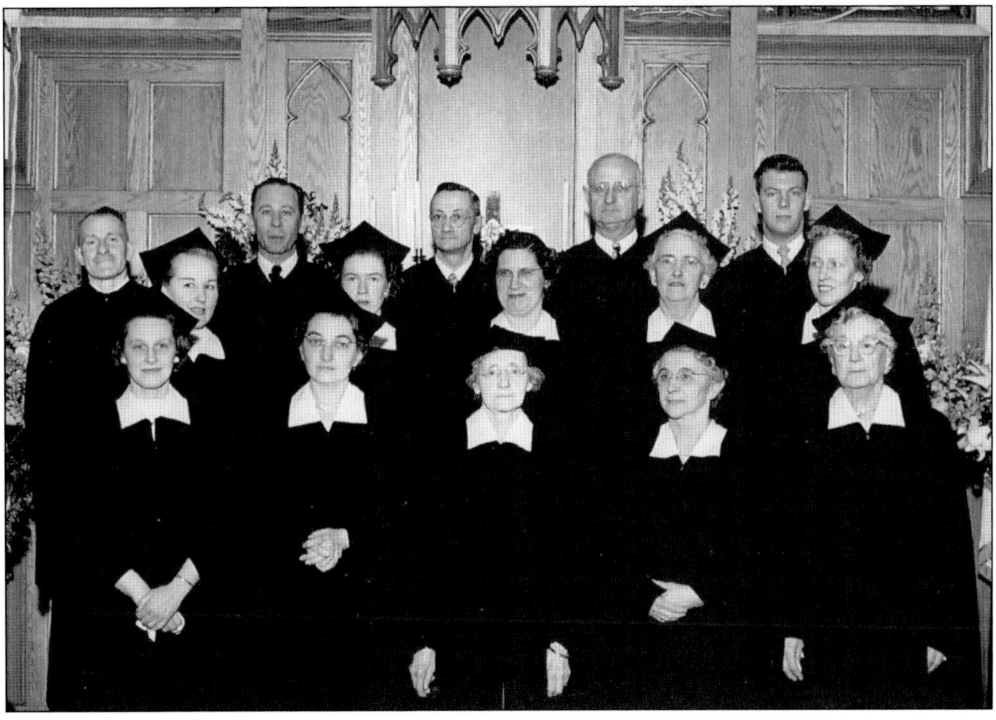

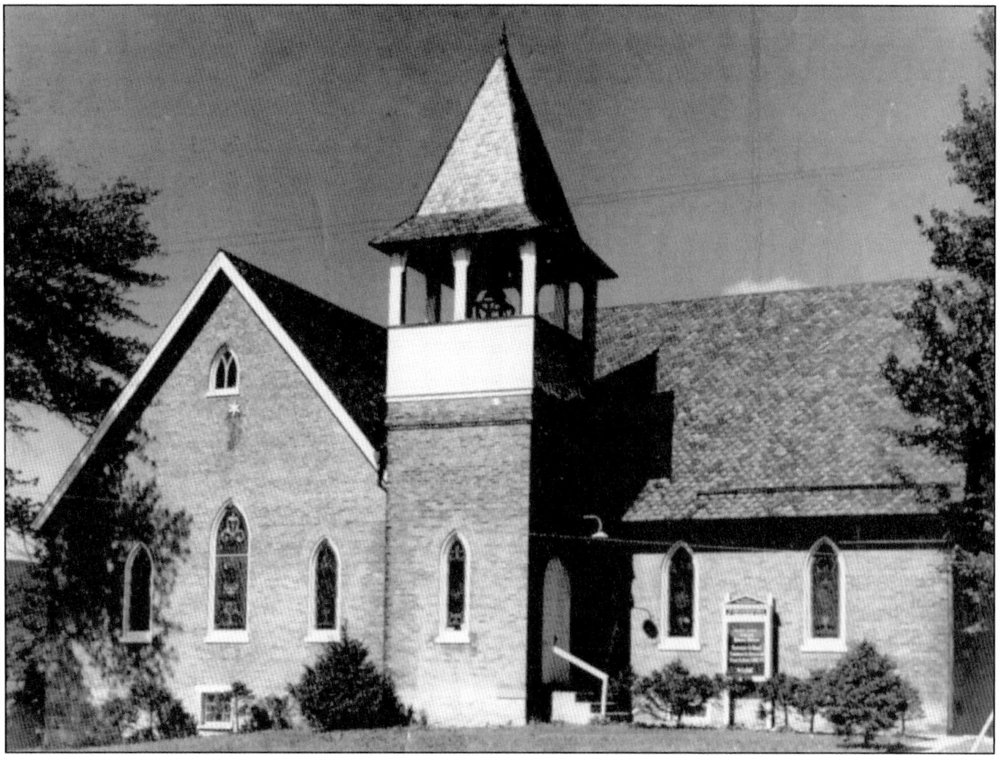

St. John Lutheran Church, locally known as the Brick Church, celebrated its 175th anniversary in 1992. The church was built from brick in 1848, destroyed by fire in 1896, and replaced within a year at the same site. (Courtesy St. John Lutheran Church.)

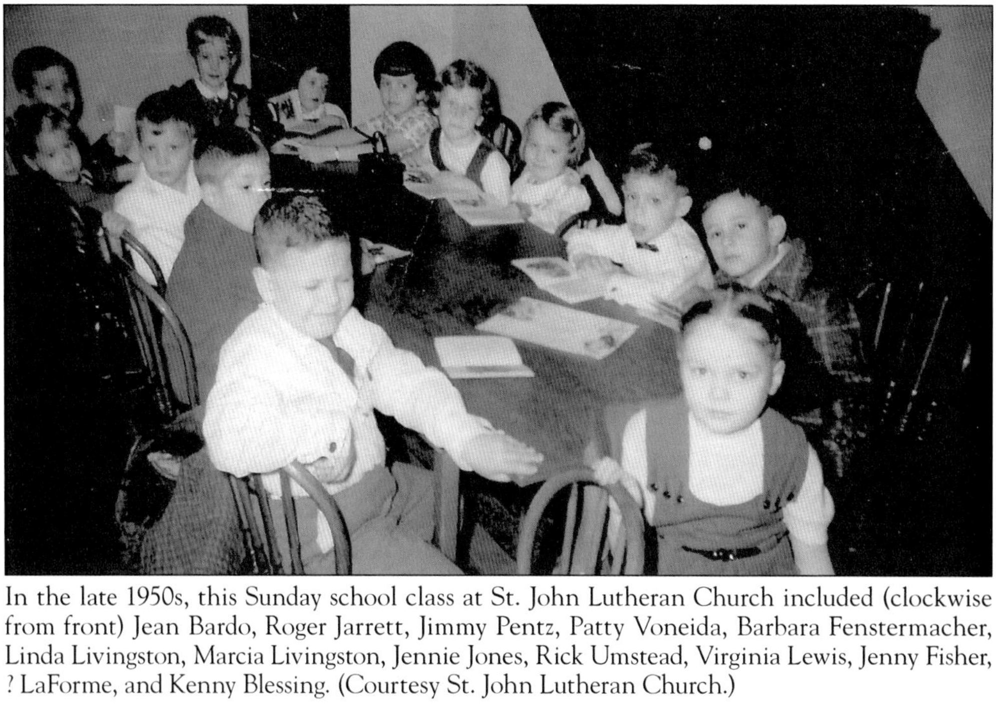

In the late 1950s, this Sunday school class at St. John Lutheran Church included (clockwise from front) Jean Bardo, Roger Jarrett, Jimmy Pentz, Patty Voneida, Barbara Fenstermacher, Linda Livingston, Marcia Livingston, Jennie Jones, Rick Umstead, Virginia Lewis, Jenny Fisher, ? LaForme, and Kenny Blessing. (Courtesy St. John Lutheran Church.)

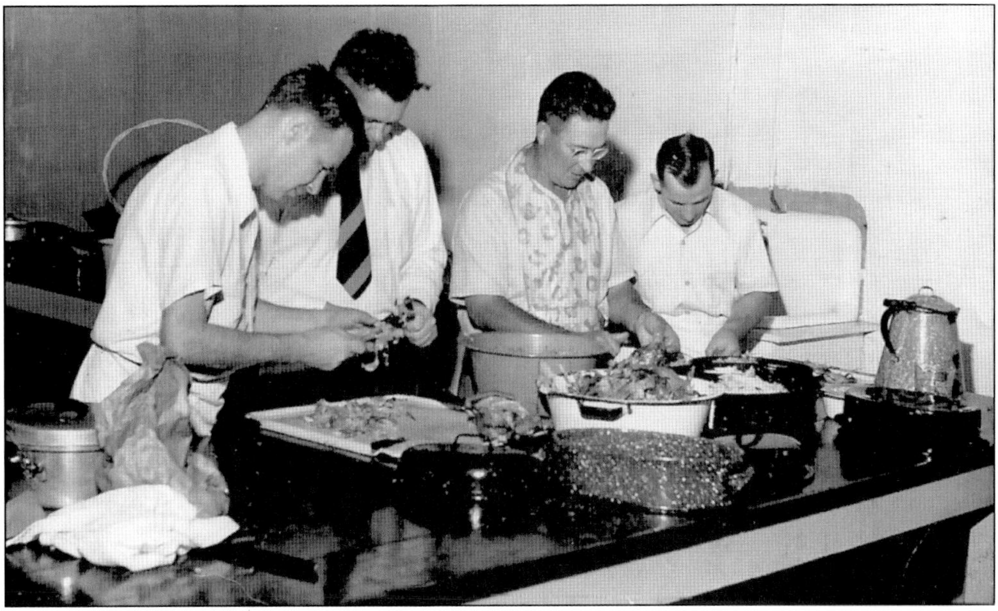

The best meals could be found in the kitchens of rural churches, where sit-down dinners and soups sales were commonly held as fundraisers. Above, these men from the Brick Church are busy deboning turkey in preparation for a turkey-based soup. They are, from left to right, Harry Gruver, Rev. Adam Bingaman, Clarence Livingston, and unidentified. Below are members of the Missionary Society, including, from left to right (first row) Cathryn Bush, Rosie Decker, Mrs. Bingaman with son David on her lap, Reba Gruver seated behind Mrs. Bingaman, Bessie Shrey, ? Harman, and two unidentified members; (second row) Mrs. Schrader, Mrs. More, Mrs. Metzger, Mrs. Morningstar, Grace Myers, unidentified, Bess Gruver, Ocie Pentz, Inez Persun, and three unidentified members. (Both courtesy St. John Lutheran Church.)

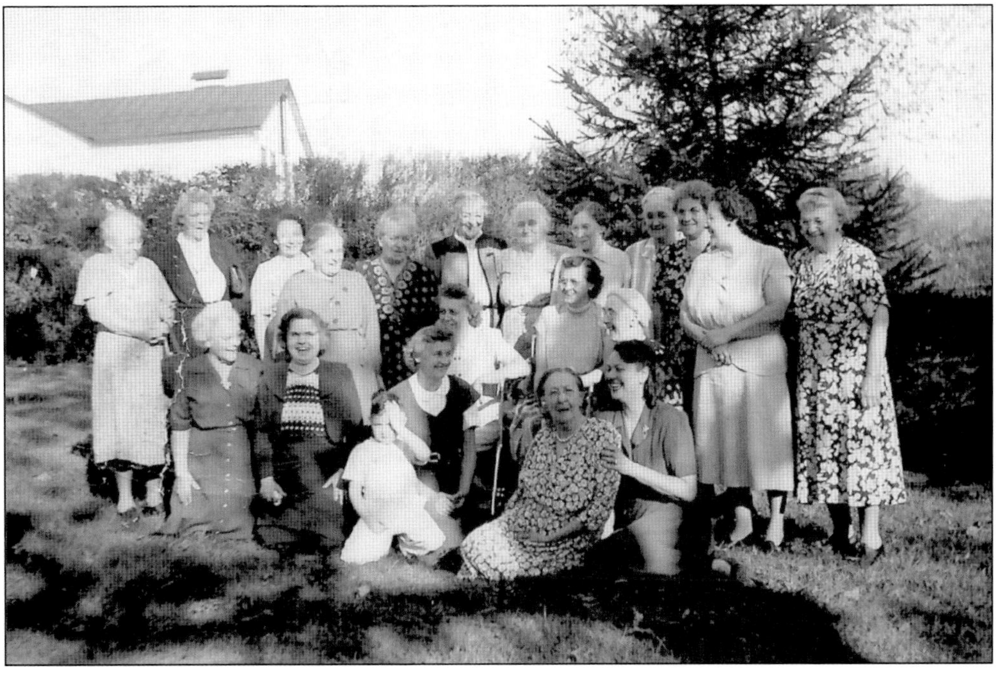

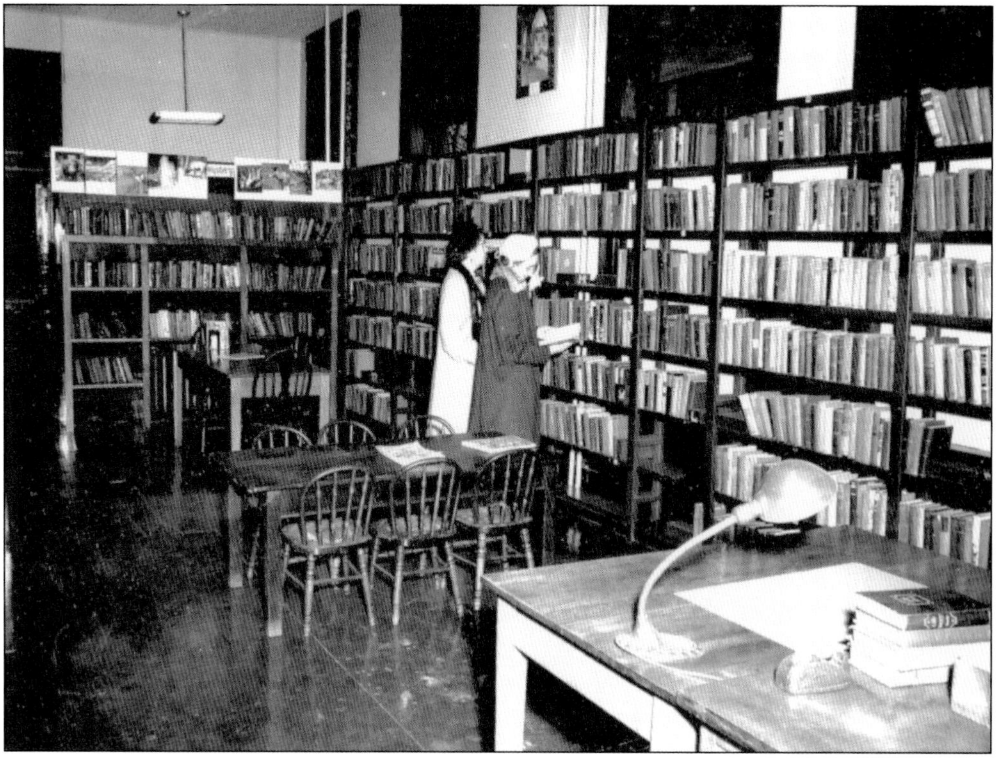

Above, Mrs. H.C. Yeager and Dorothy Shelley can be seen perusing the stacks at the Montgomery Library, located in the former First National Bank building. The Montgomery PTA founded the library in 1911 when it opened a free public library in the school library. In the summer of 1955, the Montgomery Library Association took ownership of files from the *Montgomery Mirror*, the local newspaper published between 1889 and 1944. Shown seated is Minnie Hartranft. Standing, from left to right, are Margaret Peters, Mrs. H.L. Yeager, Greta Groom, Max Mull, Roger Wertz, Beverly Christman, Kathryn Thomas, and Dorothy Shelley. (Both courtesy MAPL.)

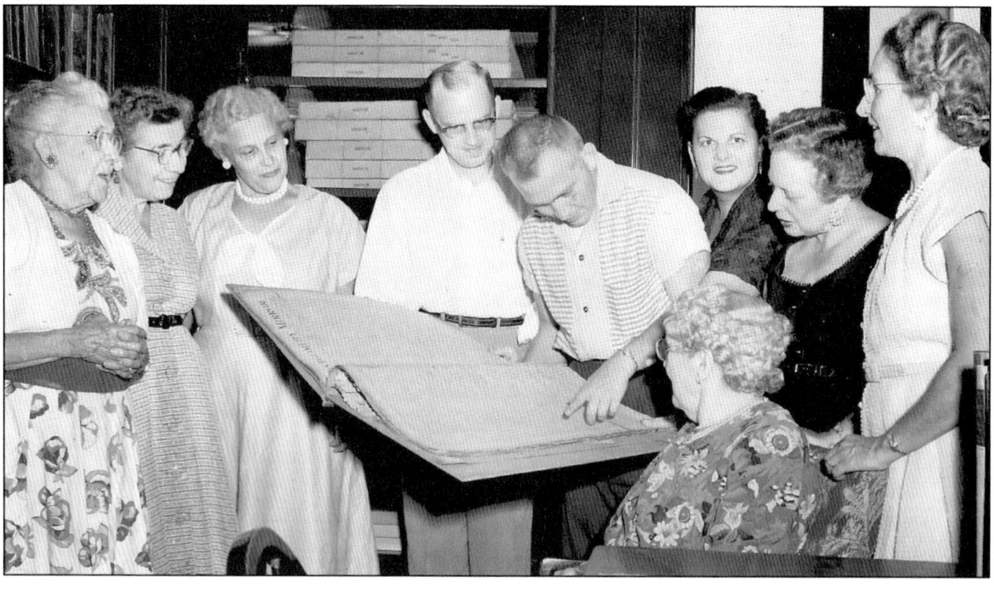

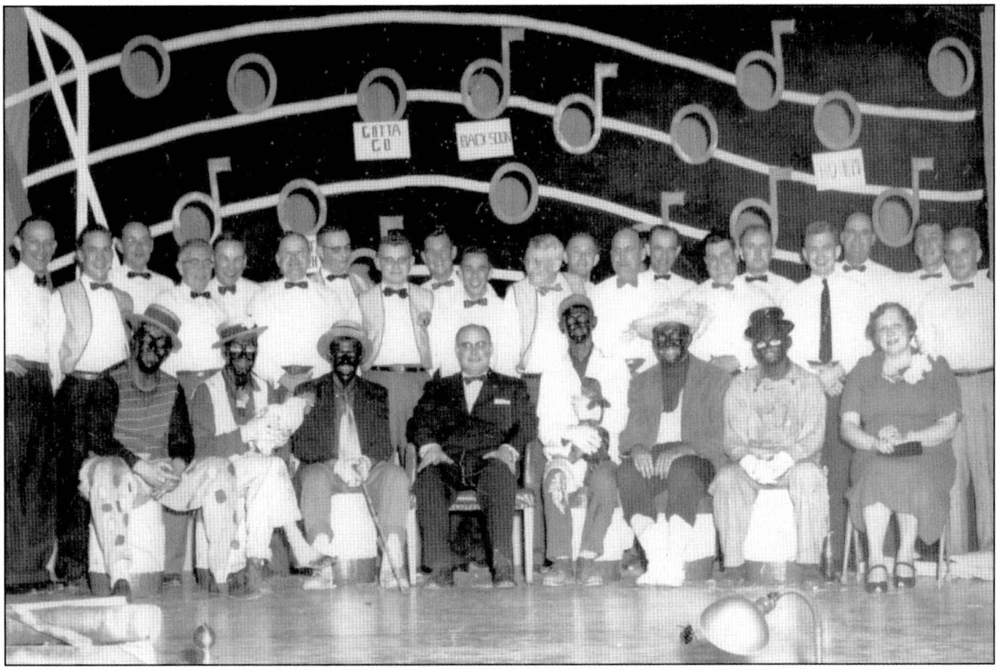

During the 1950s, the Lions Club Minstrel Shows raised money for various charities supported by the club. Pictured above, from left to right, are (seated) George Amos Smith, Clayton "Bud" Hoover, Richard Hartzell, James Pearce, William Troxell, William Creasy, William Bird, and Lillian Gramley; (standing) William Sandmeyer, Sterling "Bud" Taylor, Norman Bider, Wilbur Hall, William Young, Charles Green, John Miller, Rupert Miller, Harold Hinkle, Kenneth Hall, William Unsworth, George Deffenbaugh, Harold Emery, Raymond Gramley, Kenneth Blessing, Dunning Stamets, Roger Wertz, Joseph Farr, Delroy Schneck, and Franklin Hall. Another form of entertainment became available when the Pike Drive-In Theatre was built in 1954. Below, local company Abbey's Signs is seen erecting a neon sign that illuminated the site of the drive-in along Route 15. (Above, courtesy Montgomery Lions Club; below, courtesy Abbey Signs.)

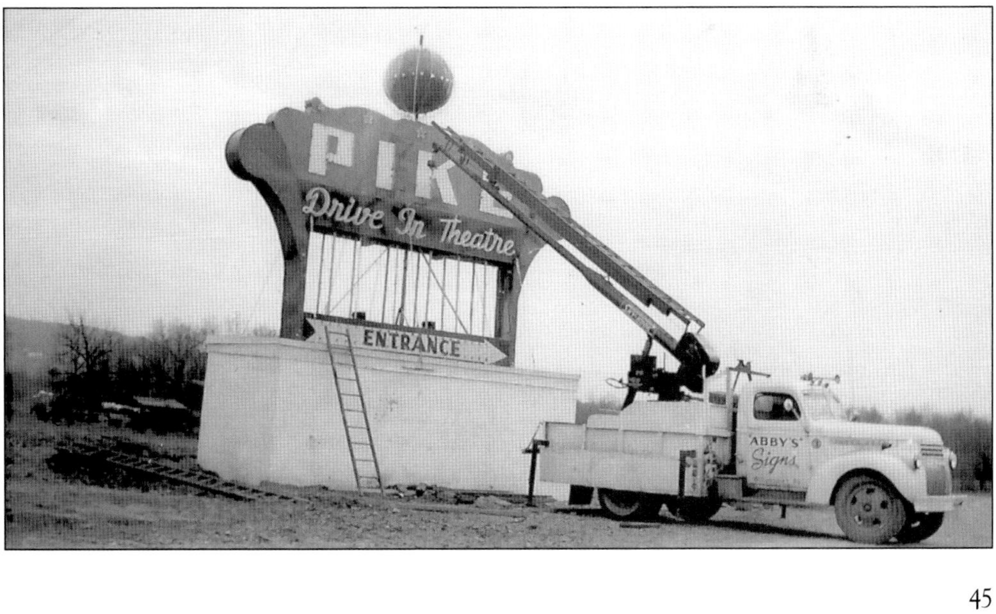

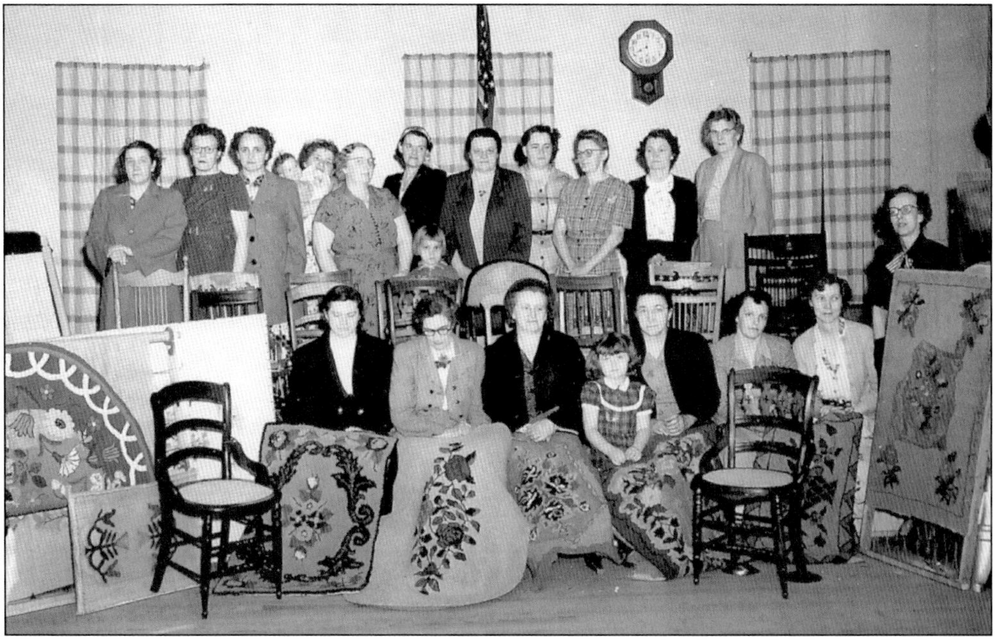

Examples of the hand-hooked rugs and re-caned chairs completed by the members of Eagle Grange No. 1 are on display above. In 1945, the family-oriented Eagle Grange organization sponsored a Juvenile Grange for children. Roxanna Hively served as matron for this group of children ranging from 5 to 16 years old. Pictured below are members of the Eagle Juvenile Grange No. 307 in 1955. Included, from left to right, are (first row) Ross Jarrett, Mary Tennant, ? Brouse, Eleanor McQuay, Joyce Jarrett, and Grace Vitkus; (second row) Barbara Staggert, Charles Brouse, Sidney Jarrett, Robert Brouse, Nancy Hively, Joyce ?, Dot Staggert, and Carol Hitesman. In 1966, the Juvenile Grange was known as the Junior Grange. (Above, courtesy Ralph Baker; below; courtesy MAPL.)

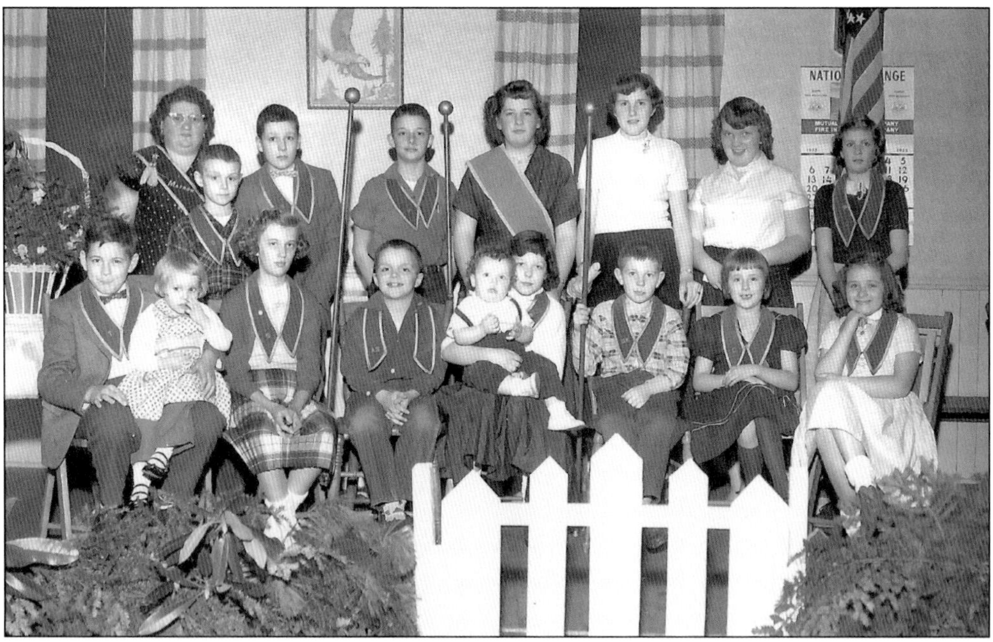

Eagle Grange members Sylvia Baker and Roxanna Hively show the before-and-after versions of caned chairs; re-caning chairs was just one of the projects the women of the Grange worked on. At the Grange's 100th anniversary in 1971, Mrs. Hively was honored for serving as Grange secretary almost continuously since 1956. (Courtesy Ralph Baker.)

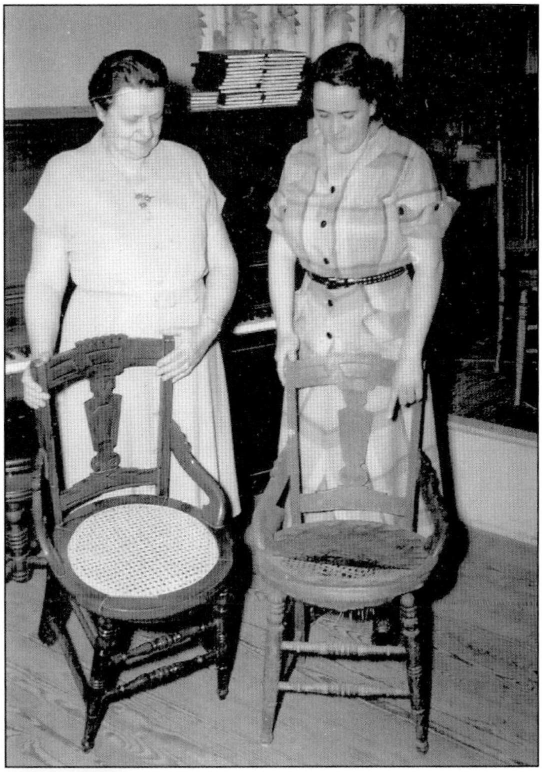

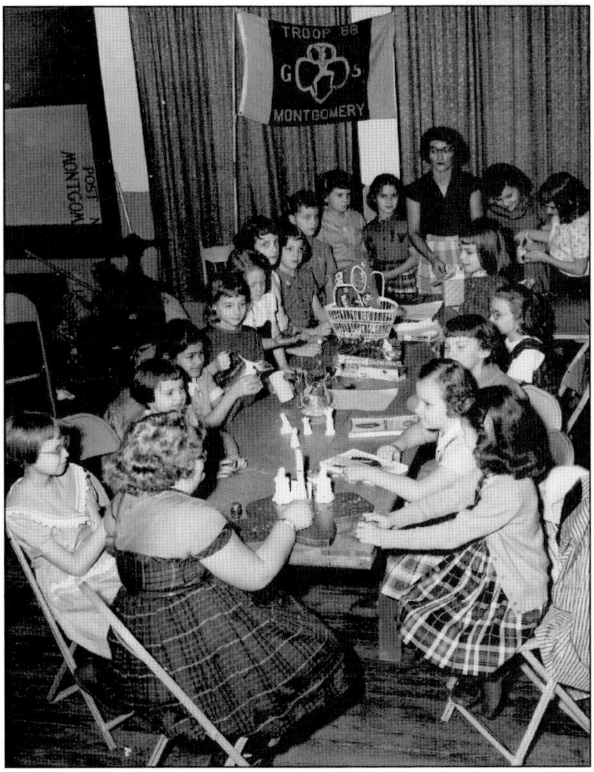

Members of Montgomery Girl Scout Troop 68 work on a project with their troop leader, Joan Taylor, looking on. The Girl Scouts organization in Montgomery began in 1940 when the borough's Junior Women's Study Group sponsored Intermediate Troop 14. By the mid-1940s, over 100 girls were involved, and by the 1960s, over 150 girls were members in all three levels of Girl Scouts troops: Brownies, Intermediate, and Seniors. (Courtesy MAPL.)

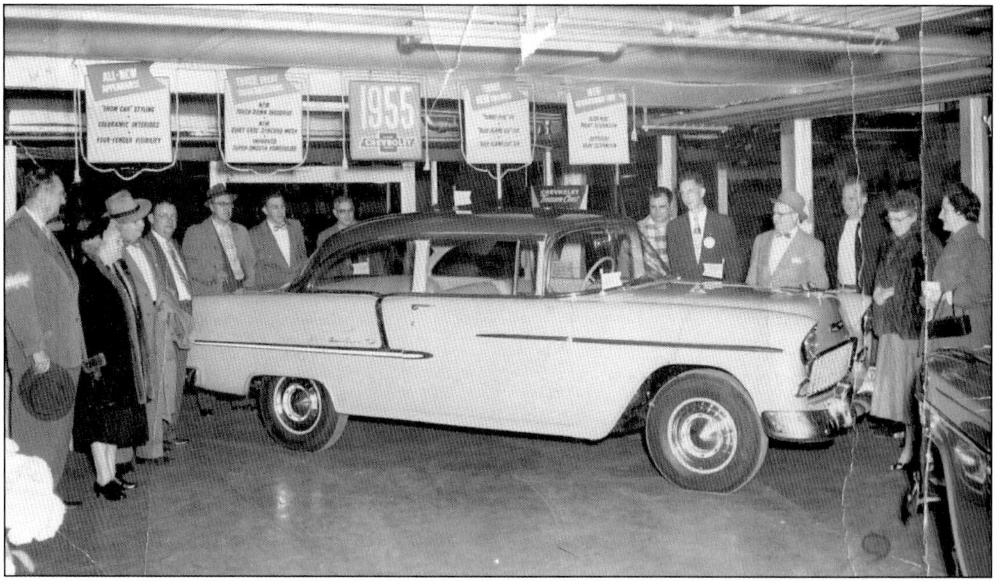

The Hulsizer Chevrolet car lot, located just north of Montgomery, held the New Car Show Day in 1955. Viewing the latest models are, from left to right, Paul Decker, Ruth Decker, Carl Stover, Bill Karshner, George Schneck, Delroy Schneck, Leo Crandel, Delbert "Bus" Phillips, Max McCarty, Lester Page, Robert Shaffer, Milly Schneck, and Grace Stover. (Courtesy Hulsizer Chevrolet.)

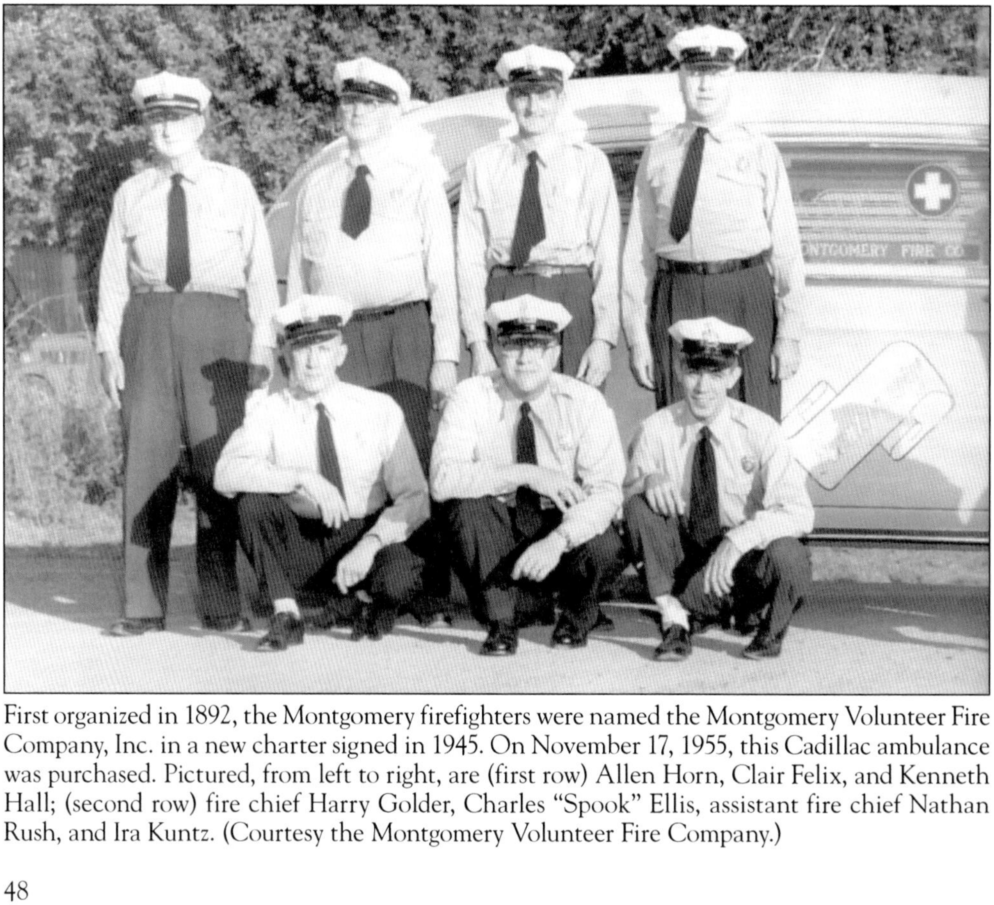

First organized in 1892, the Montgomery firefighters were named the Montgomery Volunteer Fire Company, Inc. in a new charter signed in 1945. On November 17, 1955, this Cadillac ambulance was purchased. Pictured, from left to right, are (first row) Allen Horn, Clair Felix, and Kenneth Hall; (second row) fire chief Harry Golder, Charles "Spook" Ellis, assistant fire chief Nathan Rush, and Ira Kuntz. (Courtesy the Montgomery Volunteer Fire Company.)

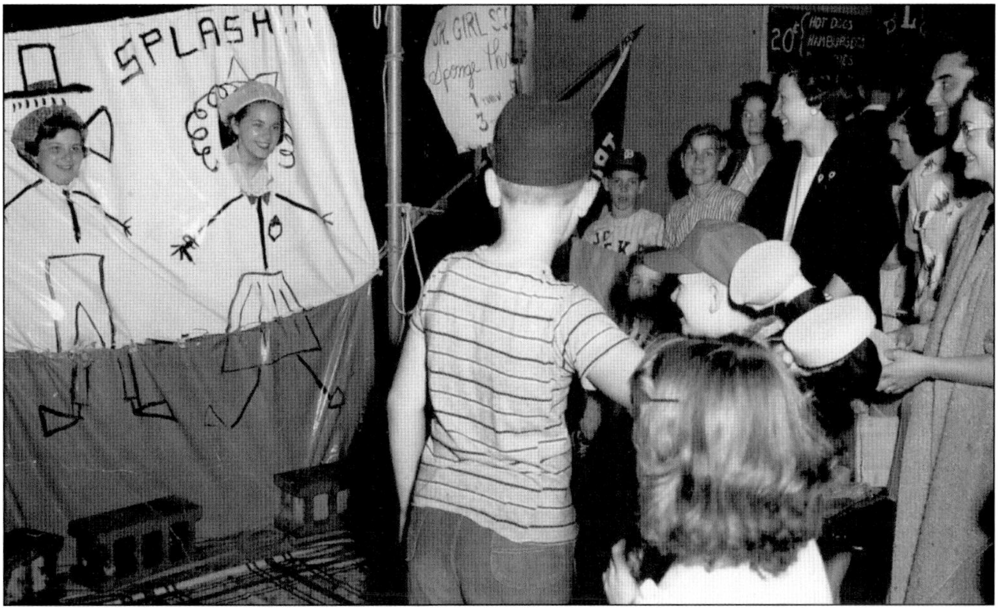

On Saturday, May 17, 1958, Montgomery hosted its first annual Crocus Festival. Part of the festivities included this sponge-throw game, sponsored by Senior Girl Scout Troop 68. Leona Dewalt (left) and Peggy Tobias encouraged participants to throw wet sponges at them for a small fee. Dot Sandmeyer, Phoebe Rodgers, and Sherry Burley can be seen in the crowd. Peggy's mother, Mary Tobias, and her sister, Debbie Tobias, are also present. (Courtesy MAPL.)

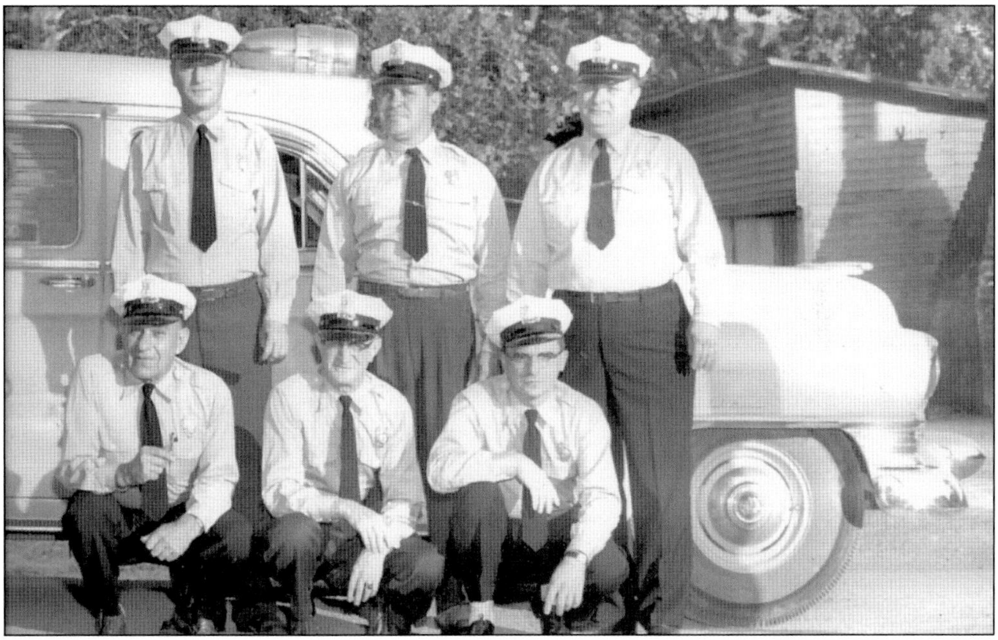

Pictured with the new ambulance the Montgomery Volunteer Fire Company purchased in 1955 are, from left to right, (first row) Myron Reichley, vice president Joseph Goldstein, and Paul Pentz; (second row) Herman Wertz, Ray Kerwell Jr., and Capt. Lehman King. In 1949, a vehicle that was used as an ambulance had been purchased from C.M. Zellers, the local undertaker. (Courtesy the Montgomery Volunteer Fire Company.)

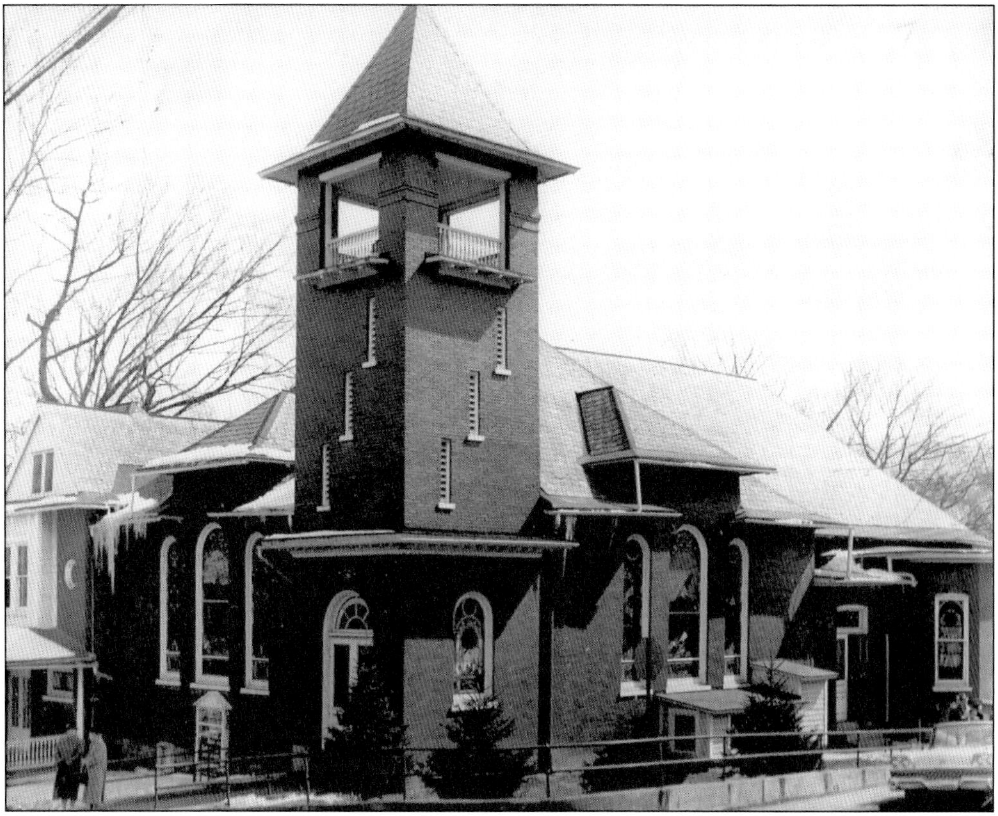

The First Methodist Church building seen above was built in 1905 at the corner of West Houston Avenue and Bower Street at a cost of $13,000. Rev. Norman Smith served as pastor at this church from 1918 to 1923; he was the first to own a car, so a garage was built to house it. The previous church and parsonage for First Methodist stood on the Hulsizer Chevrolet property and for years, the church building had been used as Hulsizer's service department. Below, Lillian Dunn Starr (wearing white hat) is assisted by Leona Dewalt in a Sunday school class at First Methodist. (Both courtesy Stamets family.)

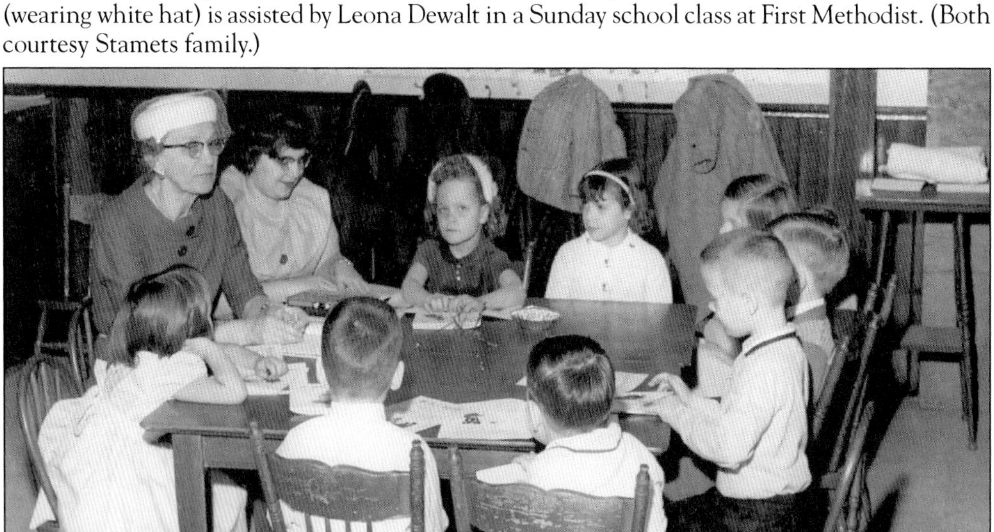

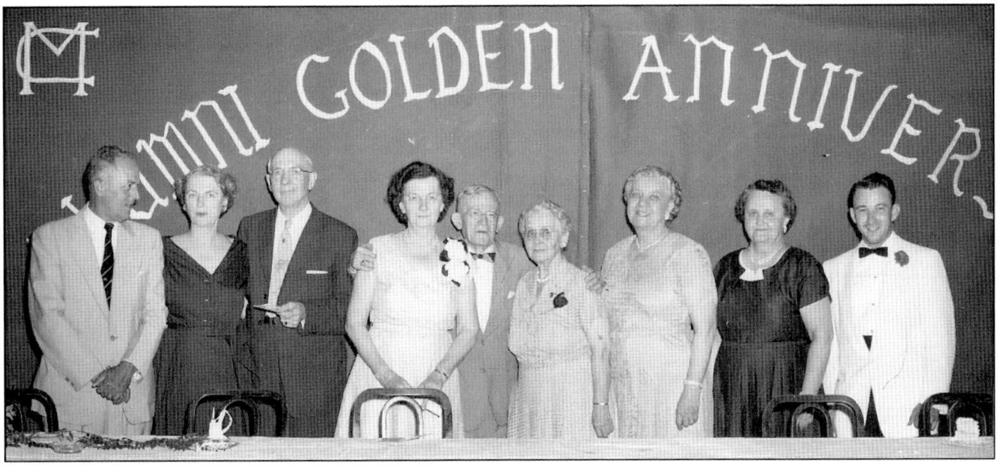

The Montgomery Alumni Association celebrated its Golden Anniversary in June 1955 at the Benevolent and Protective Order of Elks (BPOE) ballroom on West Fourth Street in Williamsport. Representing the first graduating class of 1905 was Hullda Piatt, who ceremoniously cut a 10-tier cake and accepted a gold trophy on behalf of her class. Also honored at the dinner were William Schnee, the first supervising principal, and Charles Potter, the principal between 1920 and 1935. Pictured above, from left to right, are Glenwood Crist (supervising principal, 1951–1970), Olive Hughes Cliff (class of 1909), Charles Potter, Hullda Piatt, William Schnee, Florence Strouse Speigelmire (class of 1907), Caroline Grittner Pauling (class of 1941), Evadne Ruggles (honorary alumni), and Byron Kilmer (class of 1943). (Both courtesy MAPL.)

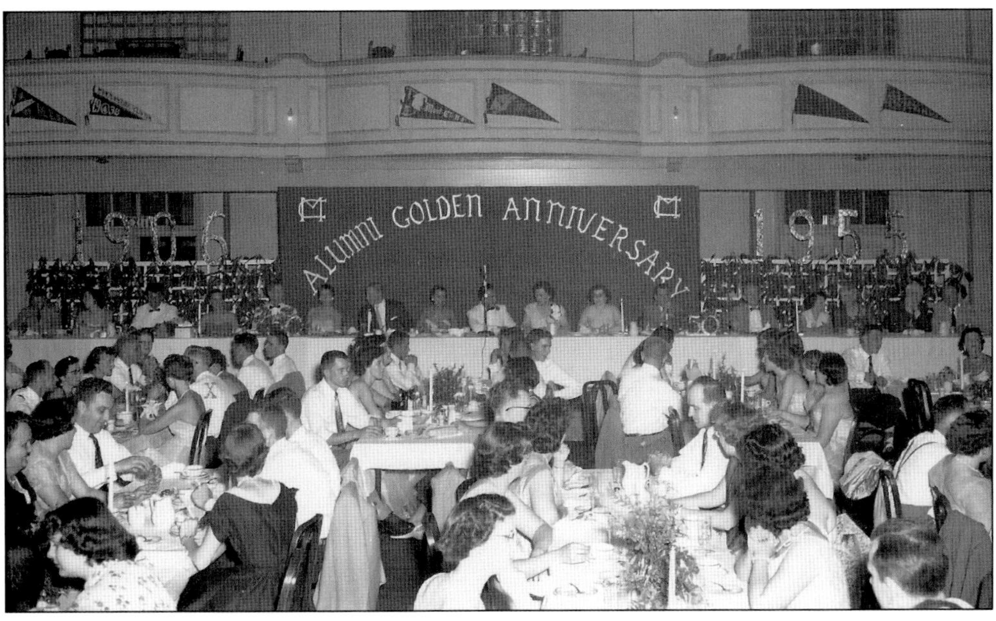

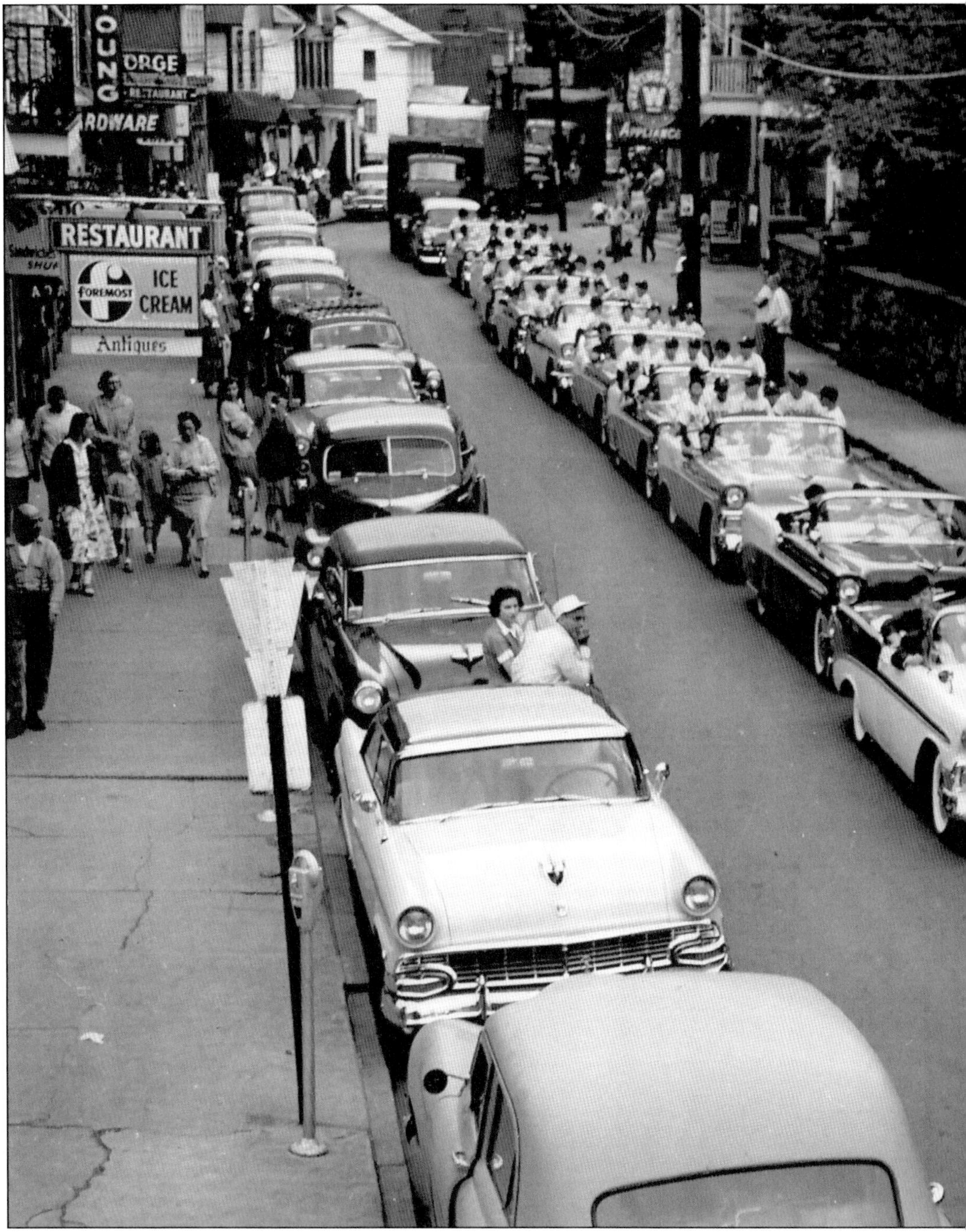

Looking north up Main Street in Montgomery, several businesses can be seen. On the left in the foreground, signs with the words *restaurant*, *Foremost ice cream*, and *antiques* advertised the location of Forrest "Ham" Bardo's Forrest Tea Room restaurant. Behind the Tea Room are W.C. Young Hardware store, Kulp's Restaurant, Charles "Spook" Ellis's newsstand, Weaver's Restaurant, and the Eagle Theatre in the background. The couple standing between the parked cars at left is identified as Irma and Harold Emery. In the background on the right, the Westinghouse appliance sign was at Hull's Appliance store. In the foreground on the right, Mrs. Bussler is standing in

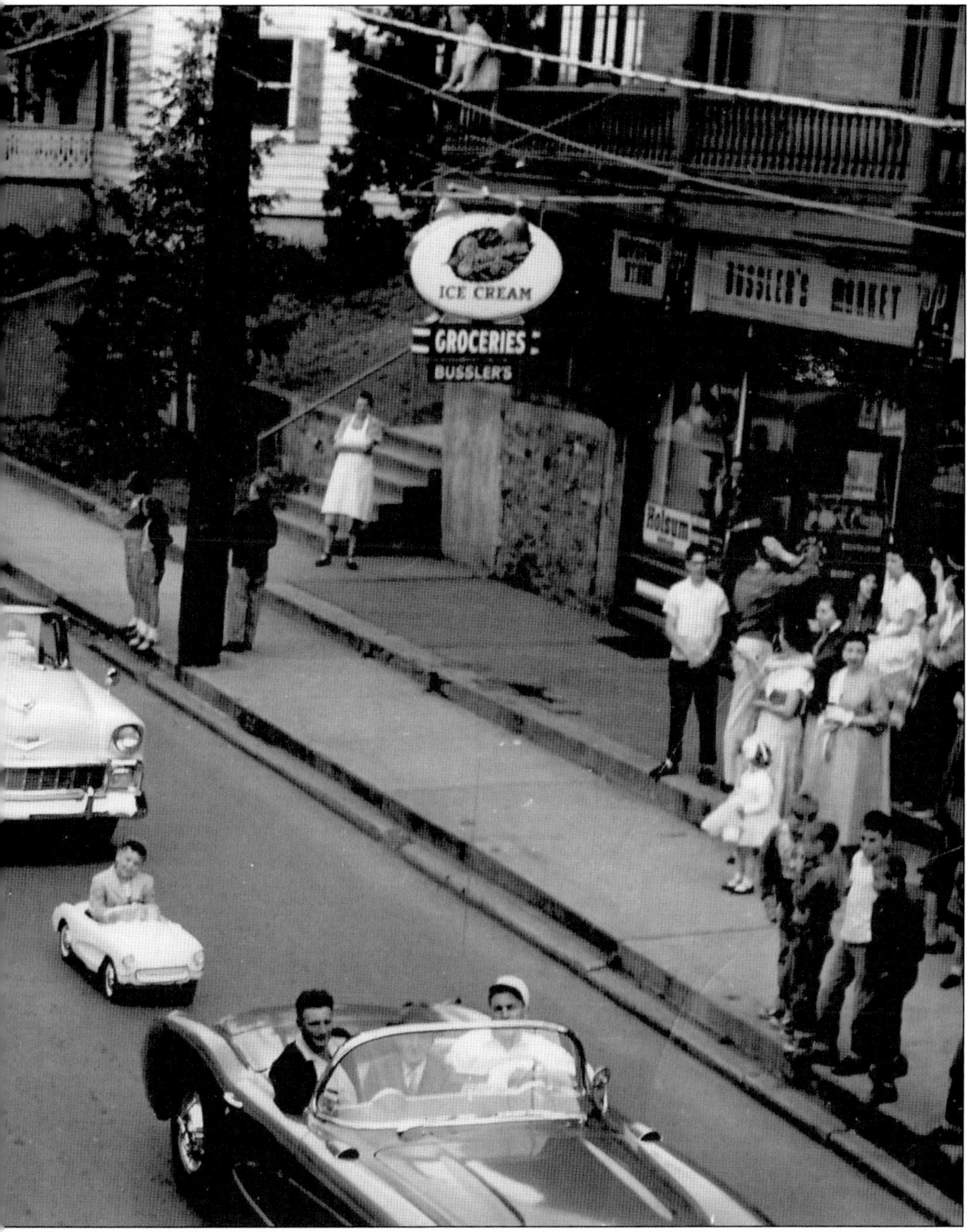

front of the stairs under the Breyer's Ice Cream sign, which is hanging in front of Bussler's Store. In the lead car, the driver is Delroy Schneck, with Burgess Ollie Housel seated next to him and Little League's President Kahle seated on the passenger side. Schneck's son Bill is driving the toy car, whose battery ran out of power just minutes after this photograph was taken. Delroy's wife, Shirley Schneck, and daughter, Cathie, are standing on the sidewalk in the front of the crowd near Bussler's Store. (Courtesy Hulsizer's Chevrolet.)

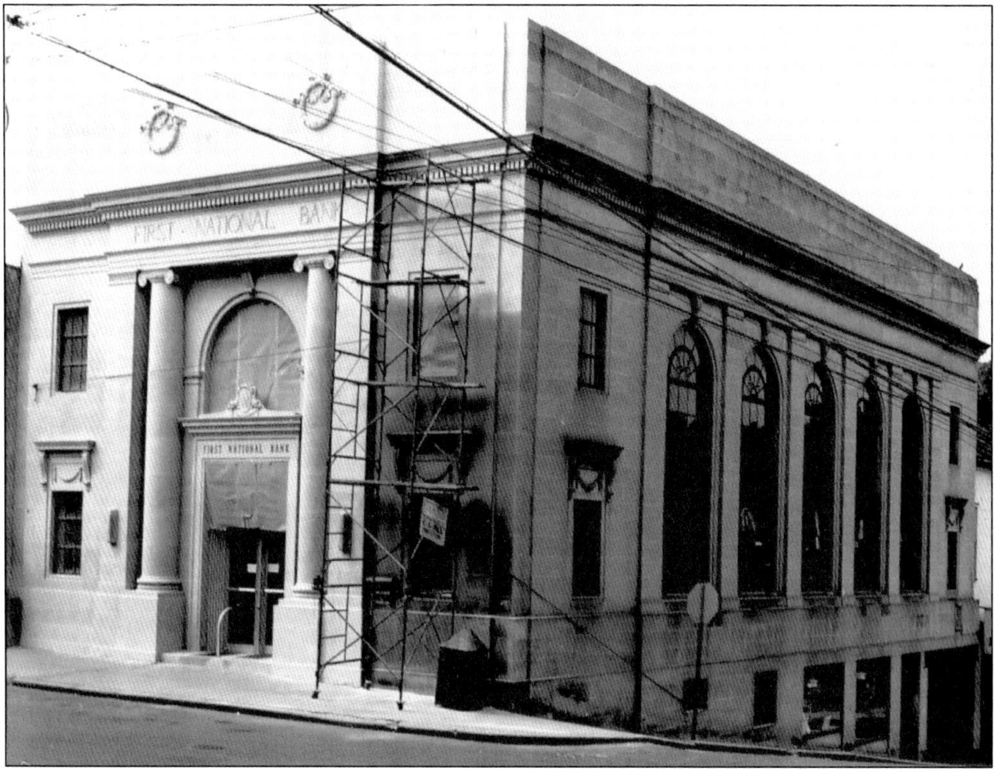

In 1959, the First National Bank building underwent renovations on the exterior and a modernization of the interior. Upon completion, the public was invited to an open house to view the updates. Pictured below is the updated customer lounge area located on the left as customers entered the building. Local businesses were hired for the renovation work: George Weller was general contractor with Willard Dewalt in charge of painting, Robert Shaffer handled the electrical work, and Paul Shrey took care of the plumbing. Irvin's Furniture Company, Isaac Decker, and H.E. Pysher provided furniture. Page Upholstering and Donald Hutchinson did the upholstery work. (Both courtesy MAPL.)

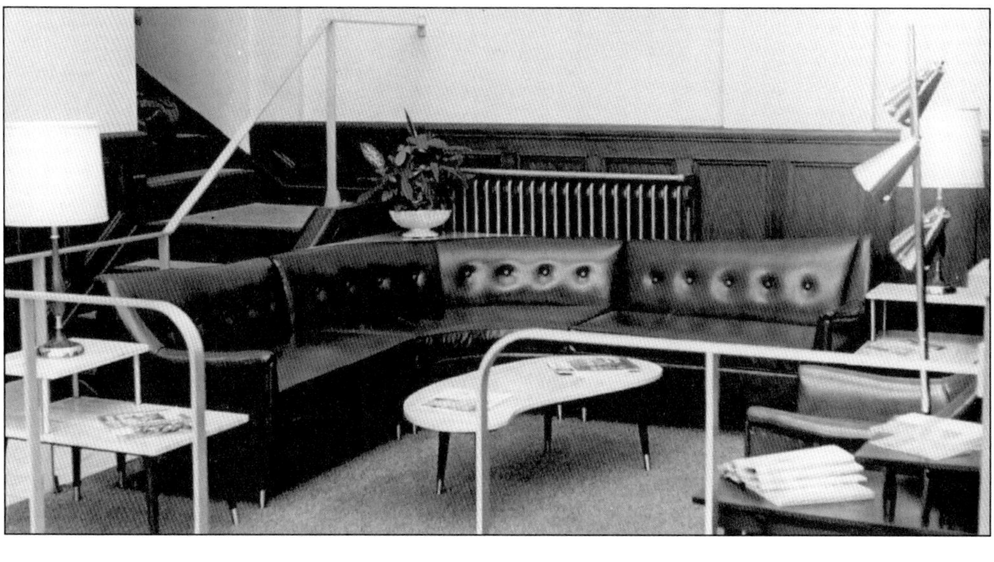

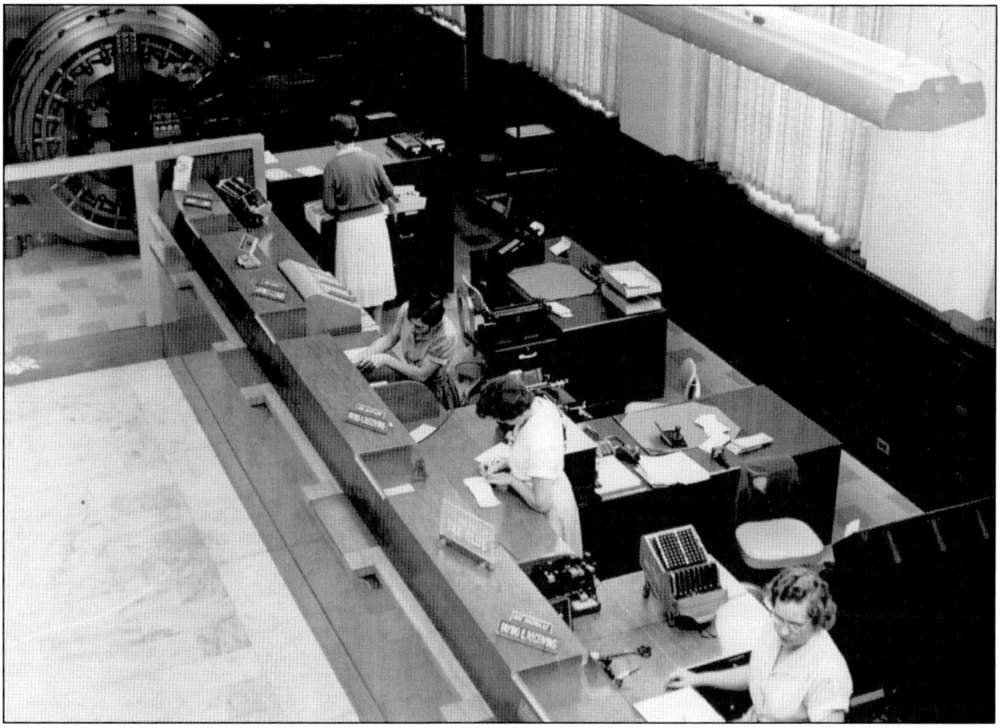

Before the renovation, the First National Bank personnel, cashiers, and tellers were partitioned behind glass walls and sliding windows. These were removed and the space was painted, tiled, refurbished, and updated with new furnishings. Pictured above at the new teller stations are, from front to back, Shirley Nicholas, Mary Bartlow, Jennie Aunkst, and Alma Wagner. (Courtesy MAPL.)

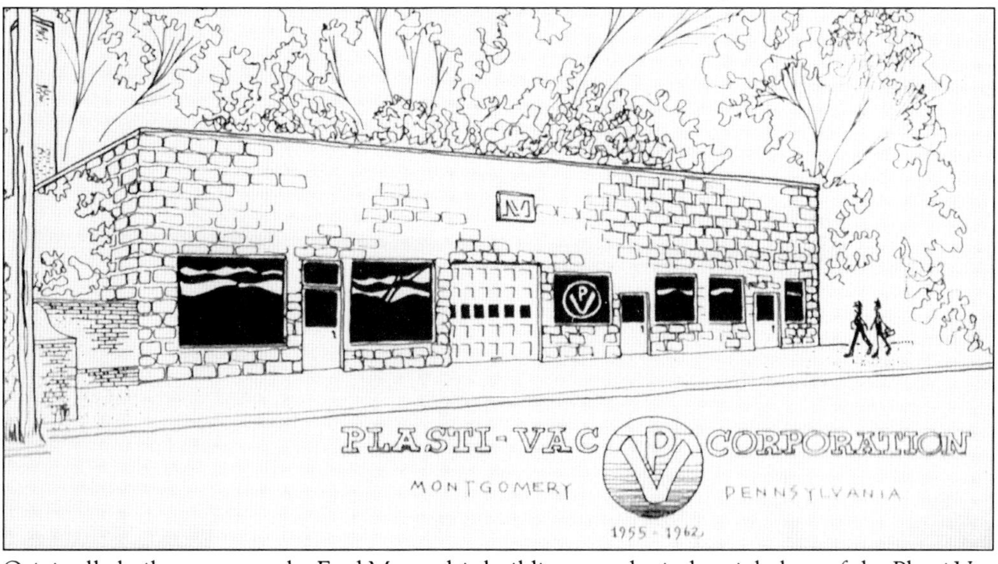

Originally built as a garage by Fred Marx, this building was the industrial plant of the Plasti-Vac Corporation from 1955 until 1962 when the company built a modern facility on Route 15 and moved its operations. Located on Montgomery Street at the site of the current fire hall, this building was sold to the borough and after remodeling, opened in 1964 as the new hall for the borough. (Courtesy Chip and Thomas Frazier.)

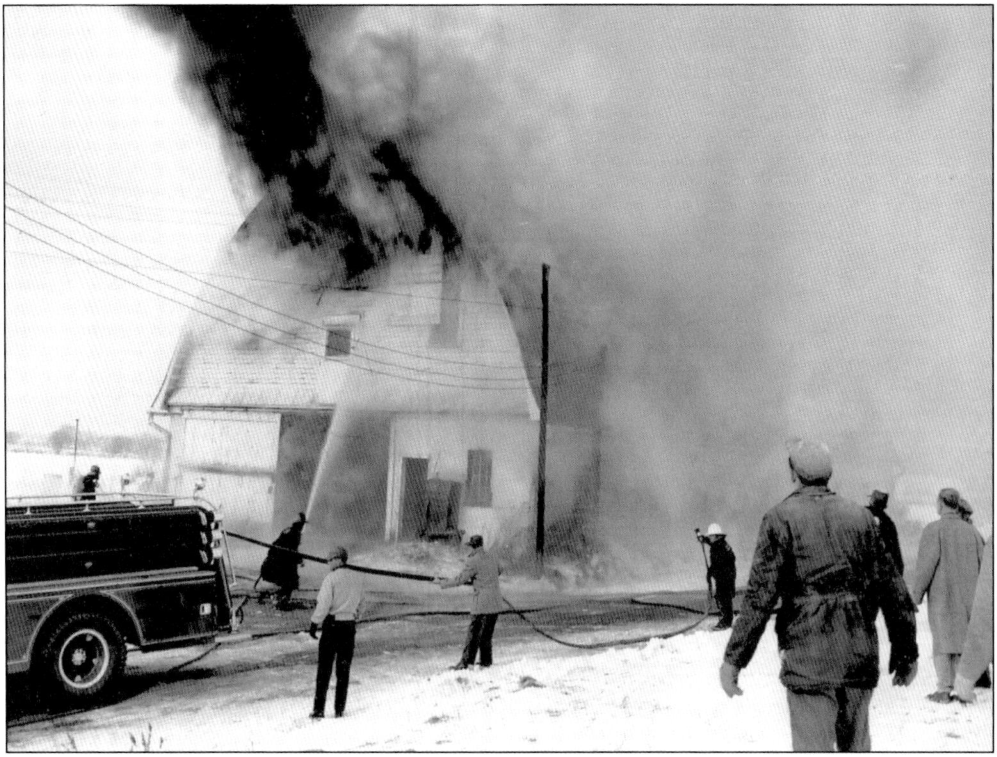

During the mid-1950s, a two-bay truck room was built as an addition on the Clinton Township fire hall to house an equipment truck purchased in 1953. Walkie-talkies and a mobile two-way radio were installed in the 1946 pumper. In 1959, the Clinton Township Volunteer Fire Company received a new Howe pumper, which was used at this fire on the Harold Bishop Farm. (Courtesy Clinton Township Volunteer Fire Company.)

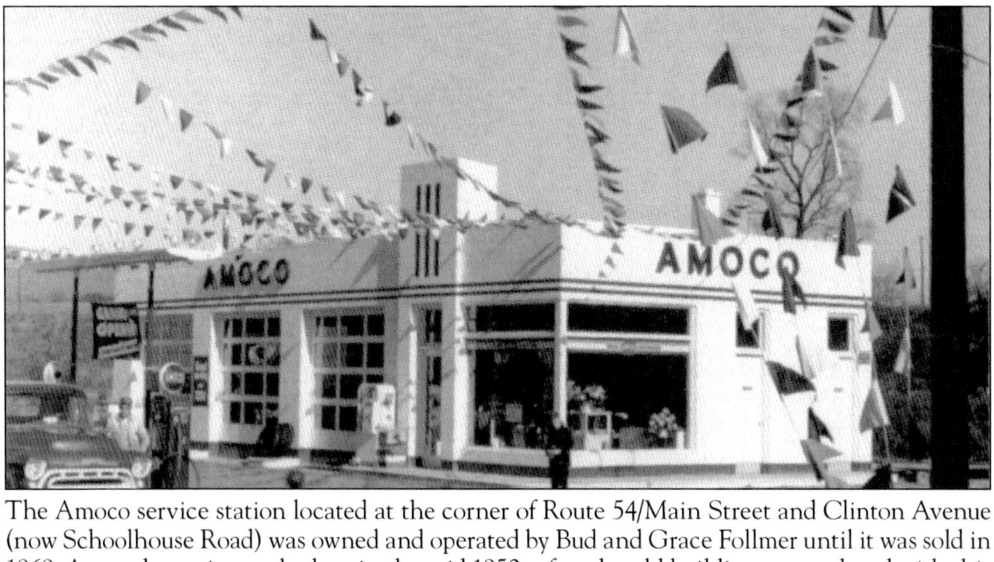

The Amoco service station located at the corner of Route 54/Main Street and Clinton Avenue (now Schoolhouse Road) was owned and operated by Bud and Grace Follmer until it was sold in 1969. A grand opening took place in the mid-1950s after the old building was replaced with this modern facility. Bud Follmer is pictured at the gas pump (left) as son Andy looks on. (Courtesy Joyce Houser.)

Three

The 1960s

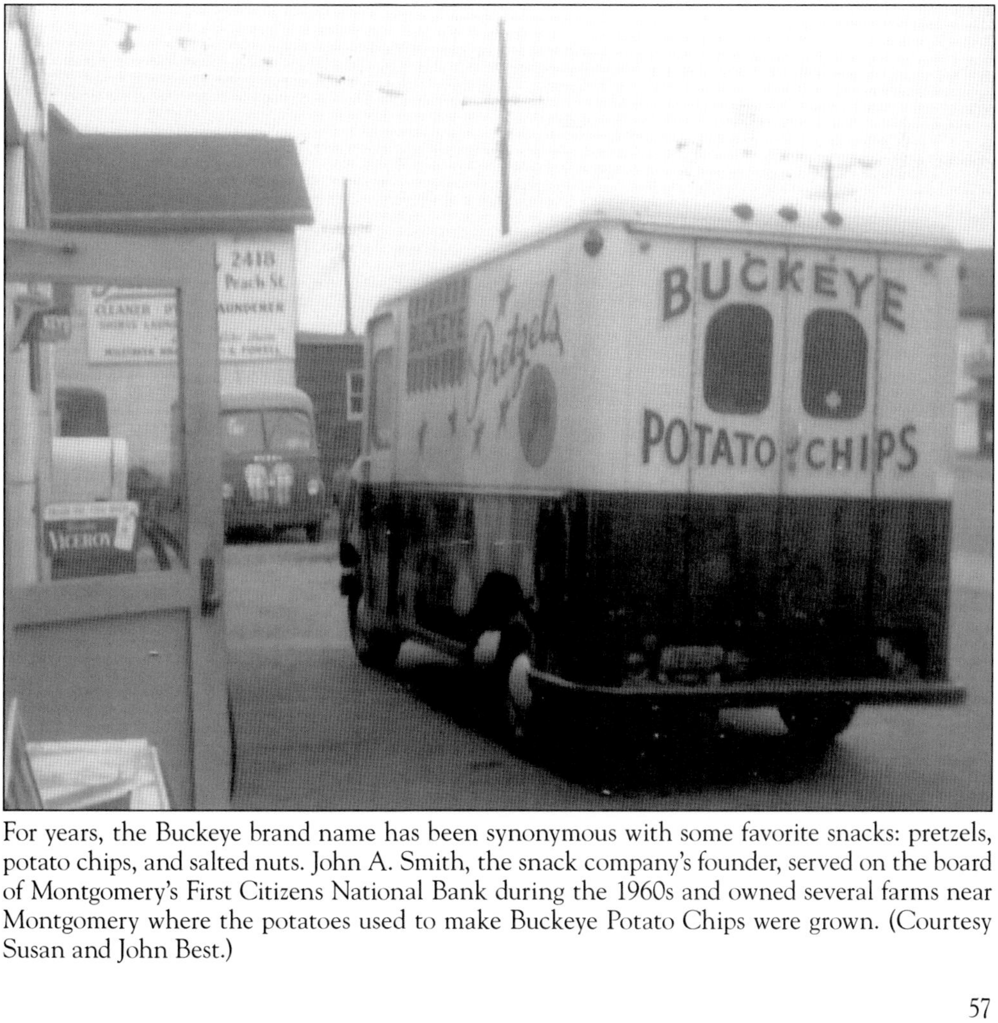

For years, the Buckeye brand name has been synonymous with some favorite snacks: pretzels, potato chips, and salted nuts. John A. Smith, the snack company's founder, served on the board of Montgomery's First Citizens National Bank during the 1960s and owned several farms near Montgomery where the potatoes used to make Buckeye Potato Chips were grown. (Courtesy Susan and John Best.)

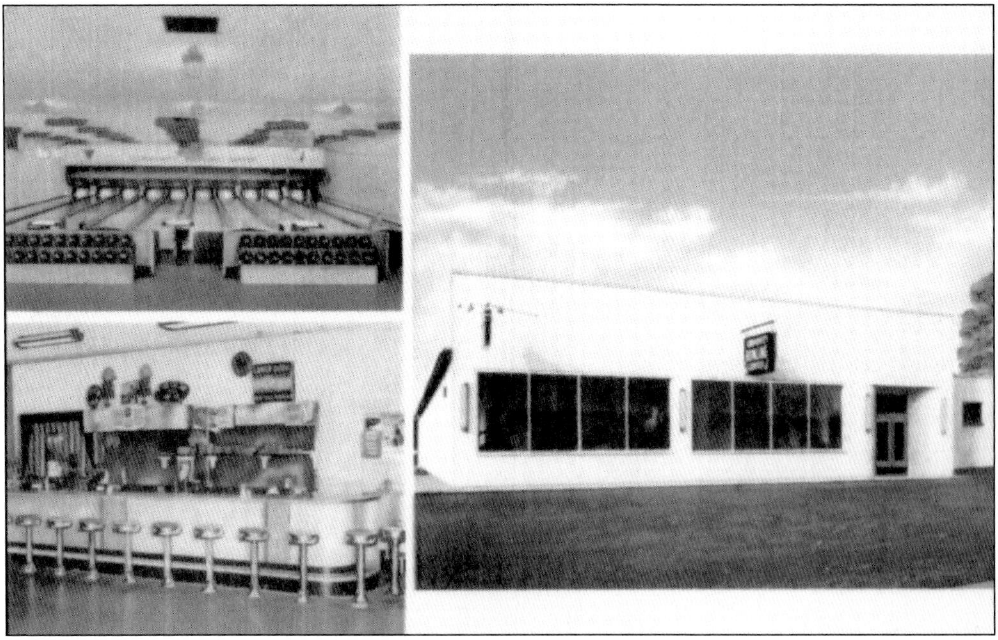

The newly renovated Community Bowling Center pictured above changed ownership in 1961 from Fred Tebbs and Max Cole, who built it in 1951, to Alem Hull, Marshall Hull, and Phillip Hall, who owned it until it was destroyed by fire in 1965. In 1969, the location became known as the Montgomery Plaza. Several shops were established including Dugan's Barber Shop, Weis Market, and the State Liquor Store; a bank branch office also occupied the space. On the other side of town, Henry Bressler operated the roadside diner pictured below. (Above, courtesy MAPL; below, courtesy Janet Bennett.)

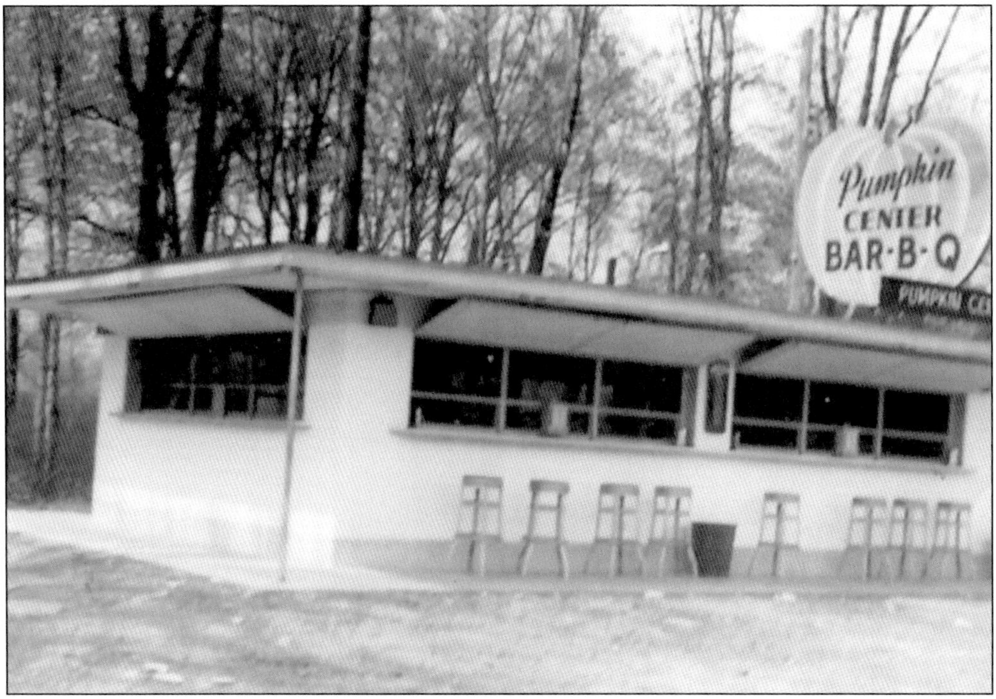

"SMOKEY" STOVER'S

USED CARS

"A little out of the way —

But a lot less to pay!"

Buy Sell Trade

Phone Montgomery KI 7-3268

Stover's Used Cars was owned and operated by Lester "Smokey" Stover from 1956 to 1980. Located at the corner of West Houston Avenue and Cemetery Hill Road, it was the only competitor with Hulsizer's Chevrolet for car sales. During the mid-1960s, the borough had about a dozen service stations and body shops. (Courtesy Joe Stover.)

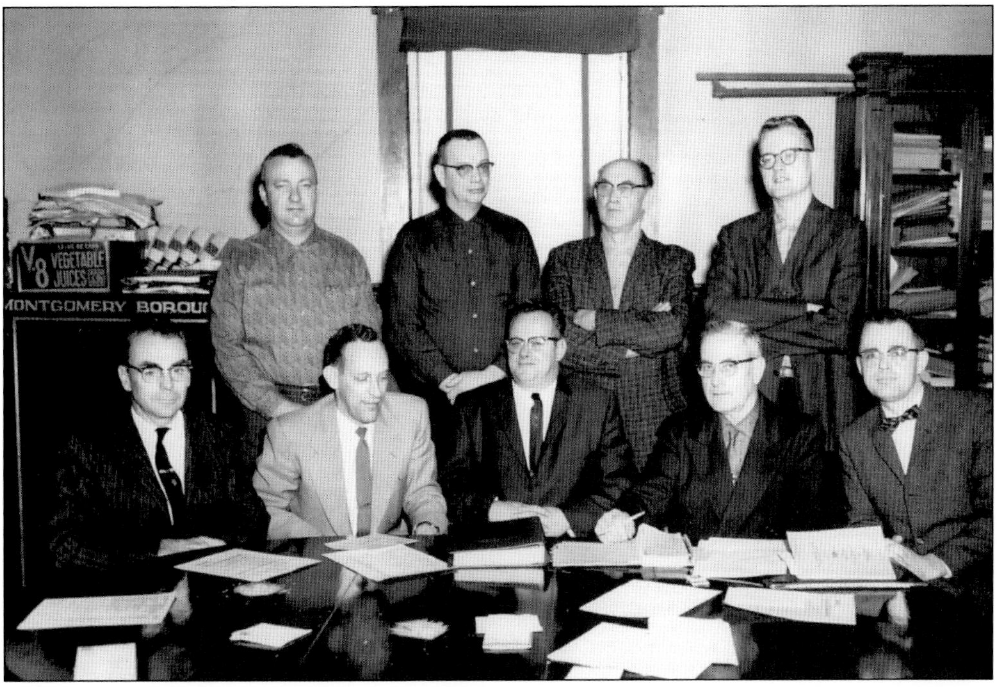

The members of the Montgomery Borough Council, pictured from left to right, are (first row) Harold Chamberlain, council president William Sandmeyer, Montgomery mayor Raymond Taylor, council secretary Leon Crandall, and solicitor Robert Wise; (second row) Paul Shrey, John Miller, council vice president Charles "Spook" Ellis, and Dr. Richard Nierle. (Courtesy MAPL.)

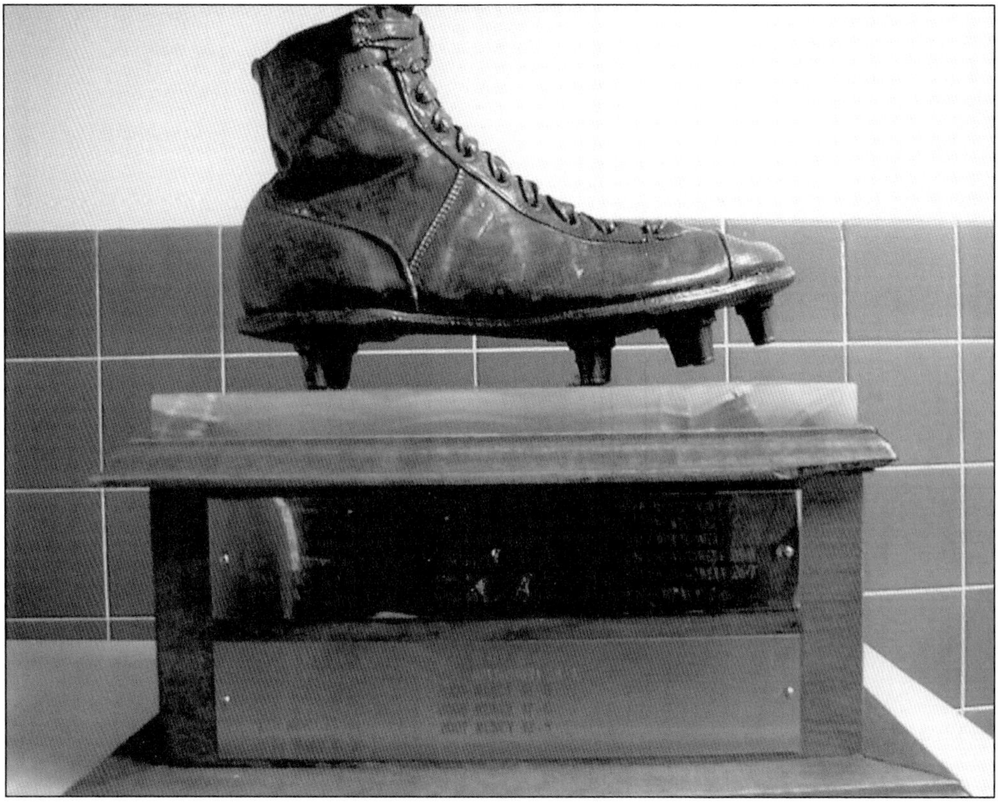

Rival football teams from Muncy and Montgomery continue to compete annually for the Old Shoe trophy. In 1967, Montgomery team members included, from left to right, (first row) coach Harold Stackhouse, Larry Miller, Gene Bartlett, Dennis Miller, Dave Drumm, Bill Hall, Jay LaForme, Tom Drumm, Curtis Barto, Tom Hinkle, Lanny Wertz, Fred Taylor, Ron Sampsell, Parvin Miller, John Lynch, Lonnie Dewalt, and Charles Fry; (second row) Doug Barto, Jack Bishop, Fred Hill, Rich Russell, Lynn Crist, Jerry Walborn, Jim Drumm, John Buck, Dan Lynch, Bob Klinger, Dave Daily, Ed Fry, Rick Kemery, Gordon Barto, Lenny Morehart, and coach Gus Spizziri; (third row) Scott Hinkle, John Hauck, Ned Neitz, Dan Pauling, Paul Shreck, Tom Fox, Perry Bullis, Bill Schneck, Rich Thomas, Steve Myers, Ken Fornwalt, Chris Wagner, Dave Ravert, Tom Baysore, and coach John Ebner. (Above, courtesy Cindy Knier; below, courtesy Hulsizer's Chevrolet.)

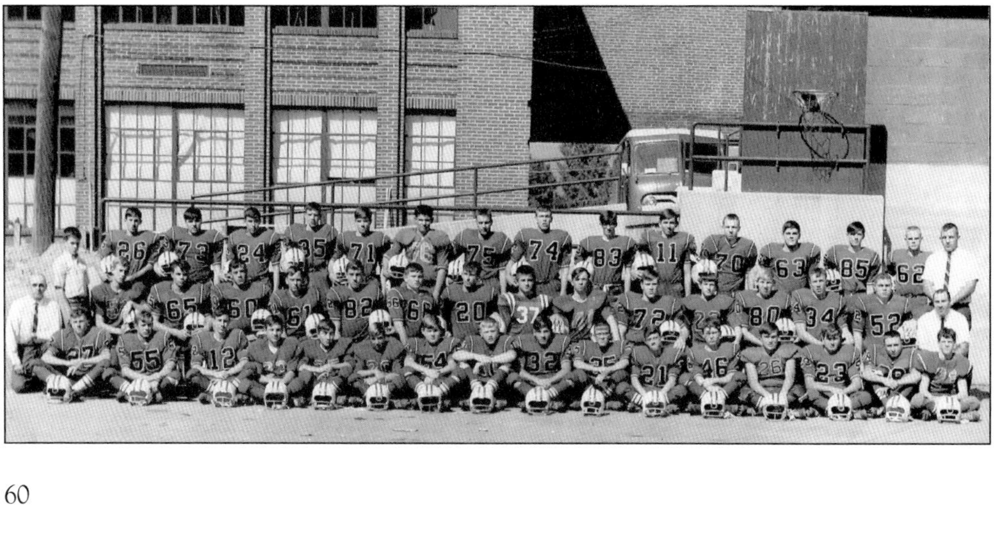

In March 1962, the planning began for Montgomery's weeklong celebration of its Diamond Jubilee, the 75th anniversary of its incorporation on March 21, 1887. The Borough Council appointed Mayor Raymond Taylor chairman of the Jubilee planning committees. Several of the committee members and other officers are pictured at right, from left to right, (first row) Joan Burchfield, Dorothy Shelley, and Joyce Taylor; (second row) John Miller, Agatha Taylor, Marion McCormick, and Effie Engleman; (third row) Frank Strickland, Robert Wise, Darius Shollenberger, and Charles "Spook" Ellis; (fourth row) Carl Chamberlain, mayor Raymond Taylor, and Rupert Miller; (fifth row) Leon Crandell, Ray Knouse, and Max Mull. Below, Mayor Raymond Taylor looks on as Bertha Kilmer, Montgomery's oldest resident, is the first to sign the official register for the borough Diamond Jubilee celebration, which began on August 4, 1962. (Both courtesy MAPL.)

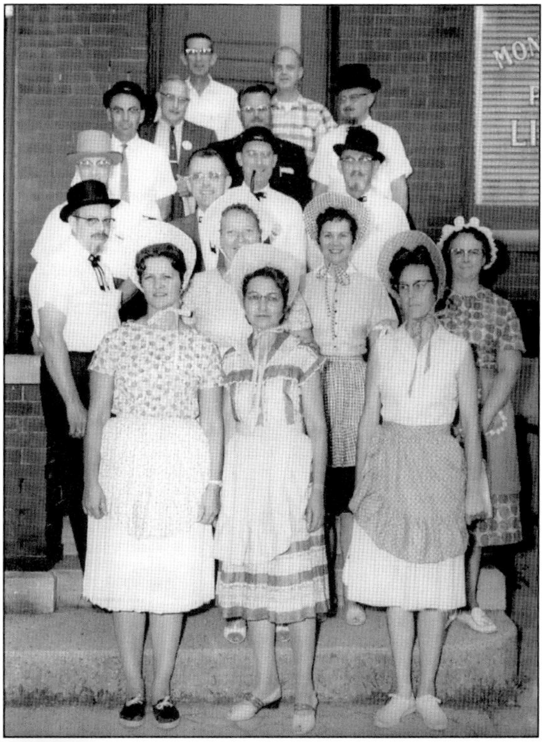

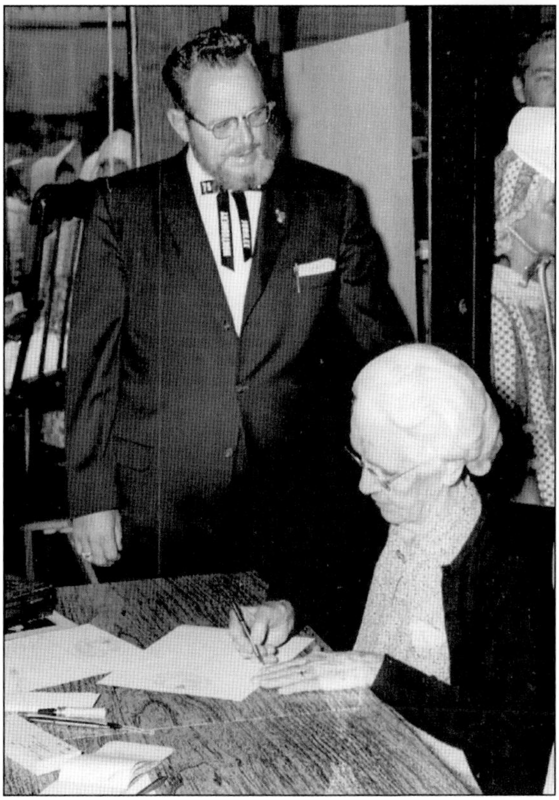

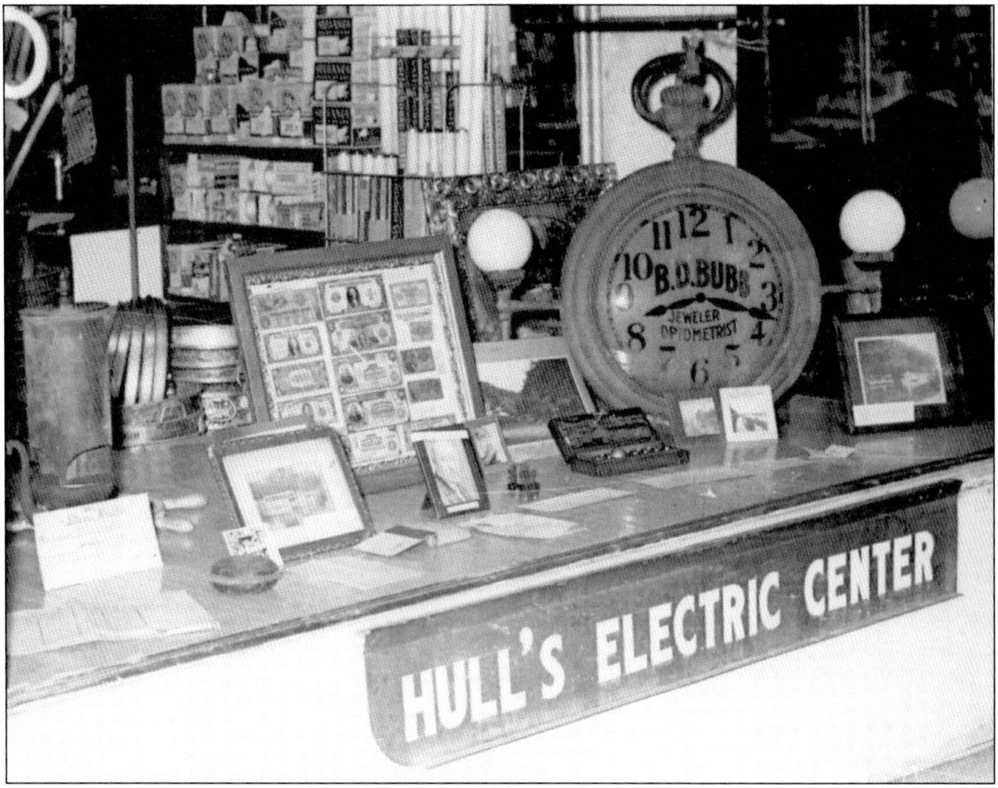

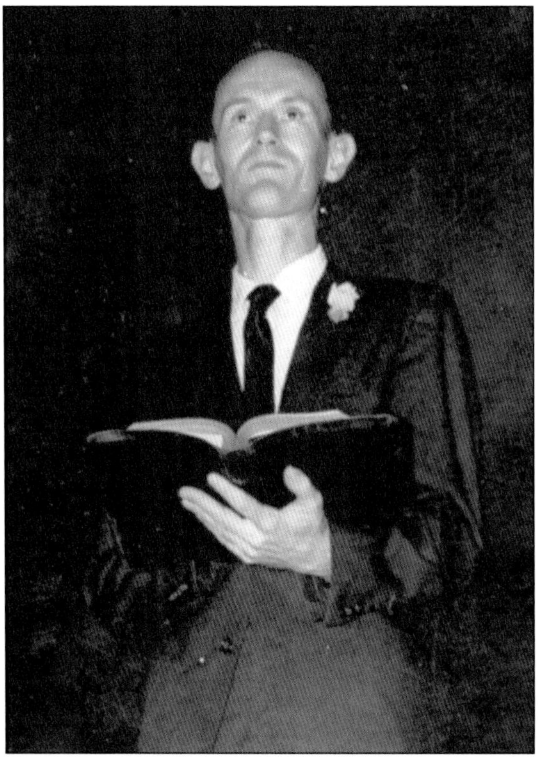

Residents and visitors were registered at the Jubilee Headquarters and historic displays were unveiled in the store windows along Main Street on Saturday, August 4. Shown above, the display in the window of Hull's Electric Center featured old currency and memorabilia, photographs of former borough residents and local landmarks, and a large clock advertising the business of B.D. Bubb, who was both a jeweler and an optometrist. The following day, August 5th, was designated as Church Day; a Union Worship Service was held at the park with Rev. Robert Berger (left), former borough resident, as the speaker. (Both courtesy MAPL.)

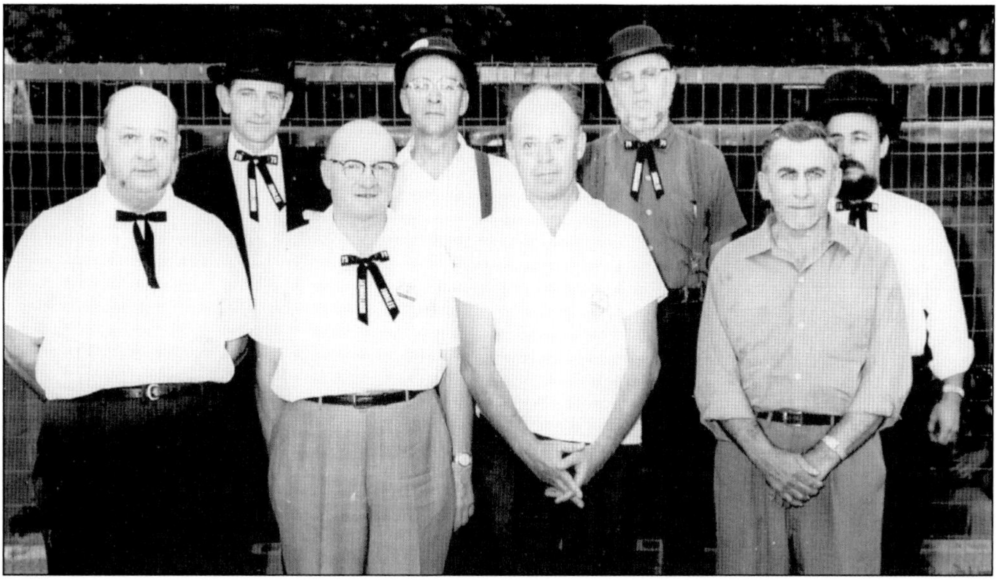

Monday, August 6 was Little League Day of Diamond Jubilee Week. The original founders of the Montgomery Little League are pictured above, from left to right: (first row) Roy Koons (sponsor of Koons Royals team), Lester Page (sponsor of Page's Upholstering team), Richard Stahl (sponsor of Stahl's Clippers team), and Dorsey Claudfelter (manager of the Stahls' Clippers); (second row) Horace "Lefty" Lovelace (manager of the Leonard's Furniture team), Harold Tobias (manager of the Koons Royals), William Grove, and Sterling Weikel. Below, the Hulsizer Little League team rides along the parade route. Pictured are, from left to right, (in front, facing camera) Dale Bennett, Craig Newcomer, Larry Pick, Roger Geiger; (in back) Mike Smith, Bill Bennett, Danny Hoover, Tim Wertz, Larry Edwards (No. 15), Bill Percival, Dave Morrison, and Jeff Burley. (Both courtesy MAPL.)

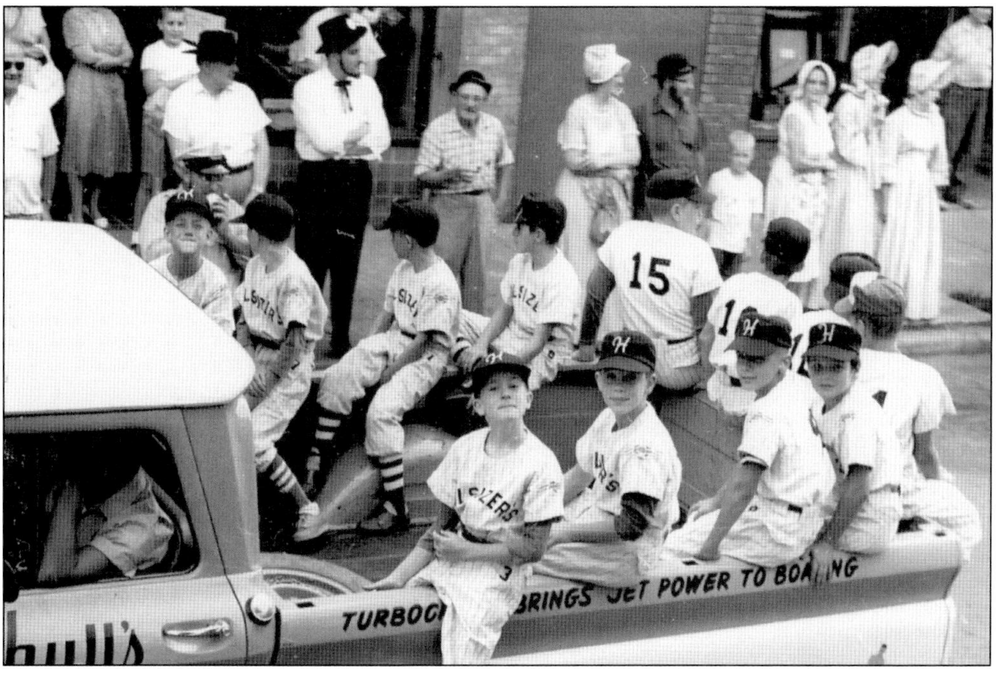

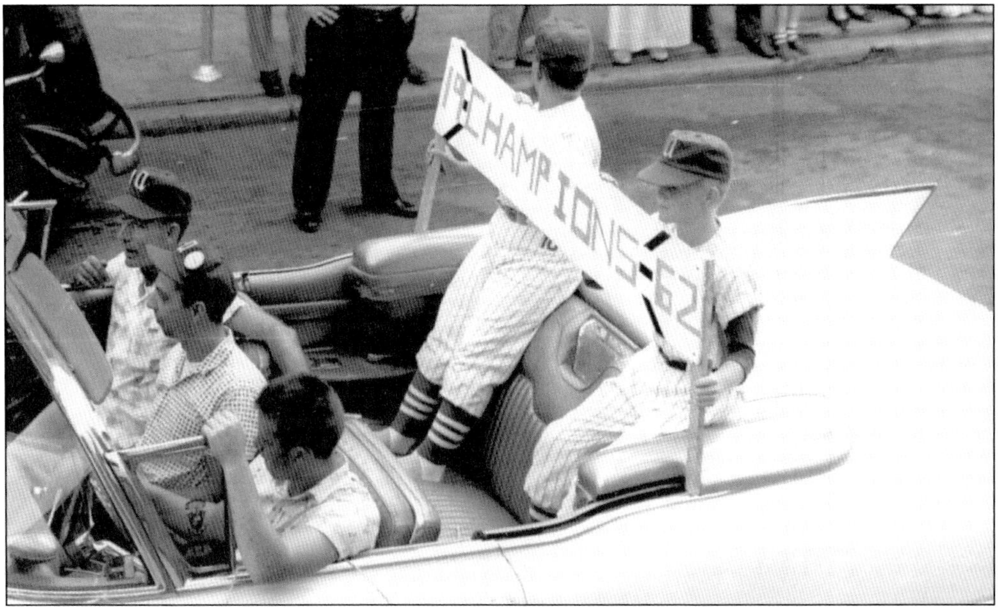

Little League in Montgomery was organized in 1946, and teams from Montgomery played in the first Little League World Series competition held in Williamsport in 1947. The team sponsored by Leonard's Furniture lost in game three to Williamsport's Brandon League team. Pictured above are (front seat) Rodney Miller (driving), Fred McCarty Jr. (center), and Lefty Foust; (back seat) Curt Barto (driver's side) and Larry Walborn. McCarty and Foust were managers for the team sponsored by Arrolet. Below, the team sponsored by Miller's Drug Store is pictured. From left to right, they are: (driver's side) Dick Miller, Jay LaForme, unidentified, Jim Reynolds, and Denny Miller; (passenger's side) Gary Yohn, Terry Miller, Ray LaForme, Kenny Harman, and Davis Ravert. (Both courtesy MAPL.)

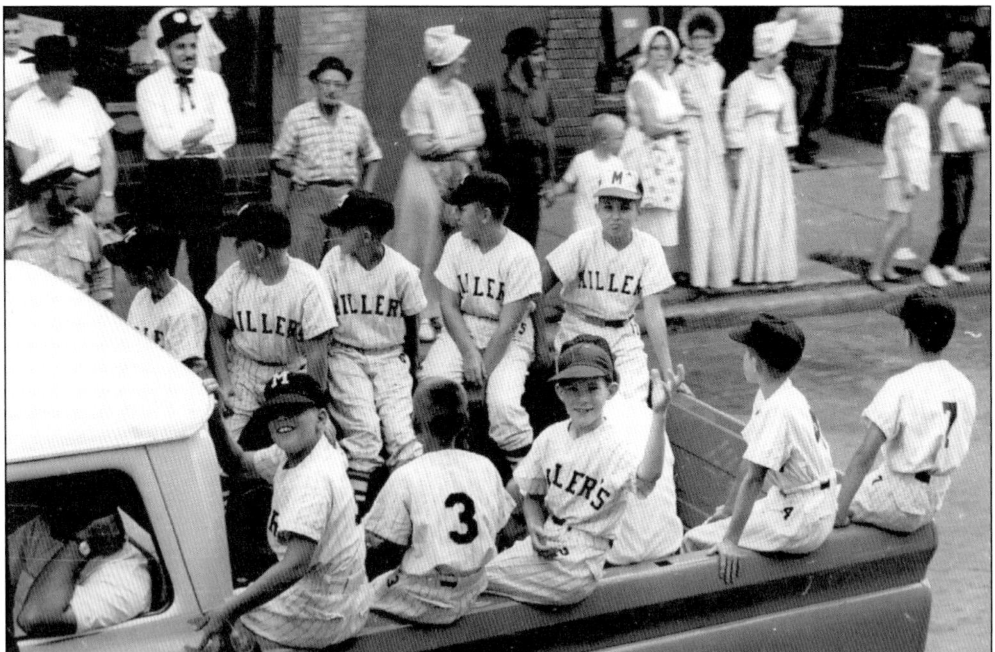

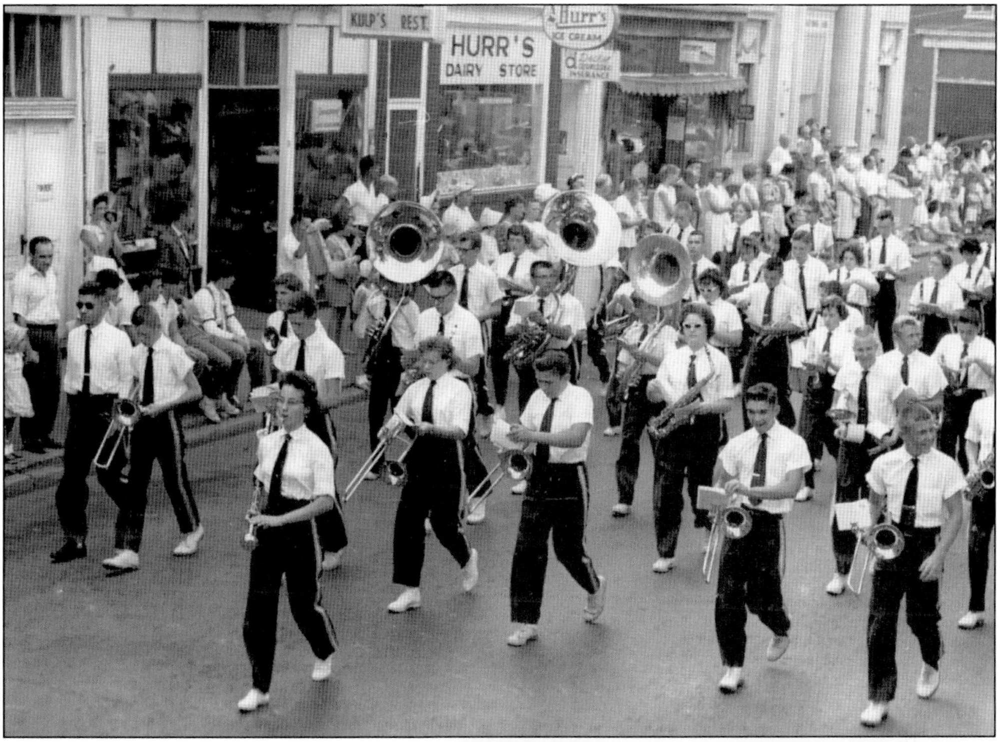

Also participating in the Little League Parade was the Montgomery High School Band, seen above. Following the parade, an all-star ballgame was held with pregame ceremonies that included the crowning of the Golden Jubilee Queen and her honor court. The queen and court were chosen through ballots submitted at local businesses and also by purchasing Jubilee bonds. Seen at right is Mayor Raymond Taylor crowning Diamond Jubilee Queen Erika Patz. Her honor court included Sandra Hain as Miss Montgomery (first runner-up), Fay Ring as Miss Clinton (second runner-up), Linda Baysore as Miss Washington (third runner-up), and Bonnie Taylor as Miss Brady (fourth runner-up). (Both courtesy MAPL.)

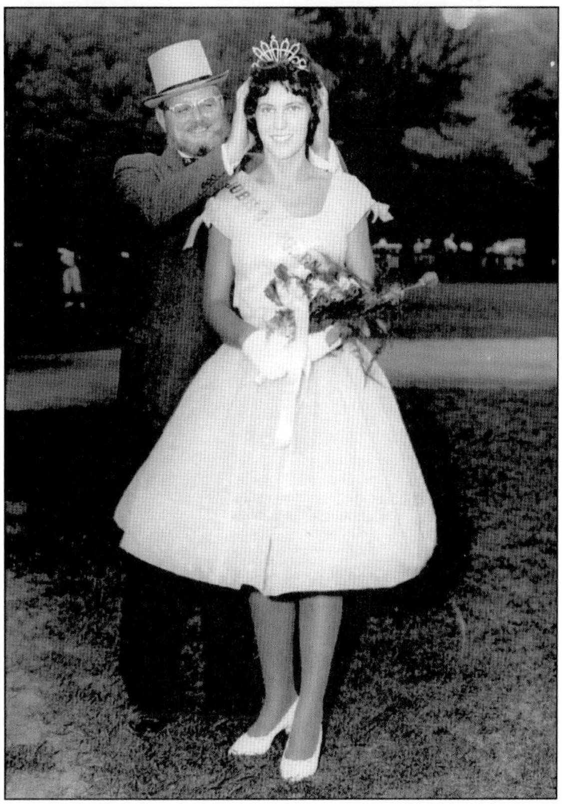

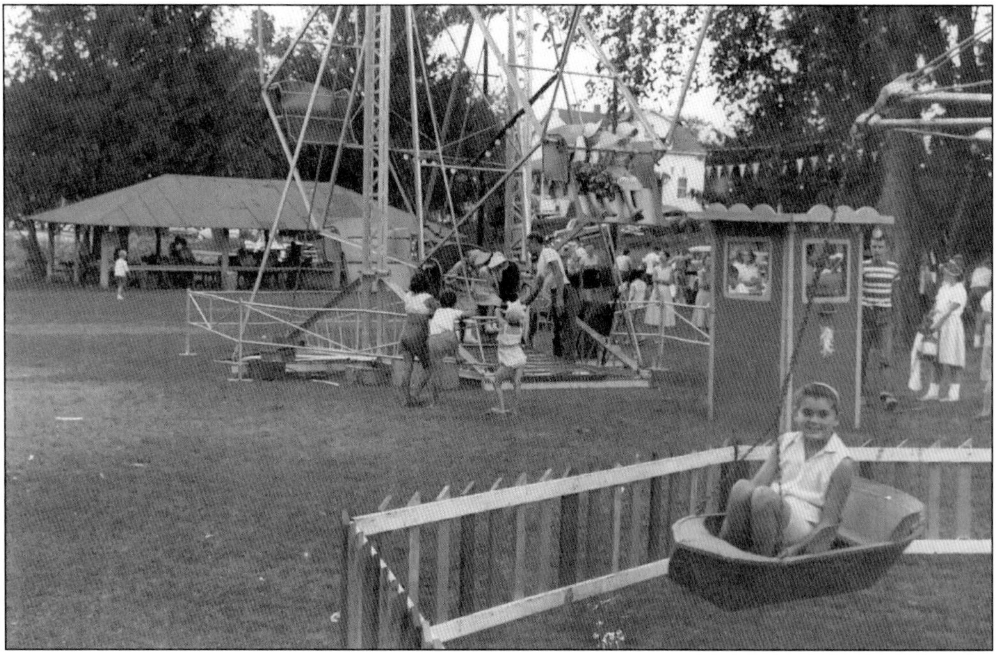

After the ballgame ended on Monday evening (Little League Day), a carnival opened on the grounds of Montgomery Park and continued each evening for the remainder of the Jubilee. Pictured above are the Ferris wheel and other rides with the pavilion in the background. Guests could purchase hot dogs served by Lions Club members, cotton candy, and other carnival fare. Another attraction at the park was the Pink Lady saloon, where teenage can-can dancers entertained the crowds. From left to right are Sharon Mowery, Sandy Mowery, Donna McCormick, Bonnie Taylor, Connie Burley, and Joanne Berger—all teens from Montgomery. (Both courtesy MAPL.)

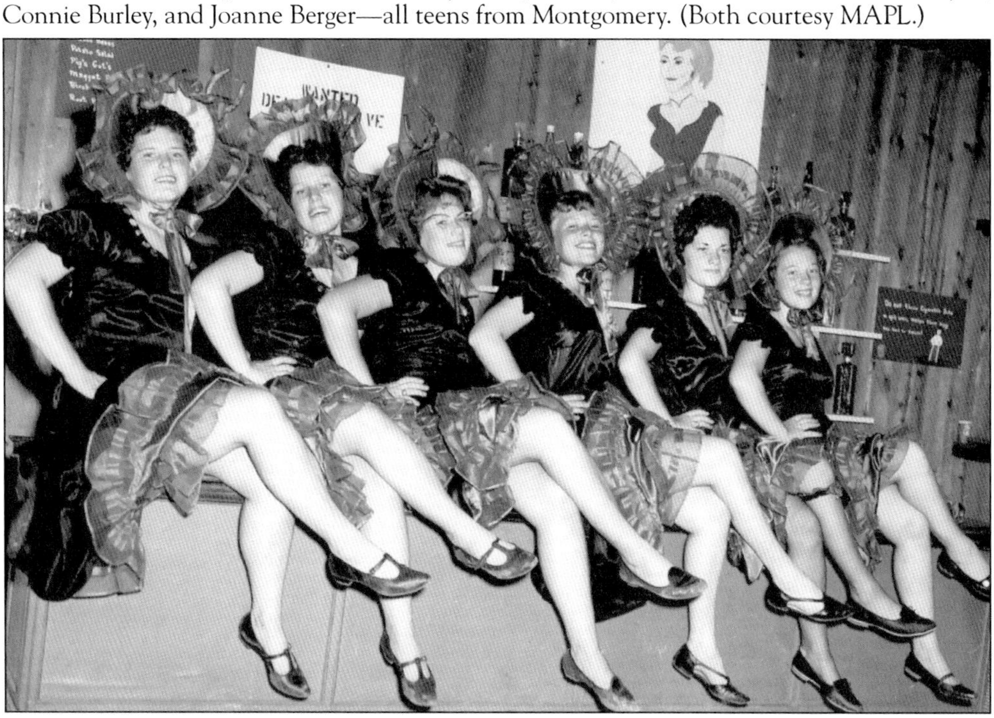

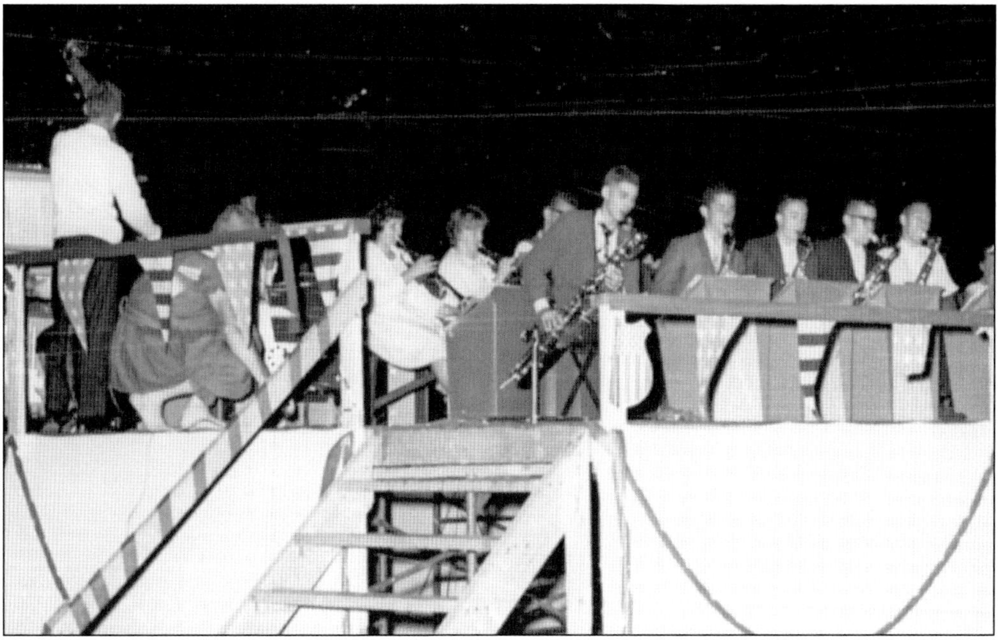

Tuesday, August 7 was designated the Diamond Jubilee's School Day with activities scheduled that would appeal to area students. A track meet was held in the afternoon, and an evening concert was held featuring the Montgomery Area High School Dance Band, also known as the Skyliners. Members of the band (above) included, from left to right, John Russell on bass, Sharon DiMarco, Joann Farley, Jim Shaffer on trumpet, Les Gruver on saxophone, Larry Ginsburg, Larry Lupold, Larry Stamets, and Jim Reaser. Also included in the entertainment was a demonstration by the Lyco 4-H Square Dancers. Pictured below, from left to right, are the following: unidentified, Sandy Mowery, Bob McCarty, Shirley McCarty, Bob More, Bill Peterman, Ross Jarrett, Janet Peterman, Terry Bastian, and Joan April. (Both courtesy MAPL.)

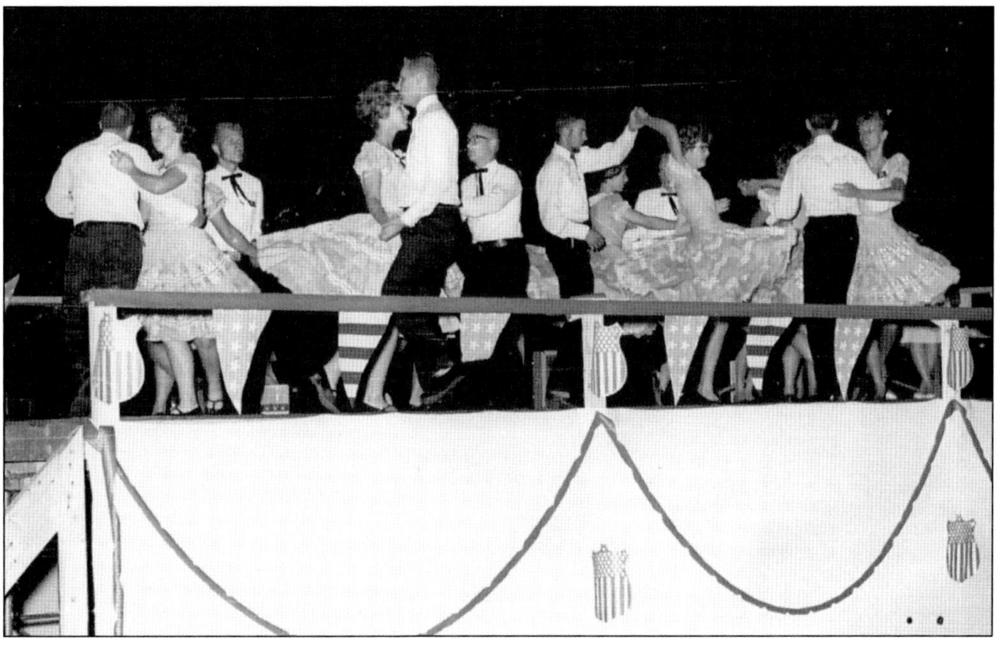

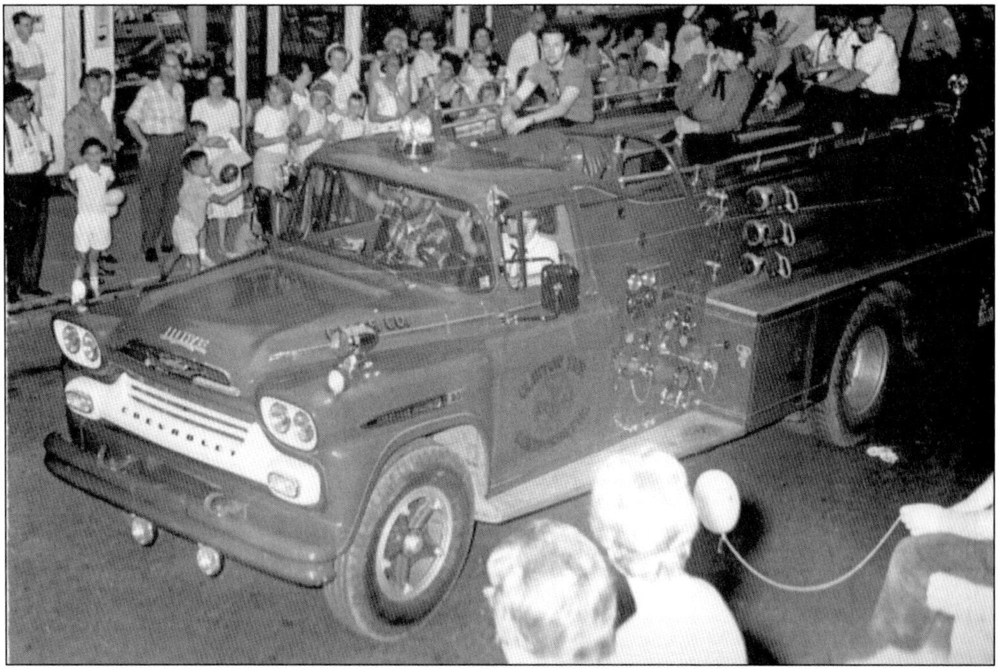

Wednesday, August 8 was Fireman's Day. An evening parade of bands, fire trucks, and equipment from Montgomery and neighboring communities was scheduled, followed by a demonstration of modern firefighting methods held at the park grandstand. Above, the Clinton Township Fire Company truck is seen along the parade route. In 1962, there were 96 volunteer firemen and 50 auxiliary members of the Clinton Township Fire Company. Below, one of Montgomery's early fire trucks is featured in the parade. (Both courtesy MAPL.)

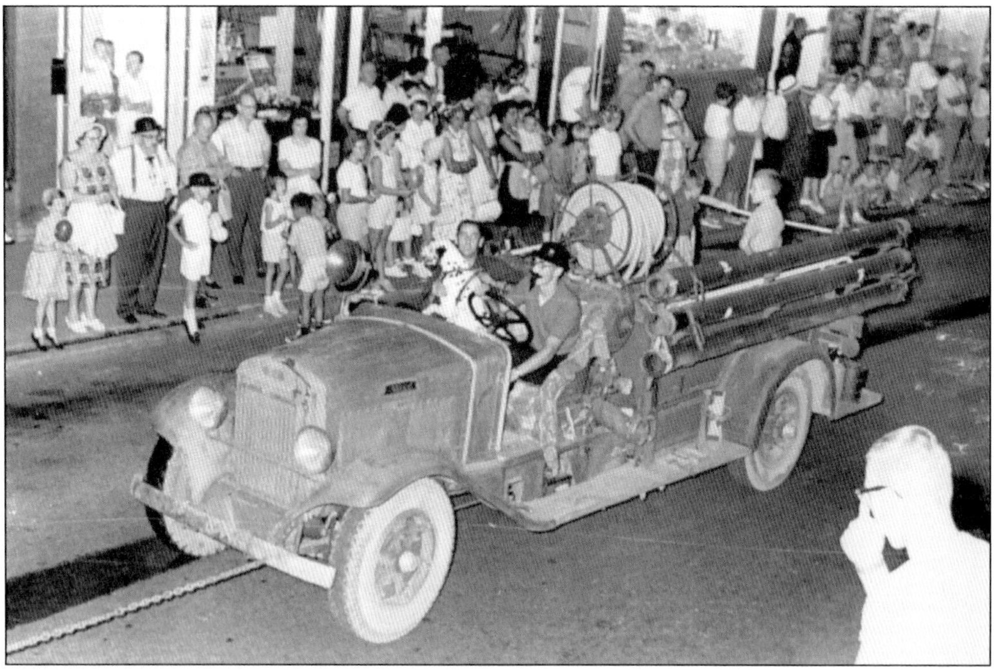

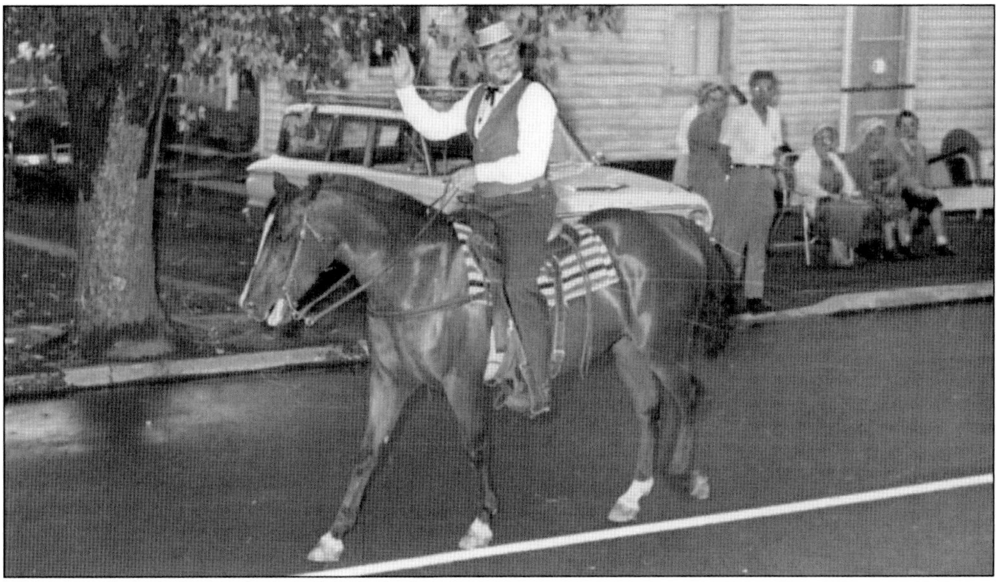

The Community Day Parade, which took place on the evening of August 9, featured horse-riding clubs, 4-H Clubs, and a variety of buggies, wagons, antique automobiles, and horse riders. The parade's marshal, borough mayor Raymond Taylor, led the way (above) with members of the Pioneer Riding Club Color Guard (below). The Pioneer Riding Club was formed in July 1960, and its membership had increased from its original 8 members to 64 in 1962. The club's purpose was to promote horse shows and rodeos; in the early 1960s, a practice show ring was located north of the borough along Route 54. Members of the riding club's color guard, from left to right, included Bill Schneck, Bob Sease (behind flag), Butch Ulolk, and Ross Jarrett. (Both courtesy MAPL.)

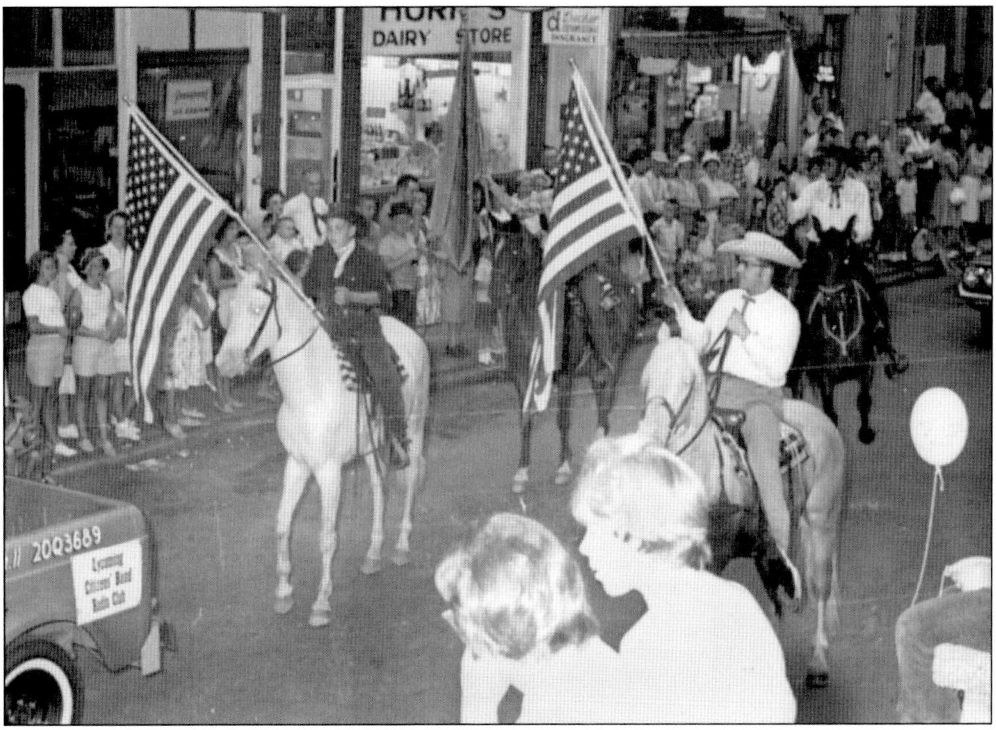

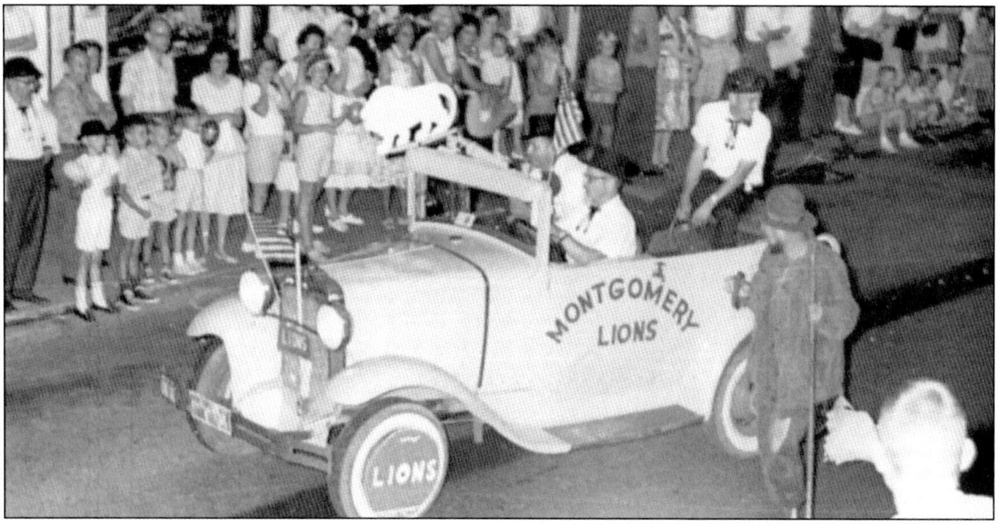

One year after its charter in 1955, the Montgomery Lions Club sponsored a program to purchase glasses for needy children in the Montgomery schools. The club also purchased an Ortho-rater machine to evaluate the vision of local school students. It held a polio clinic for vaccine administration, and rented and renovated space in the Farmers and Citizens Bank for meeting rooms used by Boy and Girl Scout troops. Pictured above in the Homecoming Day Parade held on the final day of the Jubilee is the Lions Club jitney with Rupert Miller (driver), Allen Lupold (in front seat), Delroy Schneck (in back seat), and George Amos Smith (with broom). Below, Girl Scout Peggy Tobias is dressed as Juliet Low, founder of the Girl Scouts, with a cake commemorating the 50th anniversary of the first Girl Scout meeting, which took place in 1912. (Both courtesy MAPL.)

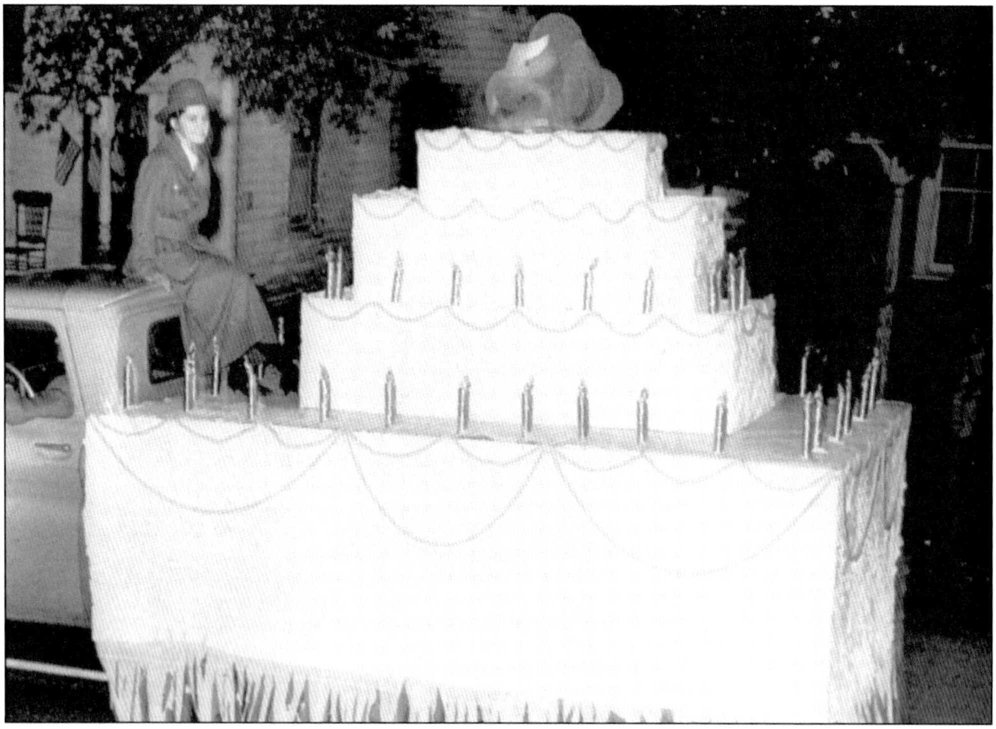

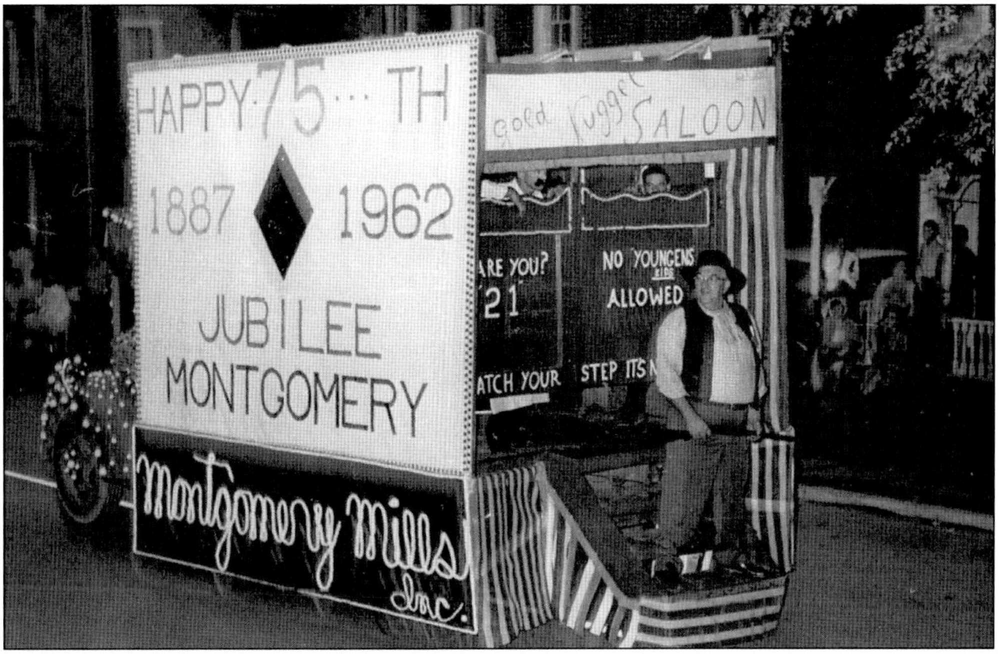

Since 1940, employees of Montgomery Mills, Inc. produced fabric trimmings in the space occupied by the former Montgomery Table Works. The float entry (above) in the Homecoming Parade was constructed of products manufactured at Montgomery Mills. Chick Adams stands guard at the entrance to the "Gold Nugget Saloon." Below is the float entry submitted by the Rochelle Furniture Manufacturing Company, which specialized in producing juvenile furniture—including cribs, high chairs, and child-size chairs—under the Babytime and Babystep trade names. The young man seated in the oversized highchair is unidentified. (Both courtesy MAPL.)

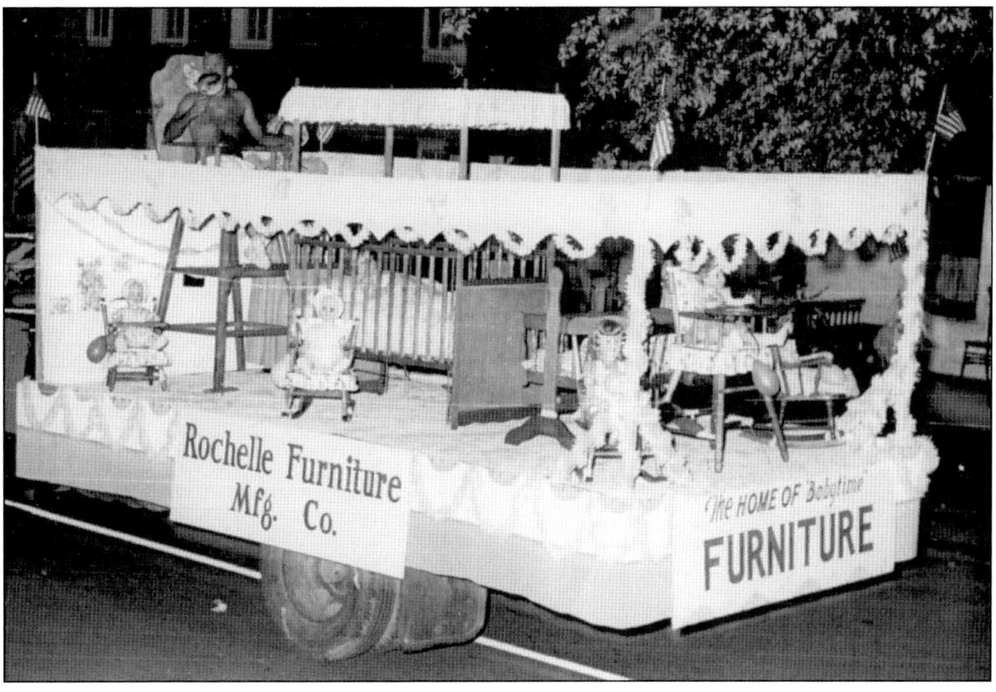

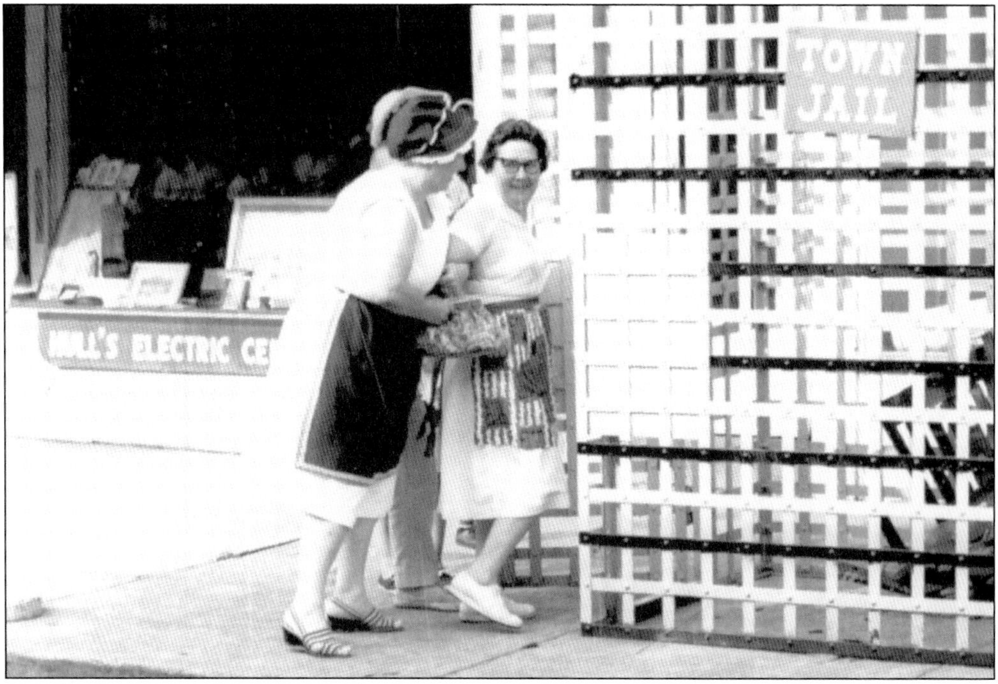

The final day of the Jubilee, Saturday, August 11, featured the grand finale of the celebration. At 1:00 p.m., the judging for the beard and apron contest was held. Seen above is June Wagner ushering Eleanor Kulp into the jail after she neglected to follow "Rule No. 1 for the Women: 'Must wear bonnet and apron.' " Below, Phil Hartranft tempts his wife as she serves time in the pokey. Assisting in the arrests of residents who violated the Jubilee rules was Montgomery police chief Bill McClintock assisted by Sterling Kulp and Shorty Mattern, all in costume. (Both courtesy MAPL.)

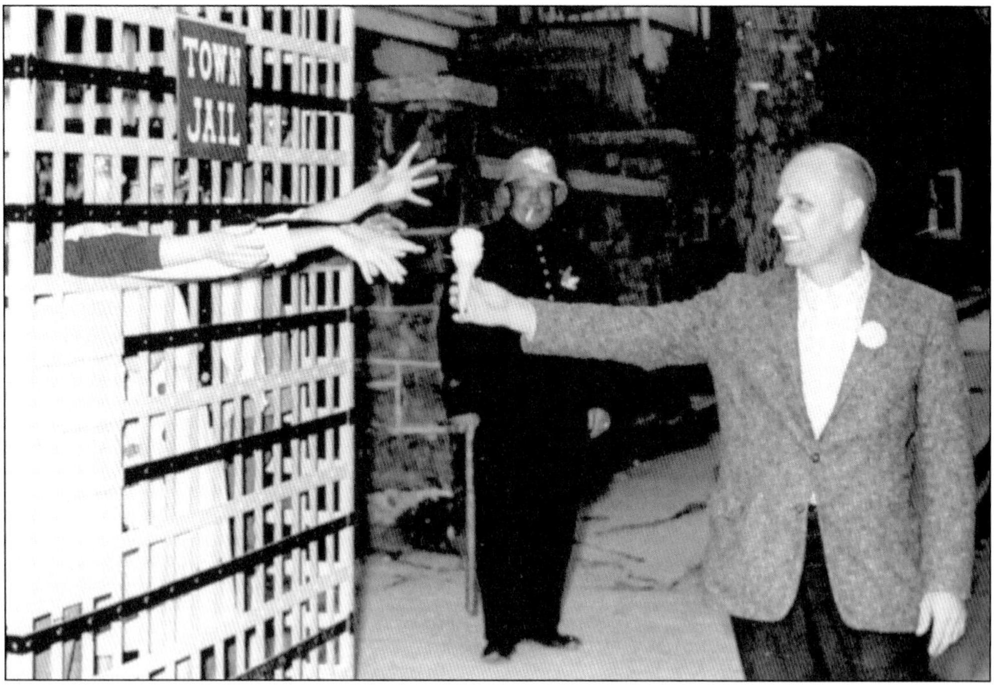

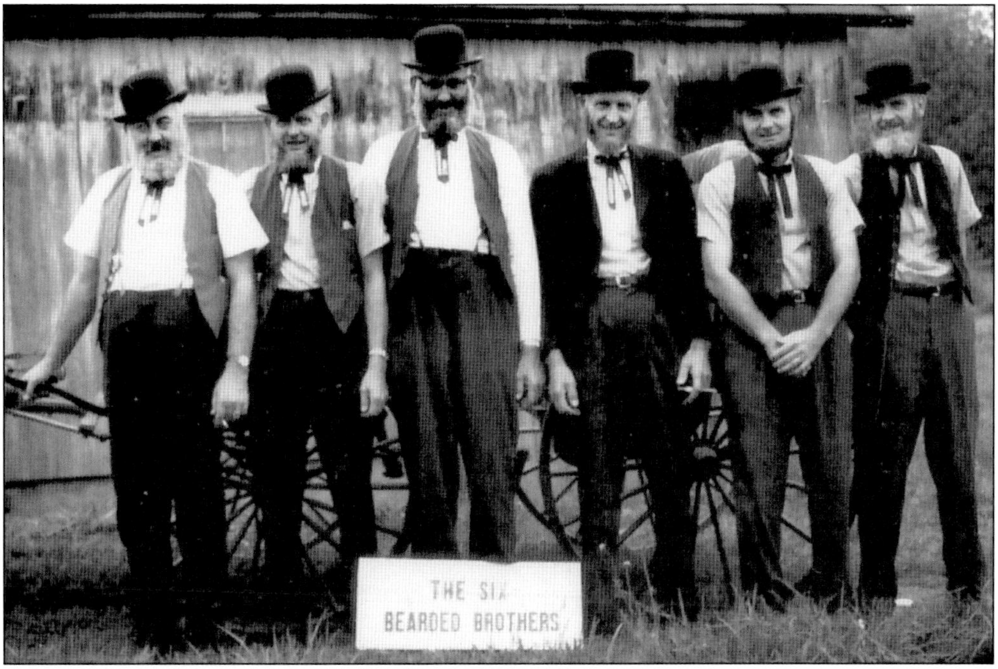

Rules for men during the Jubilee included the requirement of beards or goatees. All six Stamets brothers complied with this requirement. "The Six Bearded Brothers," from left to right, are Howard, Mike, William, Robert, Dunning, and Jack Stamets. In the Homecoming Day parade, elaborate floats, marching bands, drum and bugle groups, and drill teams were featured, including the Montgomery High School Color Guards pictured below. Members were, from left to right, (first row) Doris Yocum, Cheryl Warren, and Doris Claudfelter; (second row, holding banner) Shirley McCarty and Libby Derr; (third row) majorettes Jonnie Lou Miller and Sharon Mowery. (Above, courtesy the Stamets family; below, courtesy MAPL.)

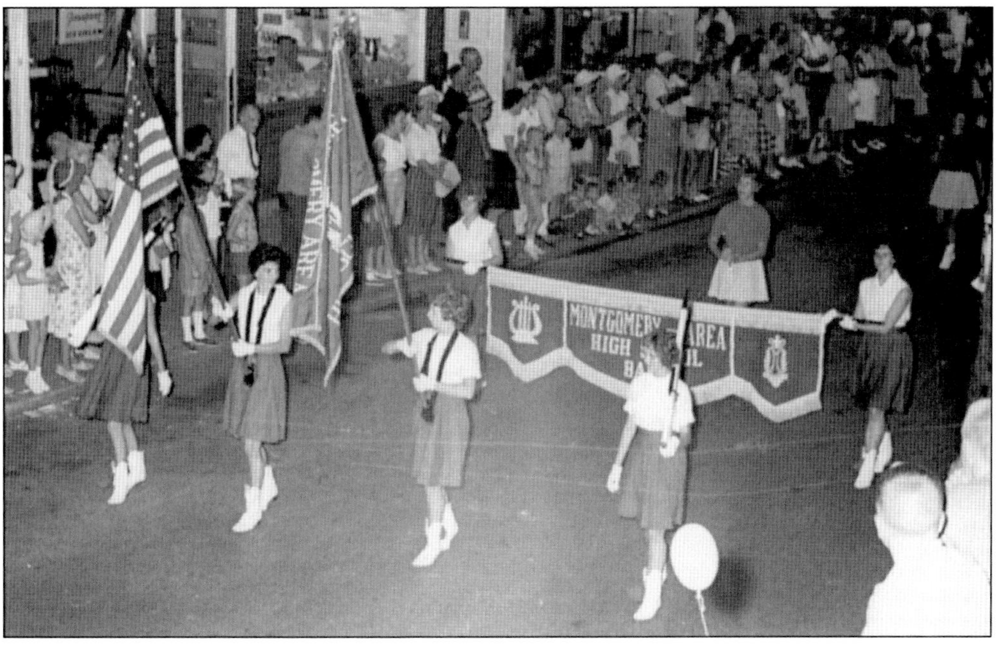

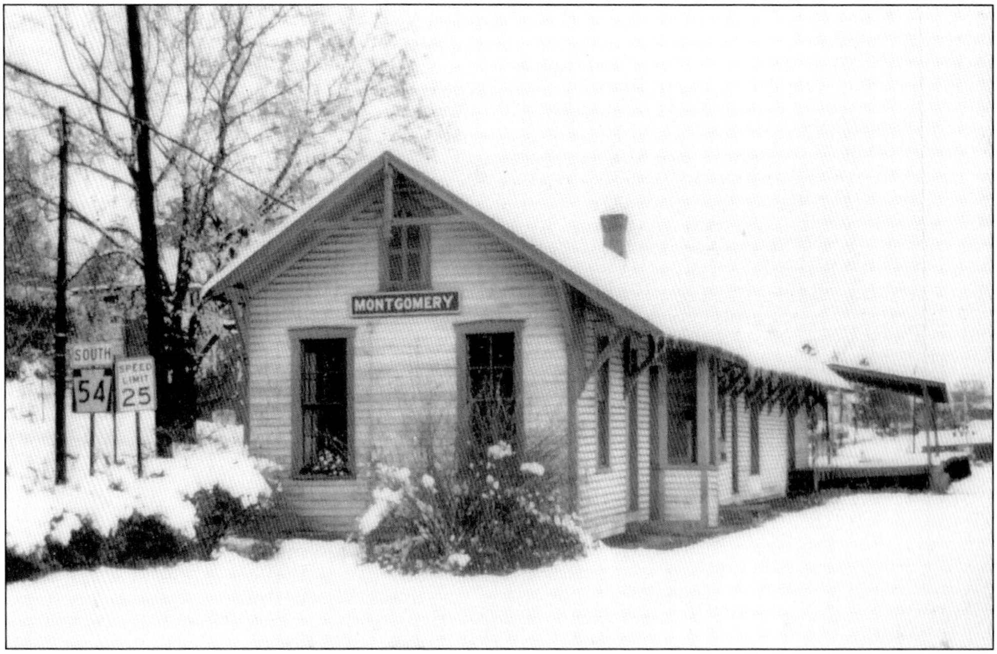

The Montgomery train station served the Philadelphia and Erie Railroad, which first laid tracks and passed through the borough in 1854. Montgomery became a regular stop when Robert Montgomery, a prosperous farmer who lived along the river, donated funds to build the station. Improvements were made in 1914 when a new waiting room for passengers was added, and an iron fence was installed between the two tracks. The station was torn down in the late 1960s, and the Reading Railroad overpass that crossed Main Street was removed in 1985. (Above, courtesy MAPL; below, courtesy Peggy and Charles Yohn.)

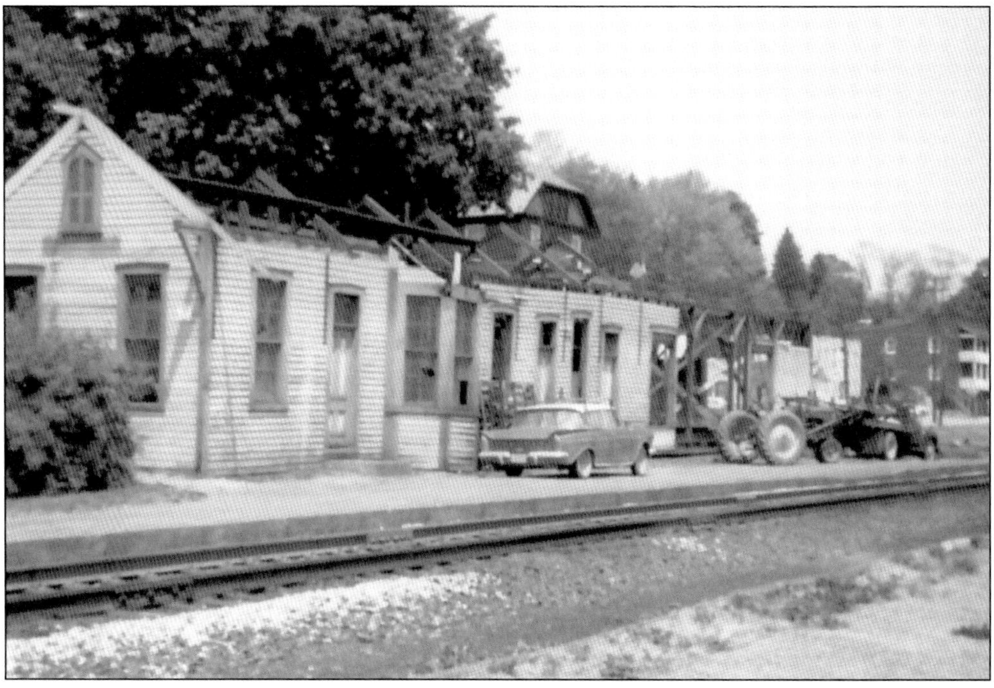

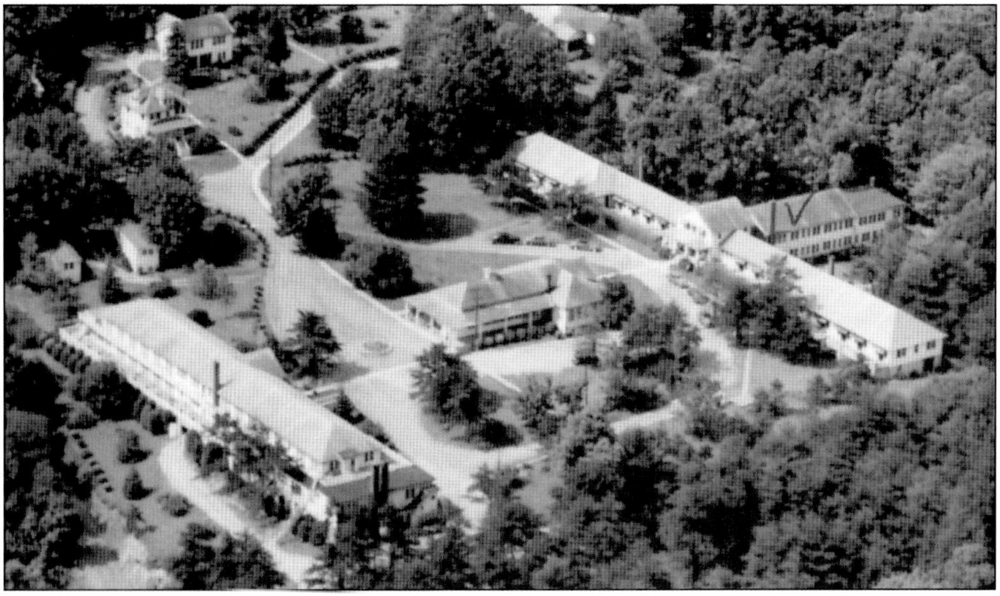

After Dr. William Devitt died in 1948, John Packard was named medical director of Devitt's Camp. After antibiotics to cure tuberculosis were developed in the early 1950s, Packard opened a unit in 1954 to treat "non-Tuberculous [sic] diseases of the chest, chronic diseases, and geriatrics." This effort was short-lived, however, as the camp's assets declined along with the number of patients. In 1956, ownership of the 220-acre property was transferred to the United Church of Christ, which established a facility for the elderly named Devitt Home. Carol "Red" Houtz, seen below, was hired in 1955 as the custodian at the Devitt Home and continued working there into the 1970s after the home closed and the White Deer Run Drug and Alcohol Treatment Center was established. (Above, courtesy Kathi Wertman; below, courtesy Carol Houtz family.)

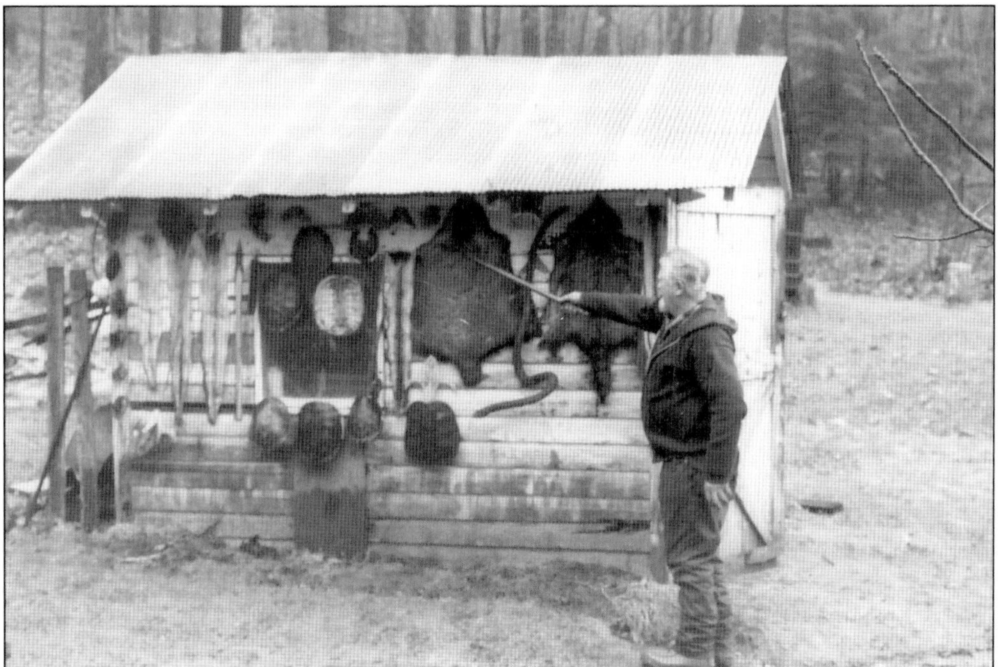

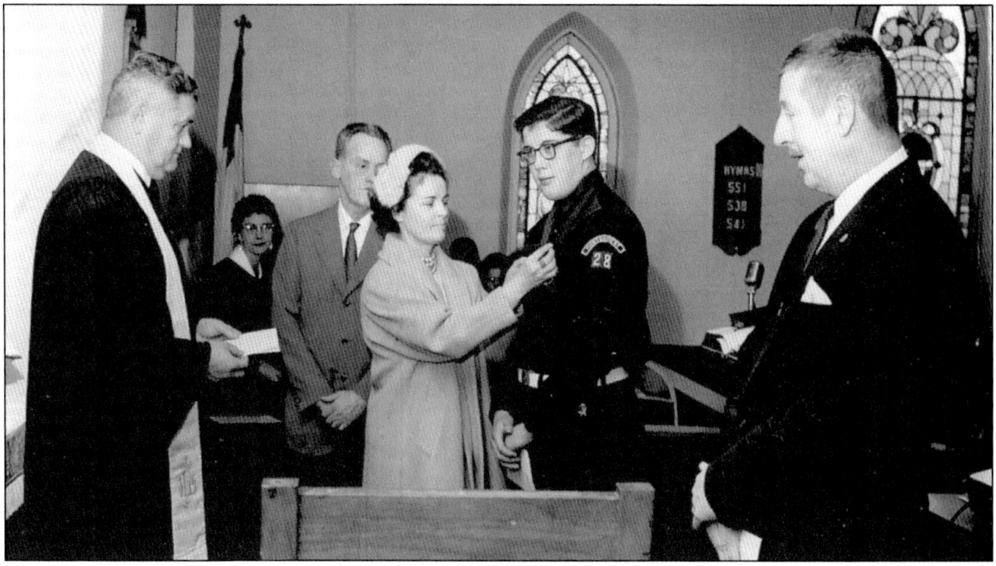

Bill McFadden receives the God and Country award in Scouting from his mother, Mary, as his father, William Sr. (behind his wife), Rev. Adam Bingaman (left) and George Amos Smith look on. Smith was the high school physical education teacher and the Boy Scout and Explorer advisor who assisted young McFadden in earning this award. Below, Montgomery Boy Scout Troop 28 and Lions members are, from left to right: Glenwood Crist, Bud Taylor, unidentified, Art Miller, Harold Hinkal, and unidentified. (Above, courtesy St. John Lutheran Church; below, courtesy MAPL.)

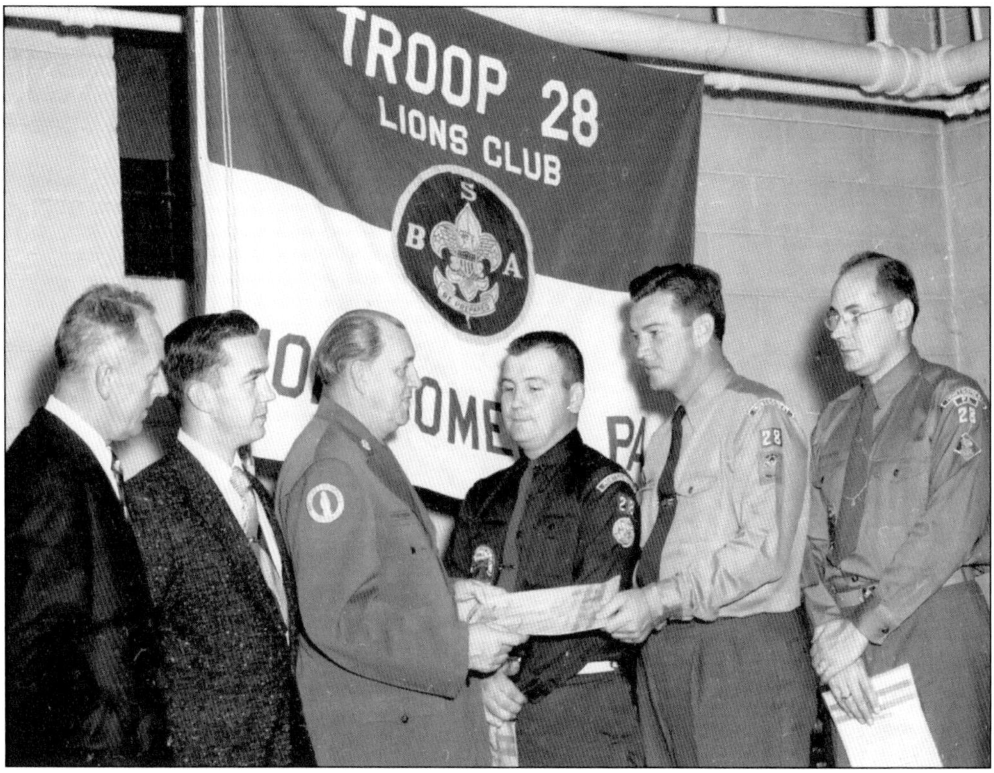

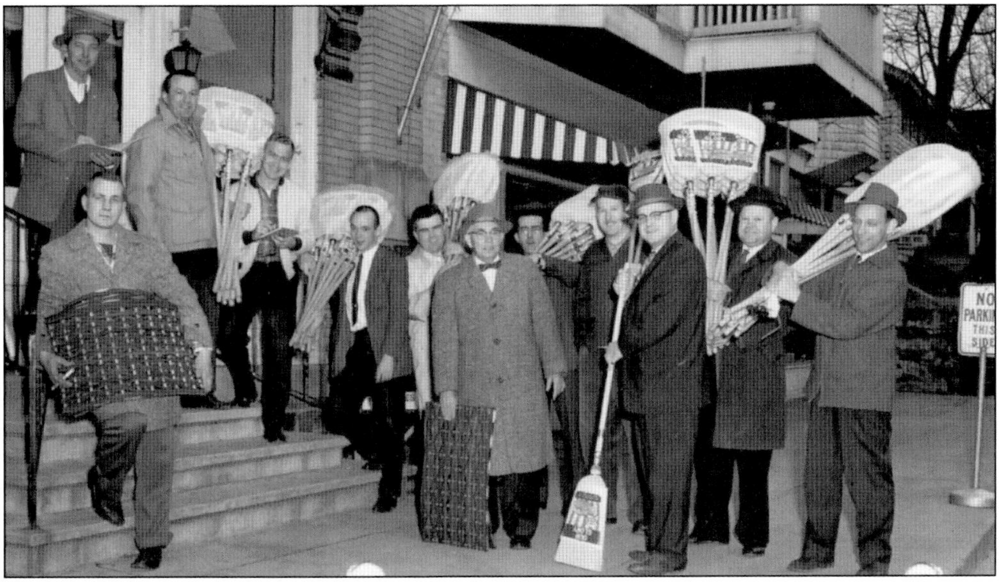

During the 1960s, members of the Montgomery Lions Club would go door to door to sell brooms for about $1.50 and door mats for about $2.50. Seen above at their Main Street headquarters are, from left to right, Bill McClintock, James Morehart (holding mat), Allen Lupold, ? Livingston, Arnold Reed, Dick Schick, Wilbur Hall, George Hulien, George Amos Smith, Jim Pearce, Charles Green, and William Sandmeyer. (Courtesy Montgomery Lions Club.)

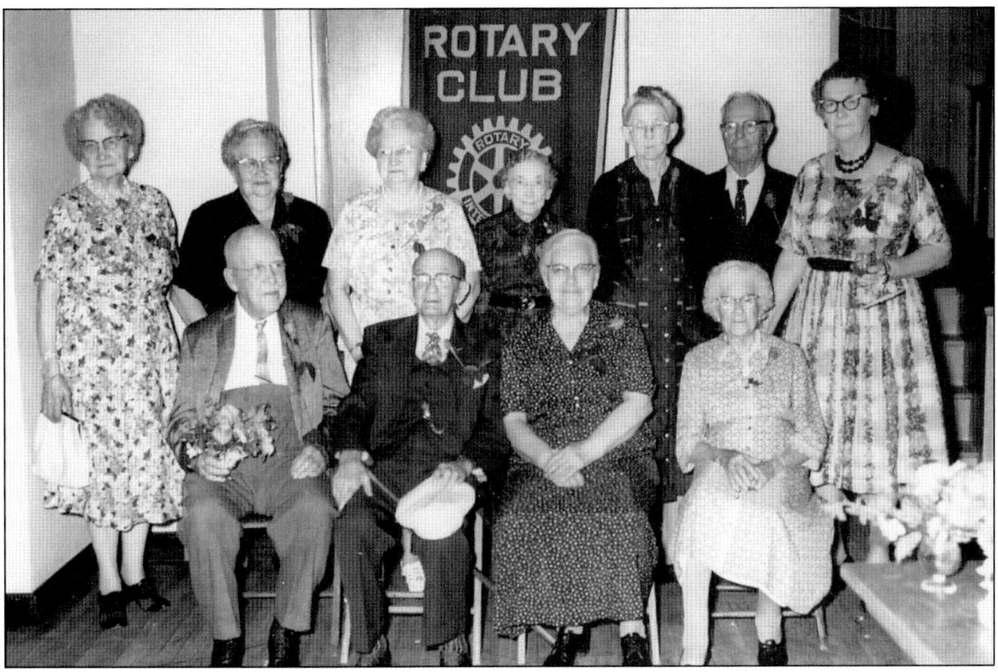

The Three-Quarter Century Club members, from left to right, are (first row) Howard Bieber, Mr. and Mrs. Elmer Kuhns, and Mrs. John Mincemoyer; (second row) Myrtle Horn, Bertha Frye, ? Mauch, Mrs. Seth Emery, Reverend Bower, and Hullda Piatt. The club originated in 1953, when the Montgomery Rotary Club honored male residents of Montgomery aged 75 years and older; the women were honored the following year. (Courtesy MAPL.)

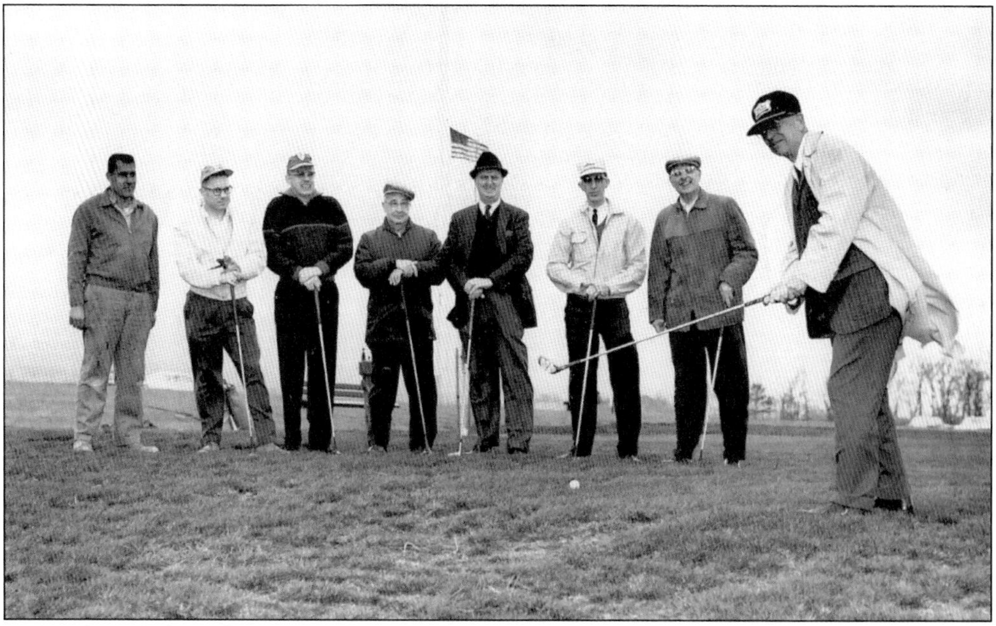

In April 1965, the White Deer Golf Course opened for business. Shown are, from left to right, Joe Cristini (golf course superintendent), Richard Eberhart (auditor), Robert Wise (solicitor), and Recreation Authority members Don Pfeiffer, Torrence Hager, Louis Nardi, and Frank Heller. Recreation Authority chairman James Axeman is teeing off. Greens fees that first year were $3 for weekdays and $4 for weekends and holidays. (Courtesy White Deer Golf Course.)

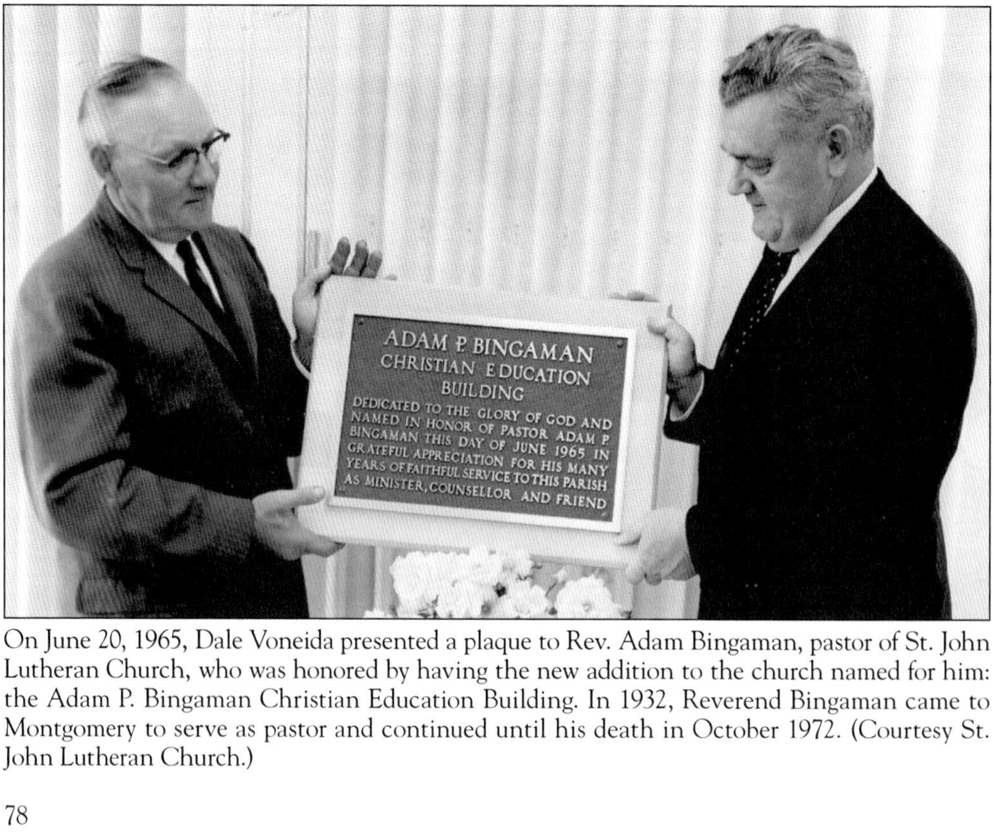

On June 20, 1965, Dale Voneida presented a plaque to Rev. Adam Bingaman, pastor of St. John Lutheran Church, who was honored by having the new addition to the church named for him: the Adam P. Bingaman Christian Education Building. In 1932, Reverend Bingaman came to Montgomery to serve as pastor and continued until his death in October 1972. (Courtesy St. John Lutheran Church.)

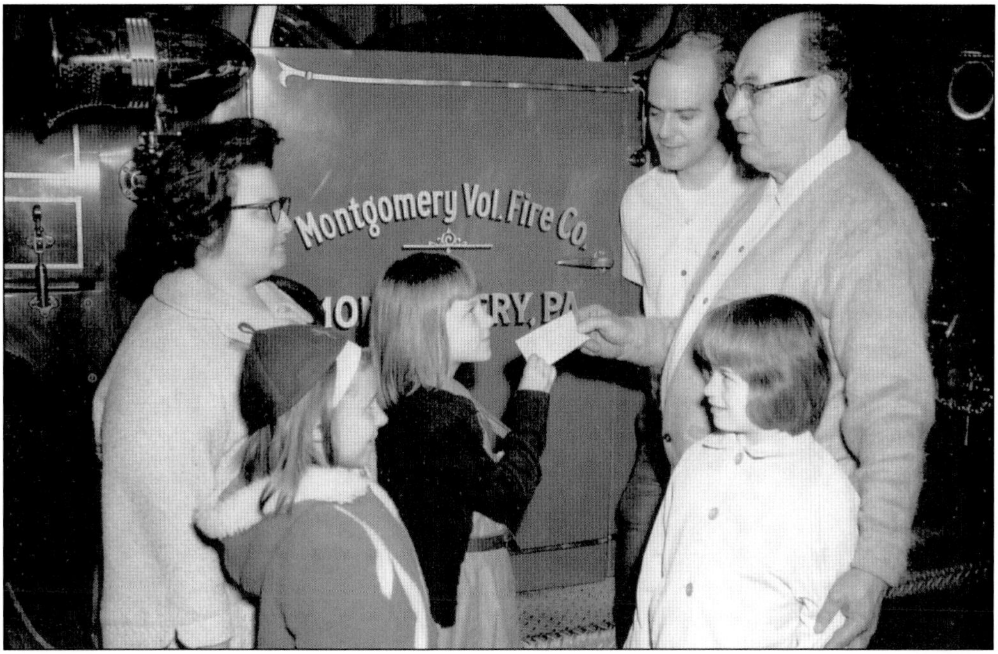

Even the smallest donation is appreciated. On May 11, 1966, Leona Dewalt (woman in glasses) accompanies local Brownie Troop members Bernice Taylor (wearing hat), Cindy Steward (holding check), and Mary Temple as they present a donation of $5 to Topper Stahl (left) and Spook Ellis, members of the Montgomery Volunteer Fire Company. (Courtesy Montgomery Volunteer Fire Company.)

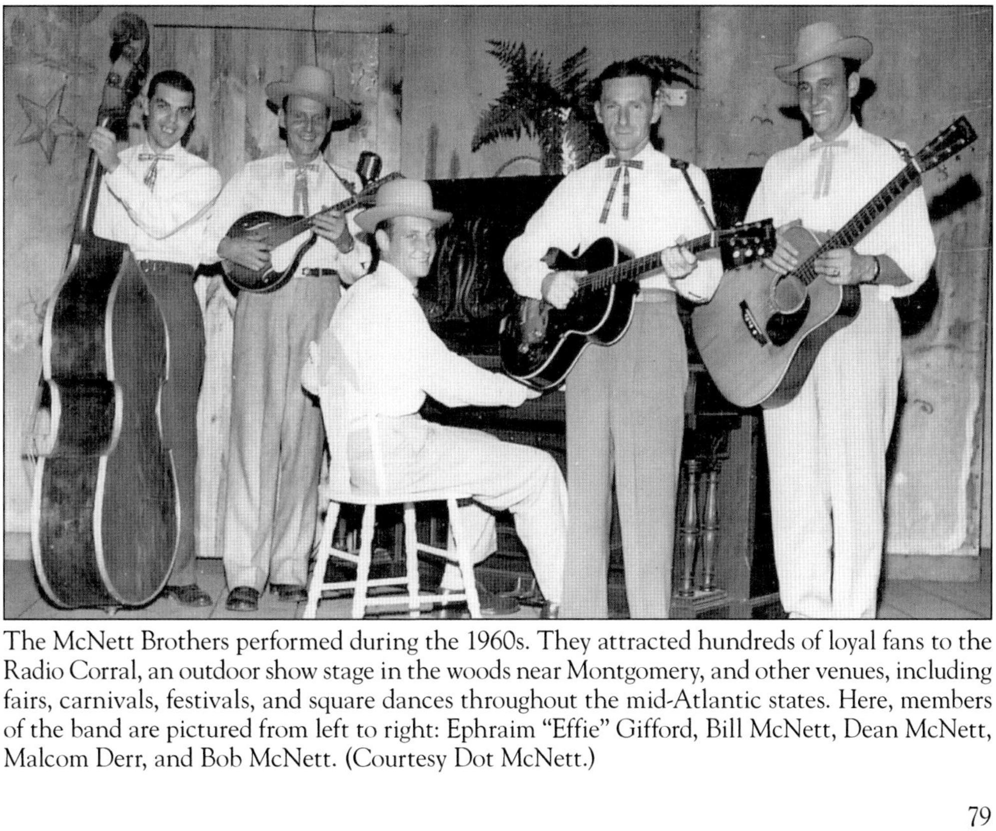

The McNett Brothers performed during the 1960s. They attracted hundreds of loyal fans to the Radio Corral, an outdoor show stage in the woods near Montgomery, and other venues, including fairs, carnivals, festivals, and square dances throughout the mid-Atlantic states. Here, members of the band are pictured from left to right: Ephraim "Effie" Gifford, Bill McNett, Dean McNett, Malcom Derr, and Bob McNett. (Courtesy Dot McNett.)

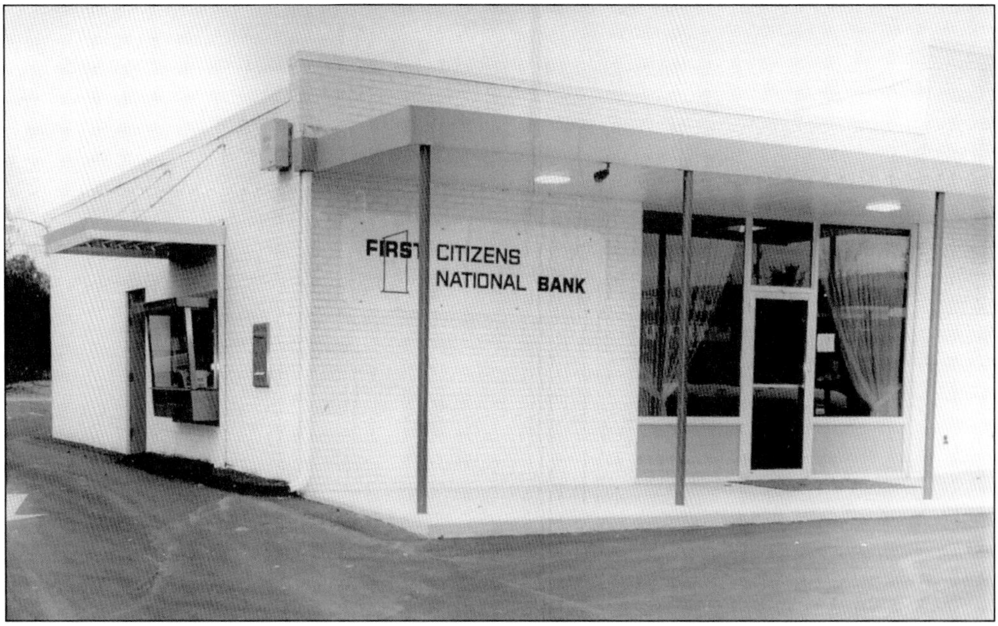

In 1969, a branch office for the First Citizens National Bank was opened at the Montgomery Plaza north of the borough. It featured a drive-through window as well as a walk-in lobby. By the mid-1980s, the name had been changed to Northern Central Bank, and in 1985, the Main Street location of the First Citizens National Bank was closed and banking operations were moved to the Montgomery Plaza location. (Both courtesy MAPL.)

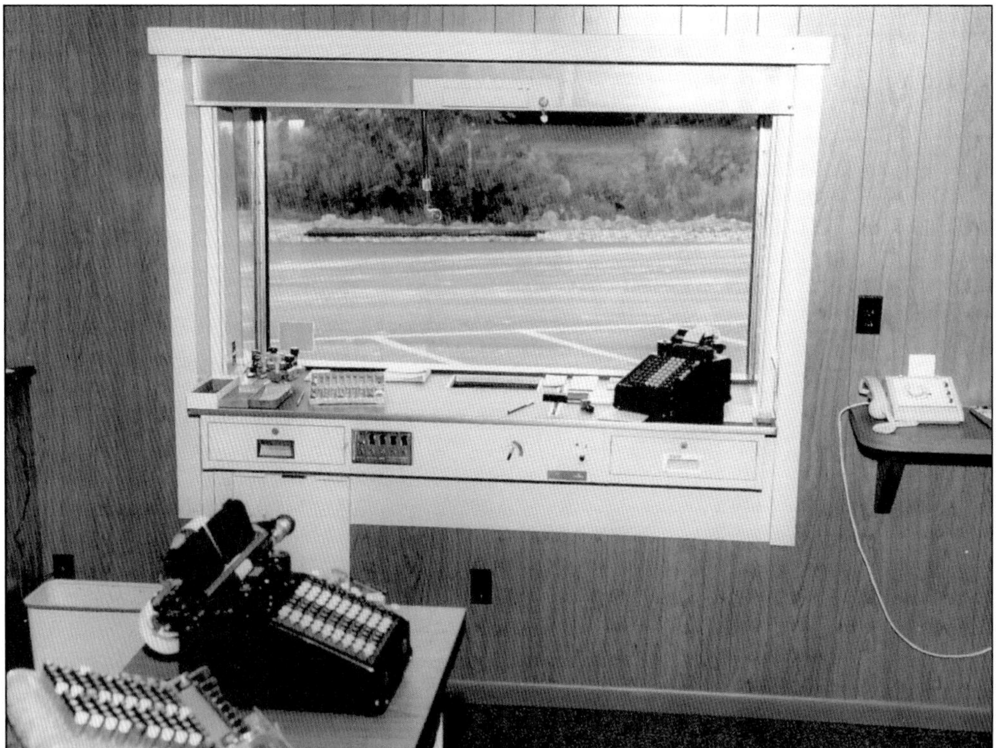

Four

The 1970s

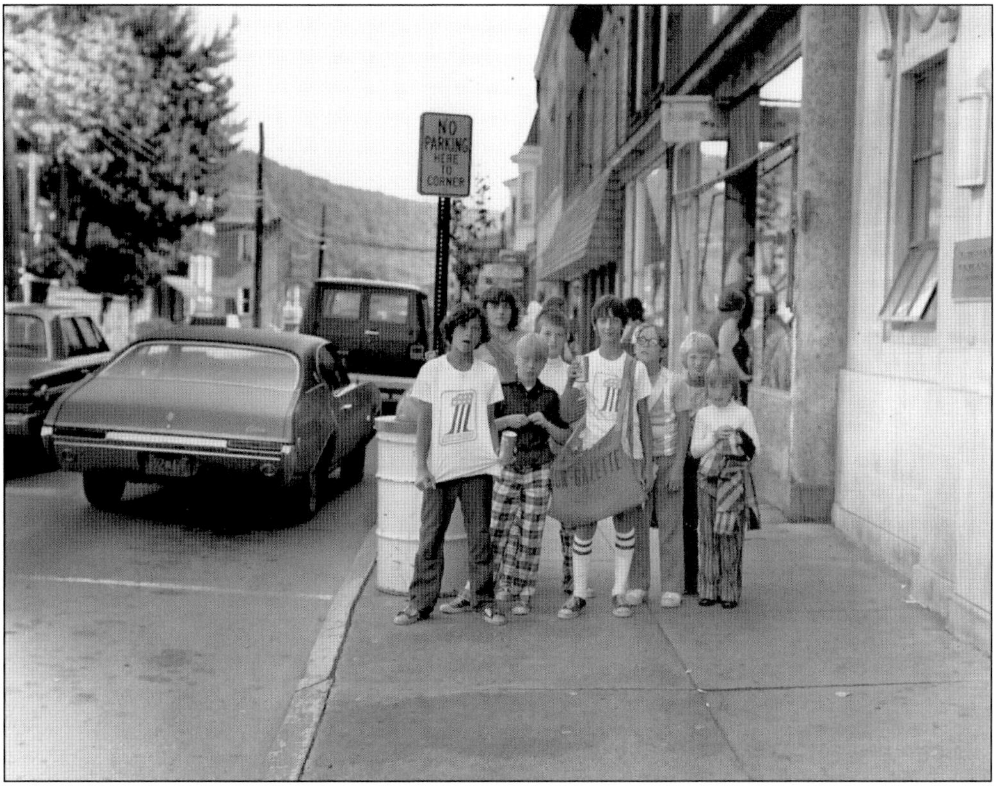

These Montgomery youngsters take a break while walking down Main Street with their friend whose part-time job was to deliver copies of the *Sun-Gazette*, a newspaper printed in nearby Williamsport. The *Sun-Gazette*, one of the oldest businesses in Lycoming County, is currently the fourth oldest daily newspaper in Pennsylvania and the twelfth oldest in America. (Courtesy MAPL; photographed by William McFadden Jr.)

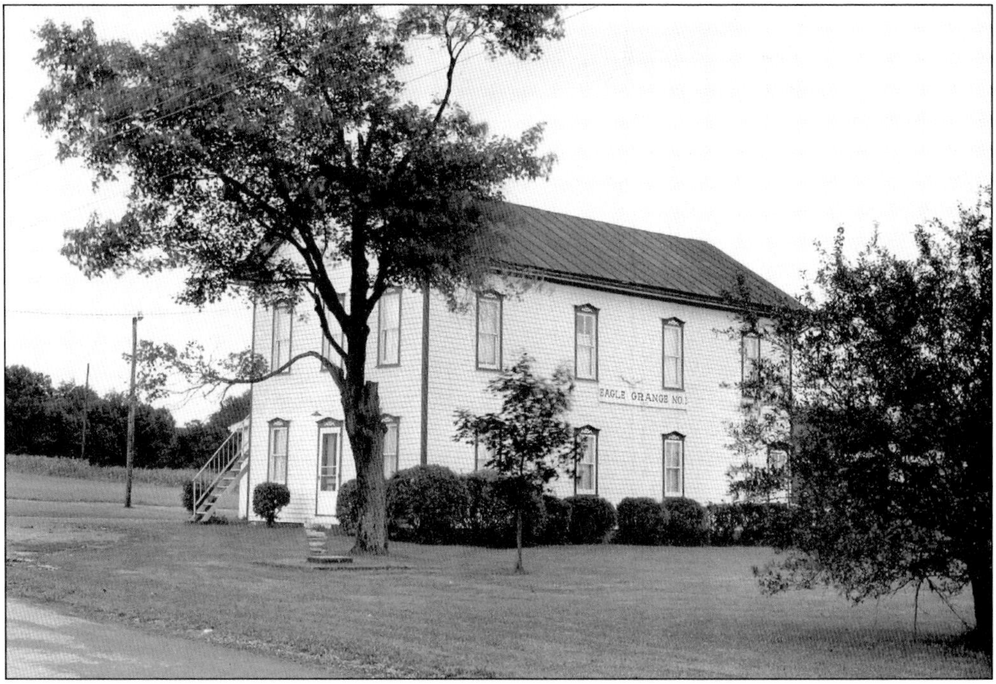

In March 1971, Eagle Grange No. 1 celebrated its 100th anniversary with an old-fashioned box social, a square dance, afternoon tea, and displays at the hall. Designated as the first grange organized in Pennsylvania, the Eagle Grange was assigned No. 1 in March 1871 after local farmer Luke Egar made application for national membership. Above is the Eagle Grange at the intersection of Route 15 and Blind Road. Below, the White Hall Grange near Elimsport is pictured before it was destroyed during the tornado in May 1985. (Both courtesy MAPL; above, photographed by William McFadden Jr.)

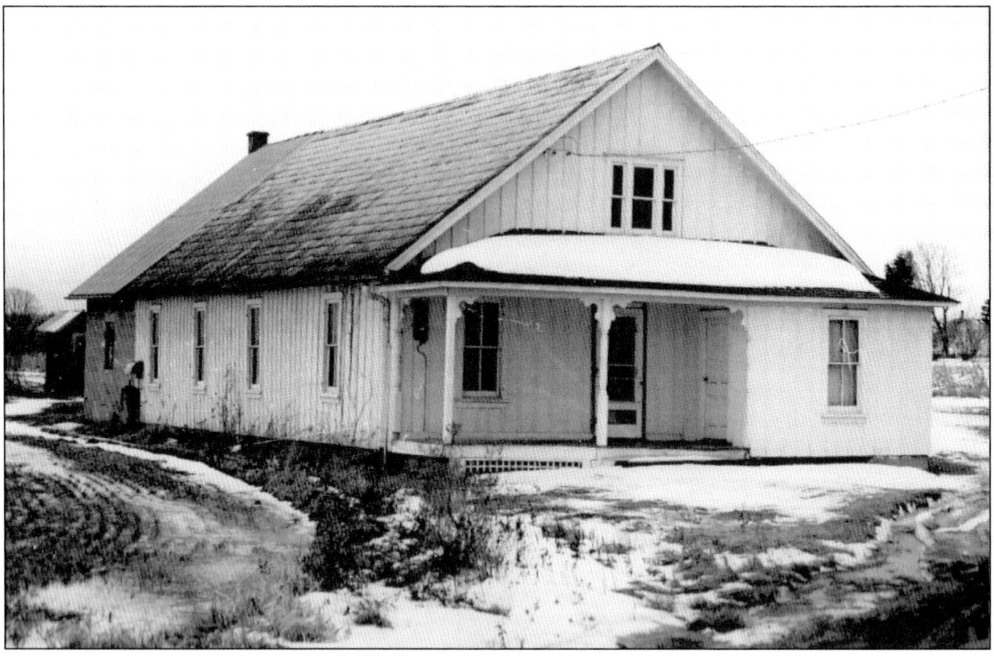

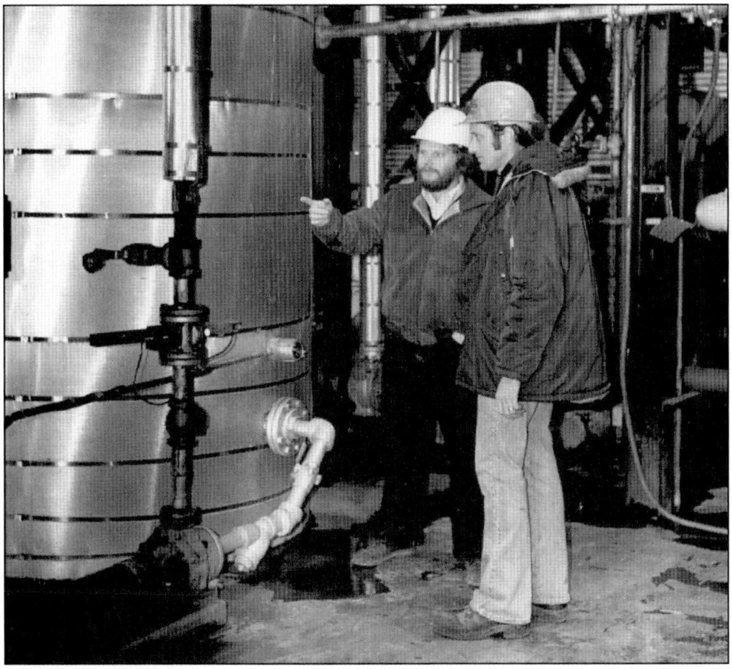

Koppers Industries, Inc., which treats railroad ties with chemical preservatives, began operation in their Clinton Township facility in 1972. By the mid-1980s, the plant expanded to include a cogeneration plant that produced electricity from burned rail ties. Pictured at a condensation tank are plant engineer Blake Housam (left) and treating supervisor Chuck Mitchener. (Courtesy Koppers Inc.)

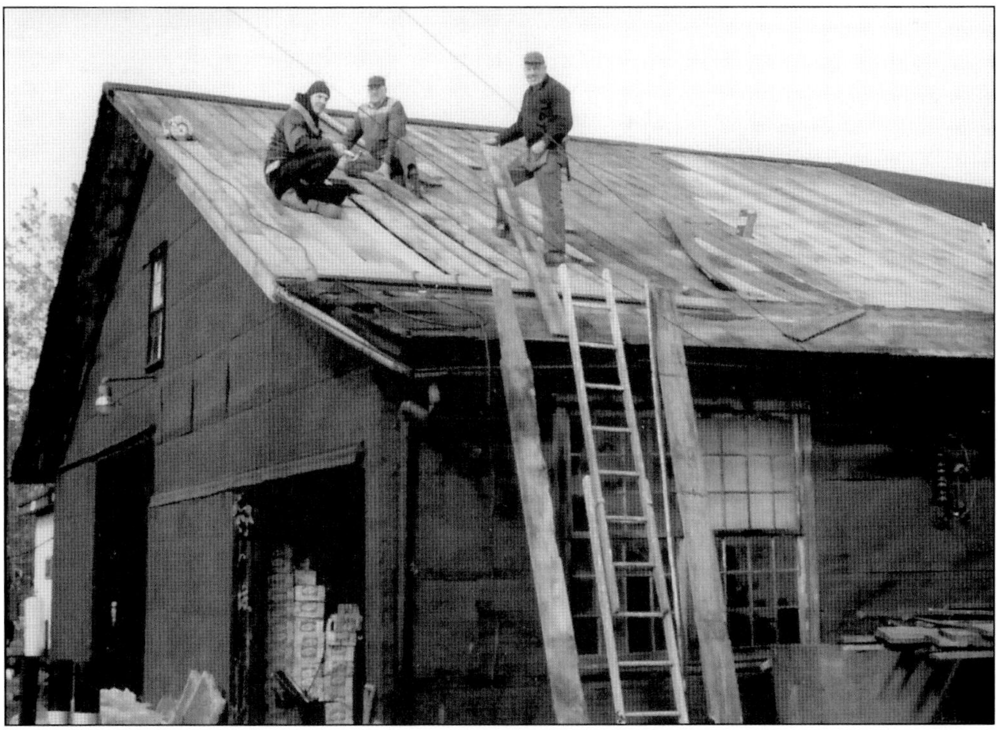

In the early 1960s, Les Gruver was appointed Montgomery's civil defense director. By 1970, Les's brother Dennis took over as director, and Les served as secretary and treasurer. In the spring of 1972, the Montgomery Emergency Management Agency (EMA) acquired and renovated a building on Thomas Avenue. Above, Ken Feaster (left), Les Gruver (center), and Don Feaster remove old shingles from the structure's roof. (Courtesy Montgomery EMA.)

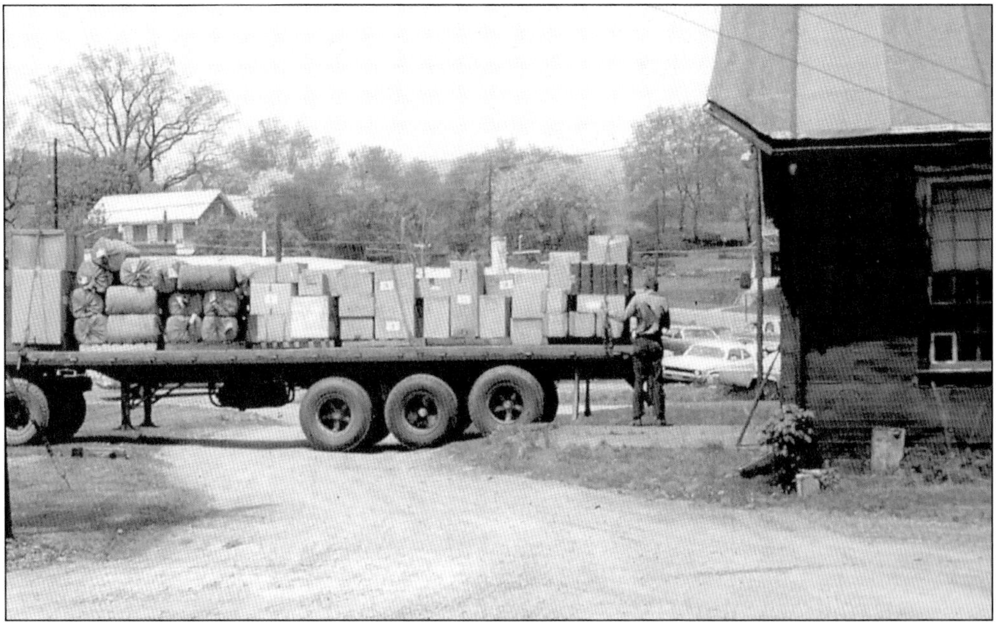

In 1972, Hurricane Agnes caused damage in Virginia, through central Pennsylvania, and up to the southern Finger Lakes region of New York. On June 22, a flash flood caused by the storm devastated the borough of Montgomery. Above, emergency hospital supplies are being unloaded from a flatbed for storage in the Thomas Avenue Emergency Management facility. Included in the boxes were splints, surgical instruments, and stretchers as well as bedpans, bandages, and Band-Aids. Below, spectators view the flooding on Second Street near Winder's Sunoco service station. (Both courtesy Montgomery EMA.)

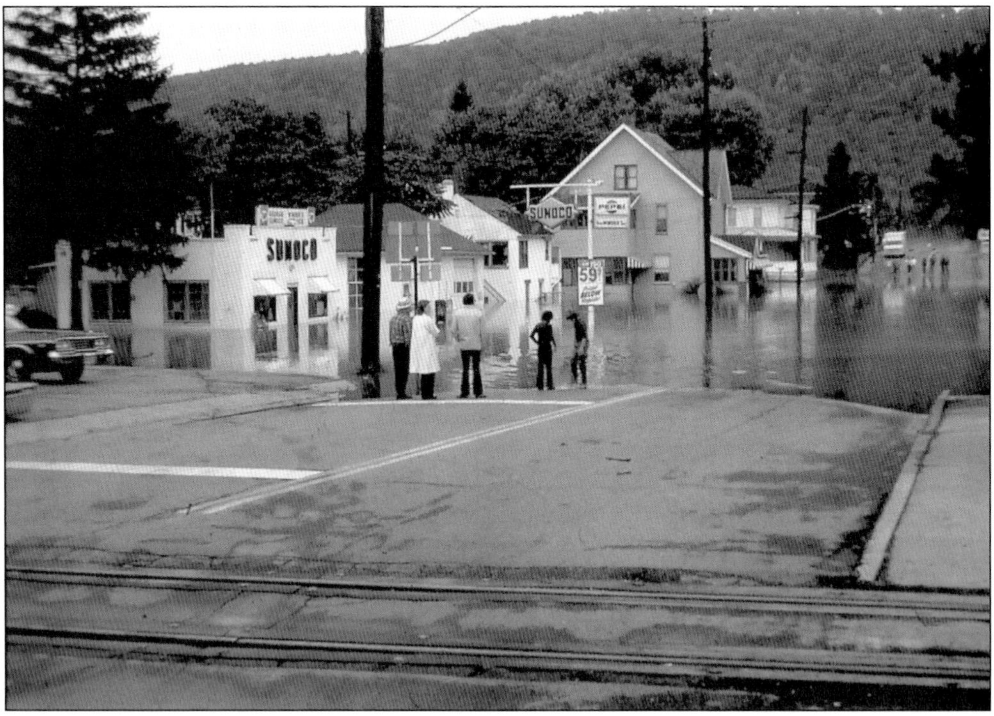

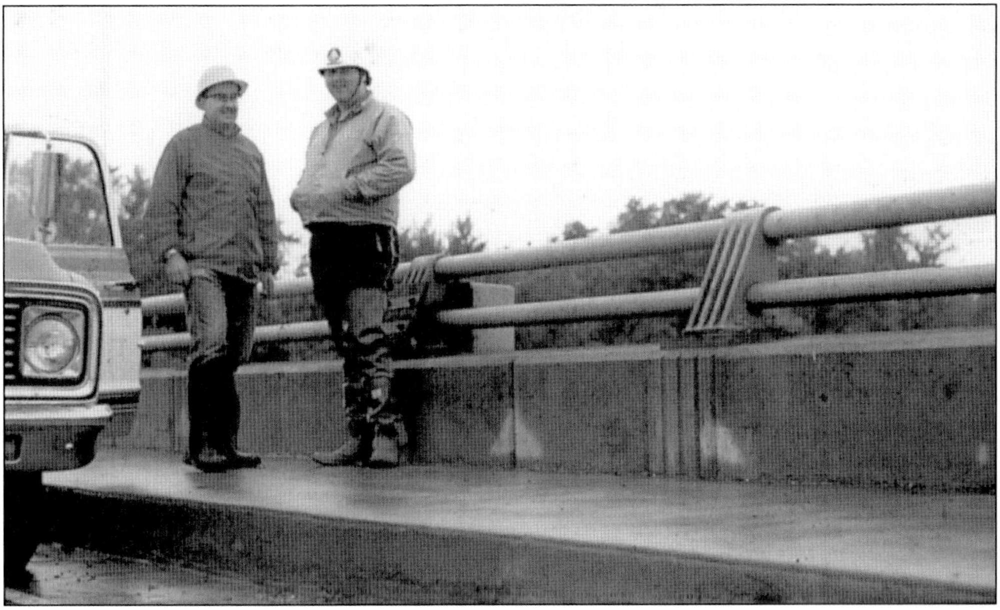

Fran Getchen and Les Gruver are seen above on the Muncy/Montgomery Bridge monitoring floodwater levels. Below, Don Feaster stands at the side entrance of the Fox home on Montgomery Street. This large house served as an emergency shelter for those who could not stay in their flooded homes. Feaster helped to distribute sanitation kits, which were cylindrical cardboard cans that contained a toilet seat, a liner, and 10 rolls of toilet paper, along with instructions for use. The Borough Water and Sewer systems were out of service due to the high water so the sanitation kits were to be used as a commode, with the liner inside and the toilet seat on top. (Both courtesy Montgomery EMA.)

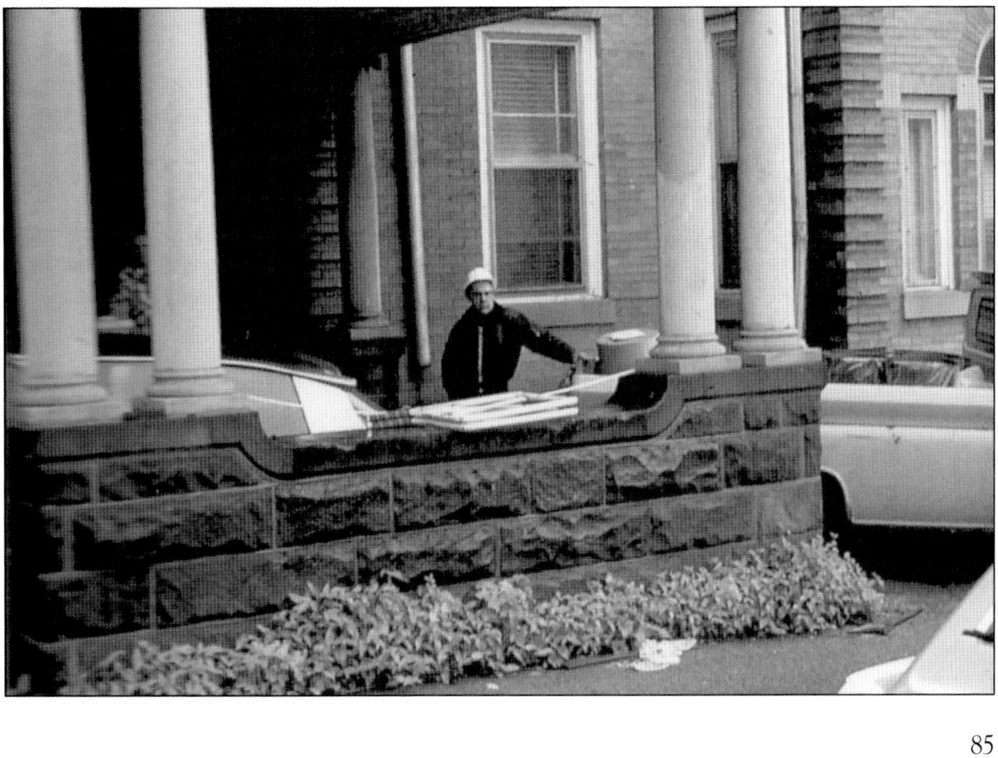

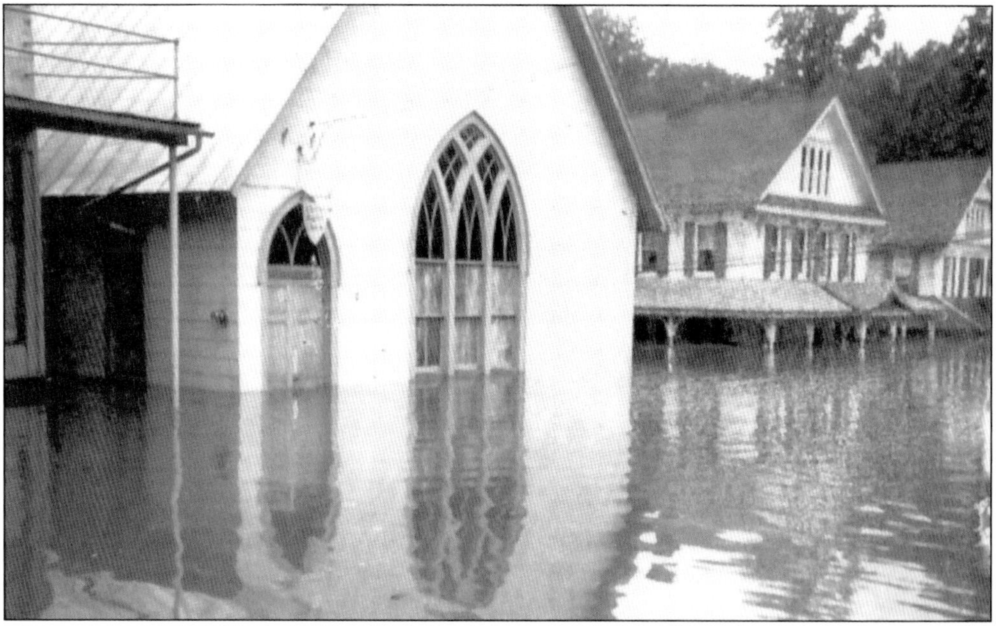

Montgomery High School was the site of the mass care center where 250 people were housed and fed for several days following the flood. Water from a well at Dorsey Creveling's residence at the top of West Houston Avenue was used to fill water cans, which were delivered to the mass care centers and placed on street corners for residents to use. The park along the river was destroyed, and the houses in low-lying areas were surrounded by water. Once floodwaters receded, homeowners returned to start cleaning up, remodeling, and repairing where necessary. Above is the Clinton Baptist Church on West Houston Avenue, and below is the railroad overpass on Main Street. (Both courtesy Montgomery EMA.)

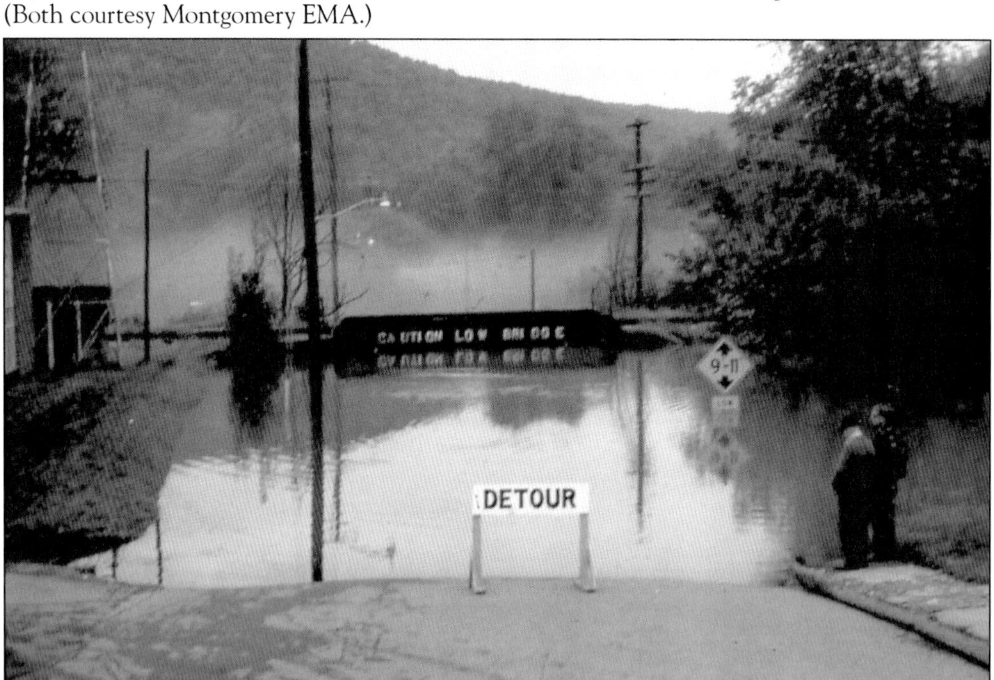

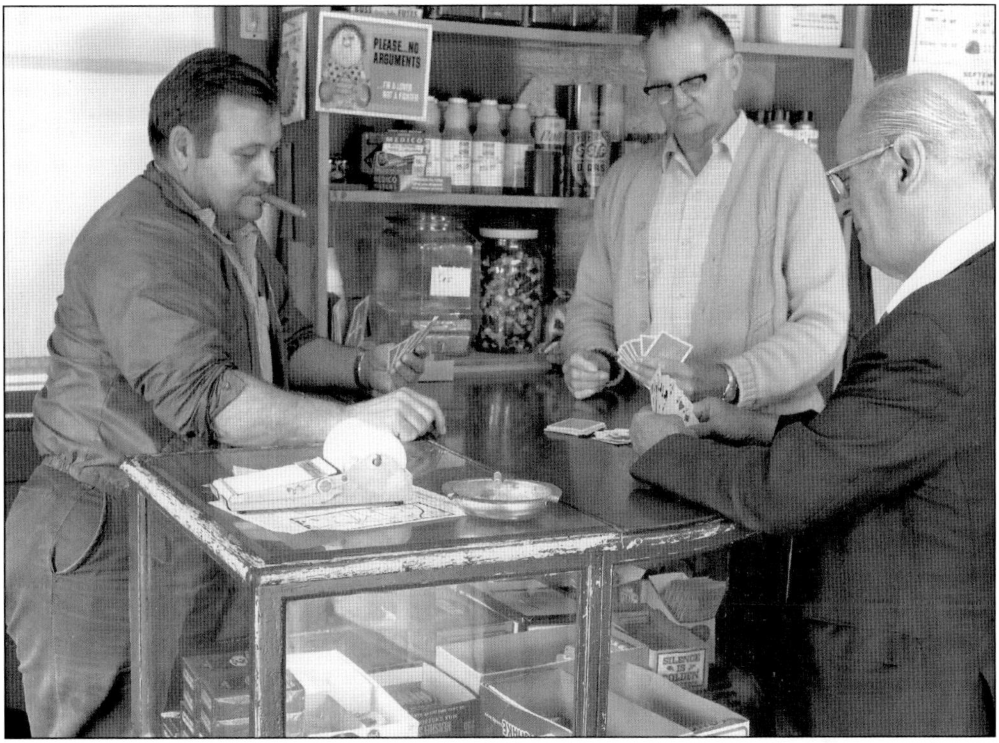

The scene captured above features Art Miller (left), Bill Grove (center), and Joe McCarty playing a card game at McCarty's Garage on Broad Street. Below is Ray and Jon's Lunch (currently the Station House restaurant), which was located at the corner of Montgomery and Second Streets near the railroad tracks. Other restaurants in the area have included the Mountain Tavern on Route 15, the Clinton House restaurant and Hotel, also on Route 15, Hoffner's Sub Shop, Kulp's Restaurant on South Main Street, Pizza Parlor on South Main Street, Jean & Ned's, Chet's Restaurant, and Ferrari's Inn. (Both courtesy MAPL; photographed by William McFadden Jr.)

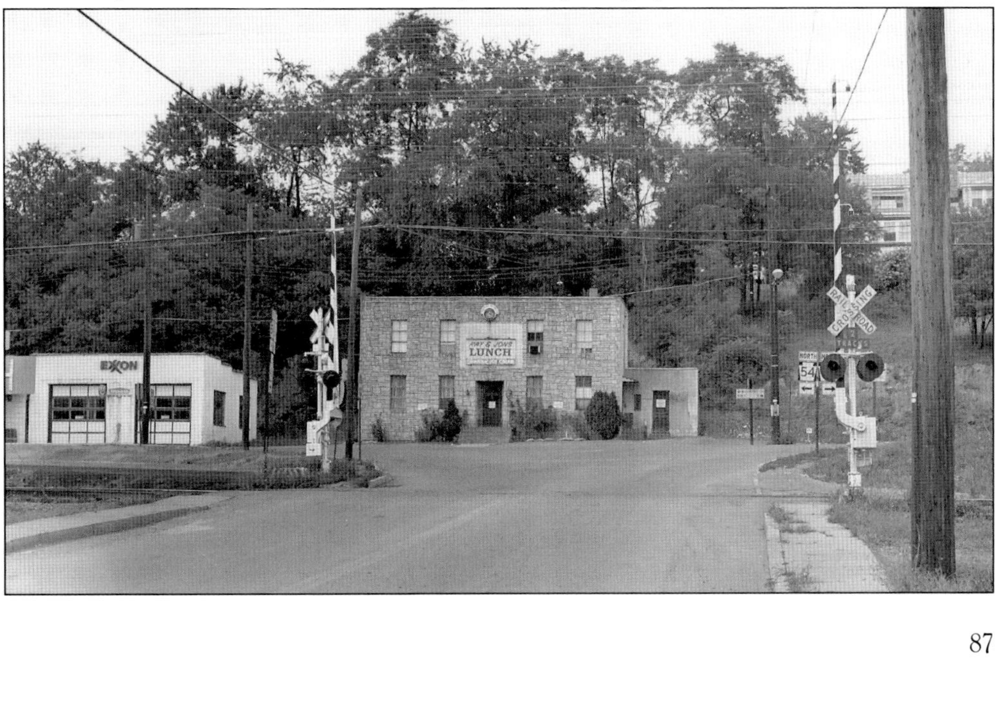

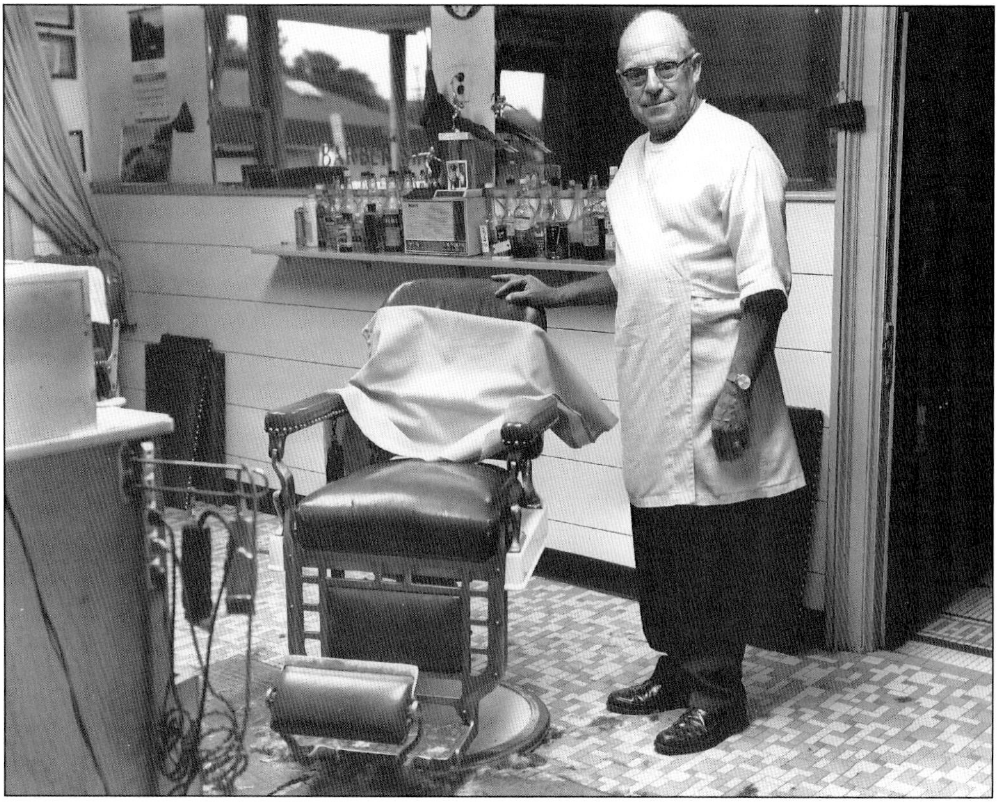

For over 30 years, Richard Stahl operated his barber shop in the Montgomery Hotel at the corner of Montgomery and Main Streets until his death in February 1975. Stahl was also one of the founding members of the Montgomery Little League, and his barbershop was the site of organizational meetings. (Courtesy MAPL; photographed by William McFadden Jr.)

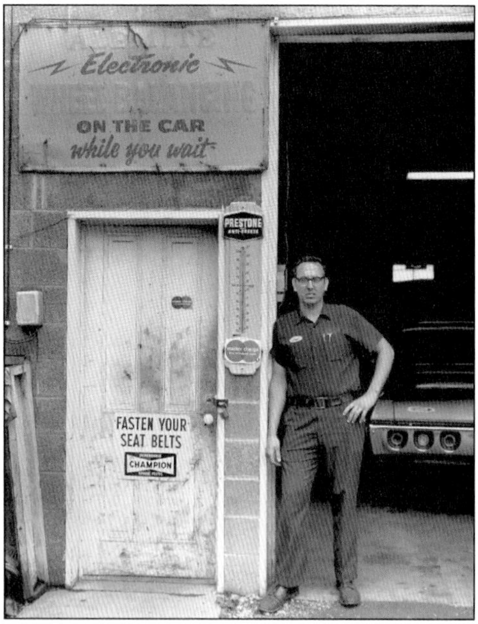

Dale Beaver stands in the doorway of his garage, which was located at 101 Third Street in the borough. Other garages in the area through the years included Canada's Garage, Follmer's Amoco, Smith's Garage, Hulsizer's, Harer's Service Station, Arthur Miller Jr., Sauer's Service Station, Stamets Service Station on Second Street, Taylor's Service Station, and Winder's on Second Street. (Courtesy MAPL; photographed by William McFadden Jr.)

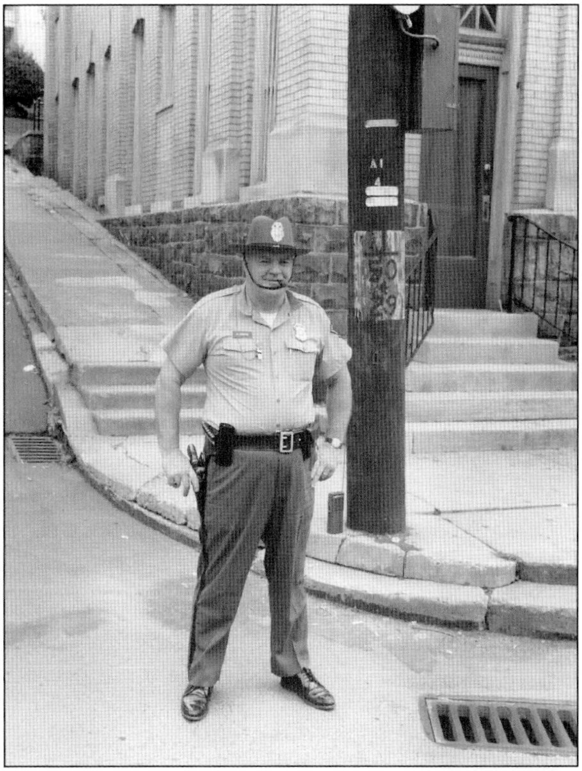

Through the years, Montgomery's police force has included police chief Charles Green during the 1950s, police chief William McClintock during the 1960s, and officer George Adams, who is shown at the corner of Houston Avenue and Main Street, ready with his pistol holstered, walkie-talkie handy, and cigar lit. Below, mailman George Waltman pauses to have his photograph taken and take a break from his daily treks up and down the hills of Montgomery. (Both courtesy MAPL; photographed by William McFadden Jr.)

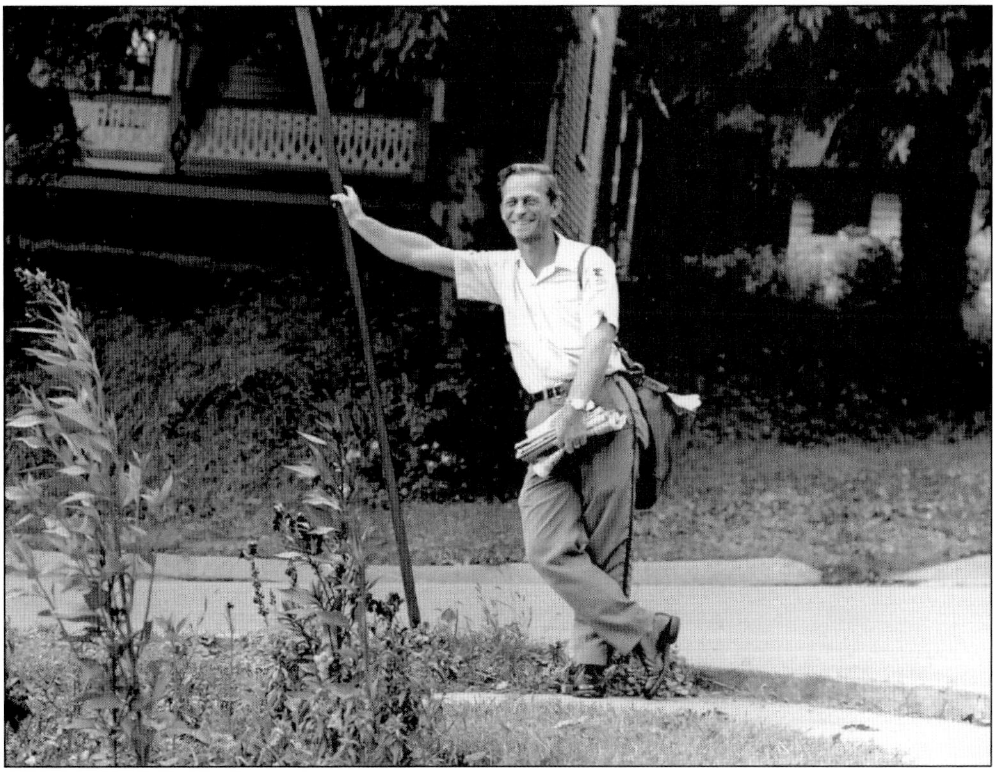

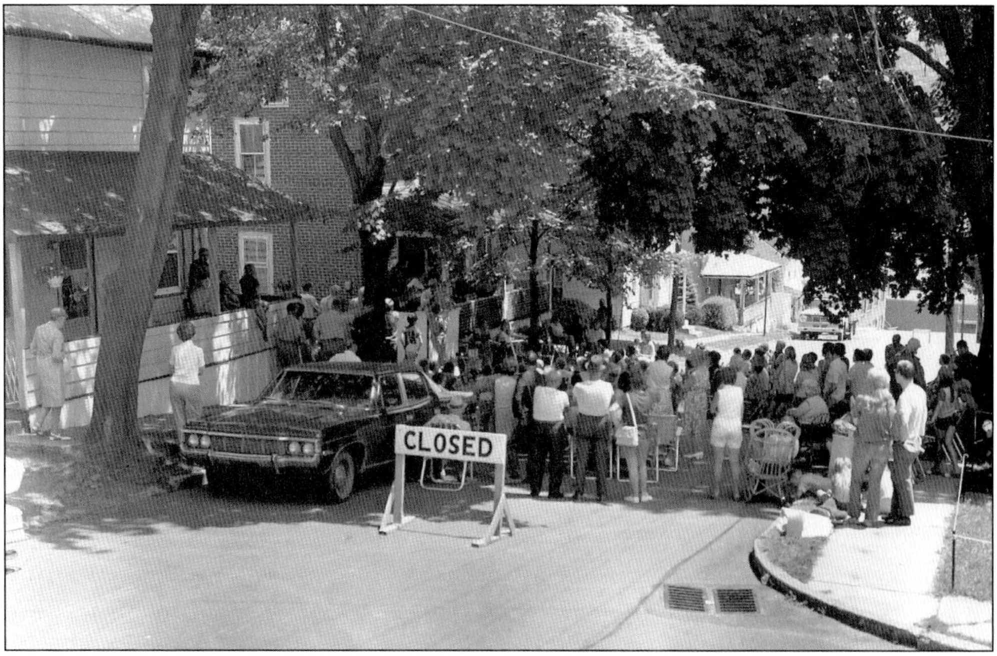

In the fall of 1974, this auction took place at the residence of Floy and Sylvia Houtz (house with brick facade) at the corner of East Houston Avenue and High Street. Barricades were erected to prevent automobile traffic as neighbors and friends gathered to help the Houtzes disseminate their belongings in anticipation of their move to a nursing home. (Courtesy MAPL.)

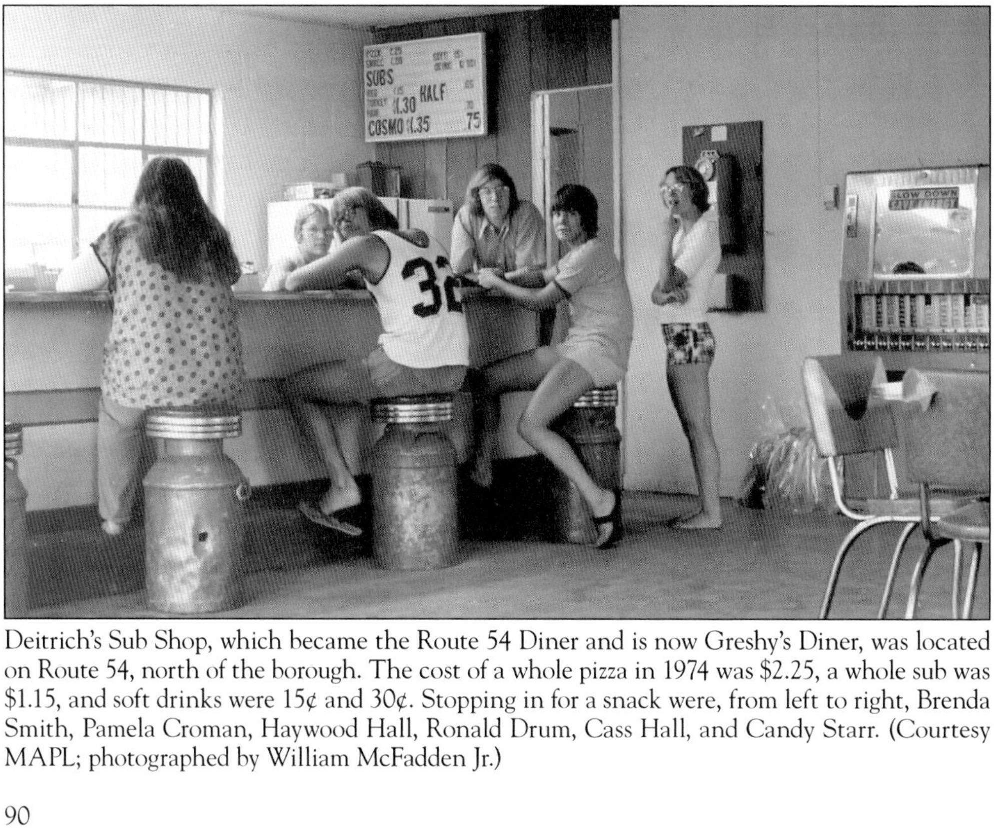

Deitrich's Sub Shop, which became the Route 54 Diner and is now Greshy's Diner, was located on Route 54, north of the borough. The cost of a whole pizza in 1974 was $2.25, a whole sub was $1.15, and soft drinks were 15¢ and 30¢. Stopping in for a snack were, from left to right, Brenda Smith, Pamela Croman, Haywood Hall, Ronald Drum, Cass Hall, and Candy Starr. (Courtesy MAPL; photographed by William McFadden Jr.)

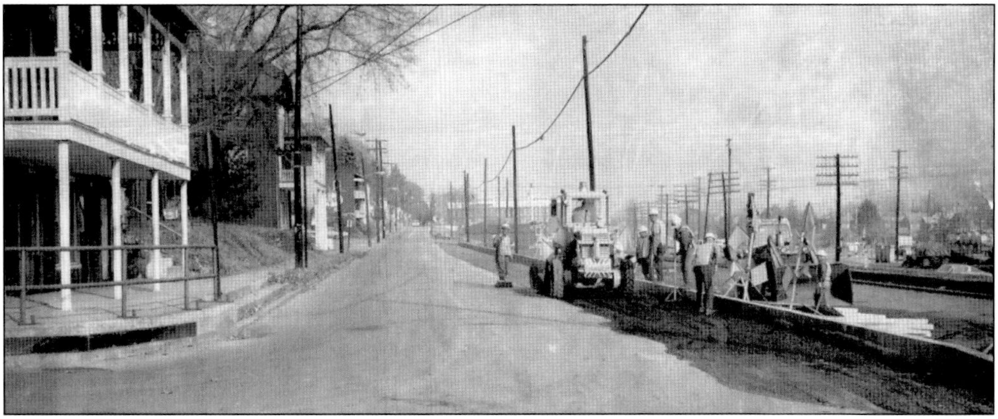

After the Pennsylvania Railroad station at the corner of Main and Montgomery Streets was demolished in 1973, Montgomery Street between Main and Second Streets was widened and a mini parking lot was made on the former site of the train depot. Above, the Montgomery Hotel appears on the left. Below, the house that had the distinction of being the oldest within Montgomery is seen before it was demolished in 1973. The house was originally built in 1852 by Henry Bower. It was razed to accommodate the construction of the Robert B. Montgomery Housing Development. (Both courtesy Montgomery Borough Historical Archives.)

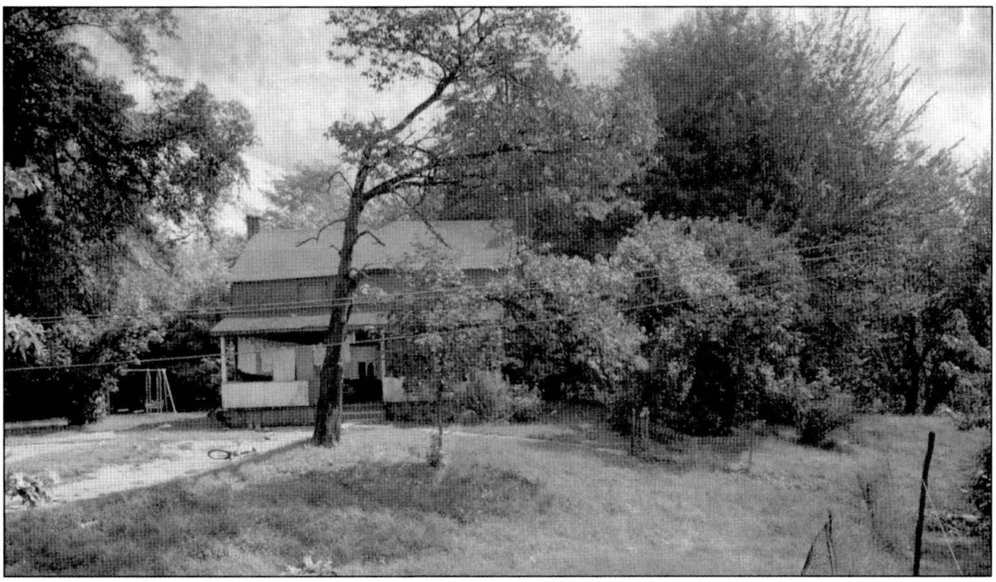

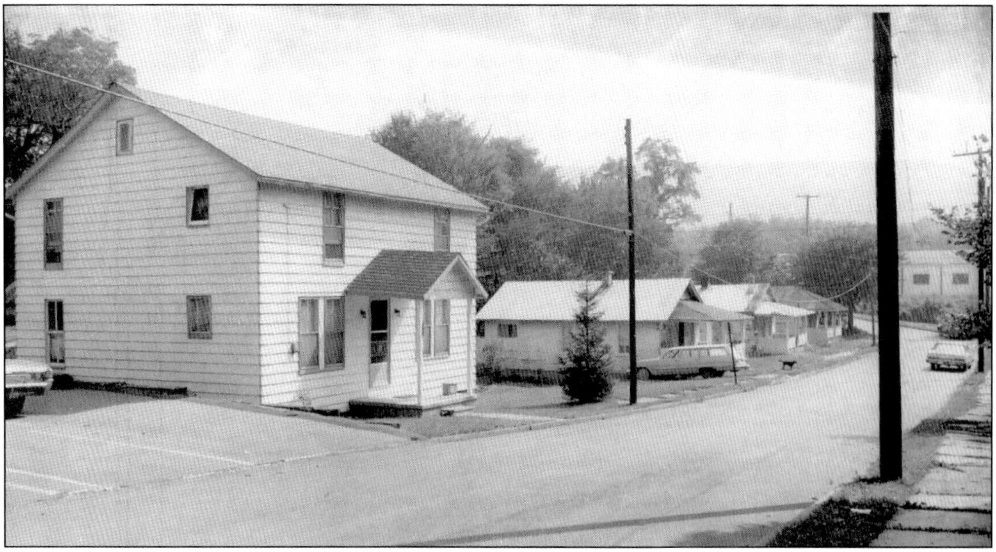

In response to the destruction of buildings and property during the Agnes Flood in 1972, an urban renewal project was initiated. Thirteen buildings located in the flood zone were demolished. The Montgomery Park and playground area, which had been destroyed in the flood, was rebuilt with funds from state and federal grants. Additionally, homes were razed on Bower Street to construct the Robert B. Montgomery Housing Development, adjacent to the First United Methodist Church property. The development made available several units for elderly housing as well as low-income apartments. (Both courtesy Montgomery Borough Historical Archives.)

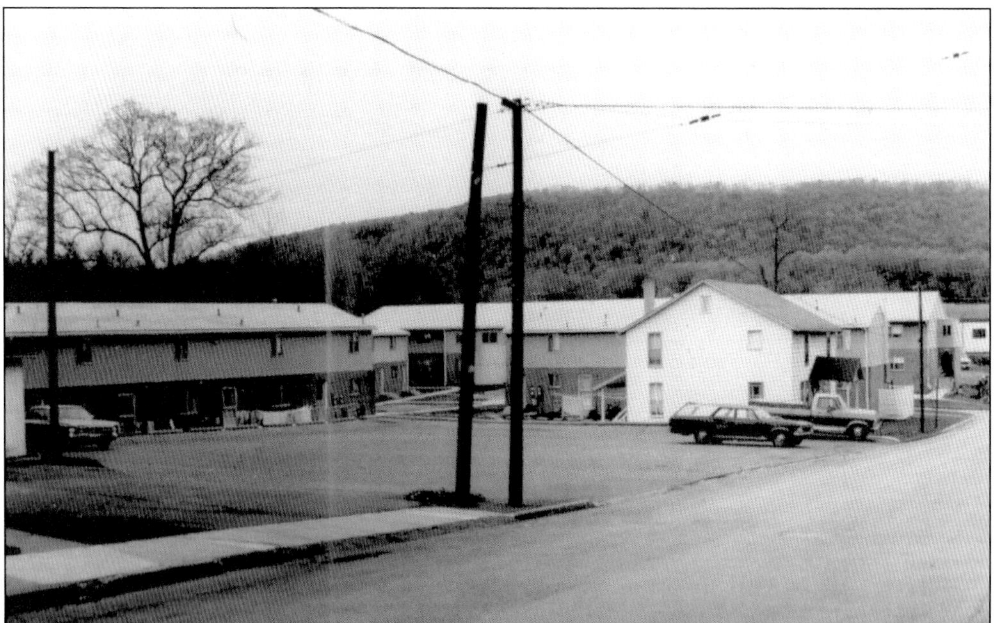

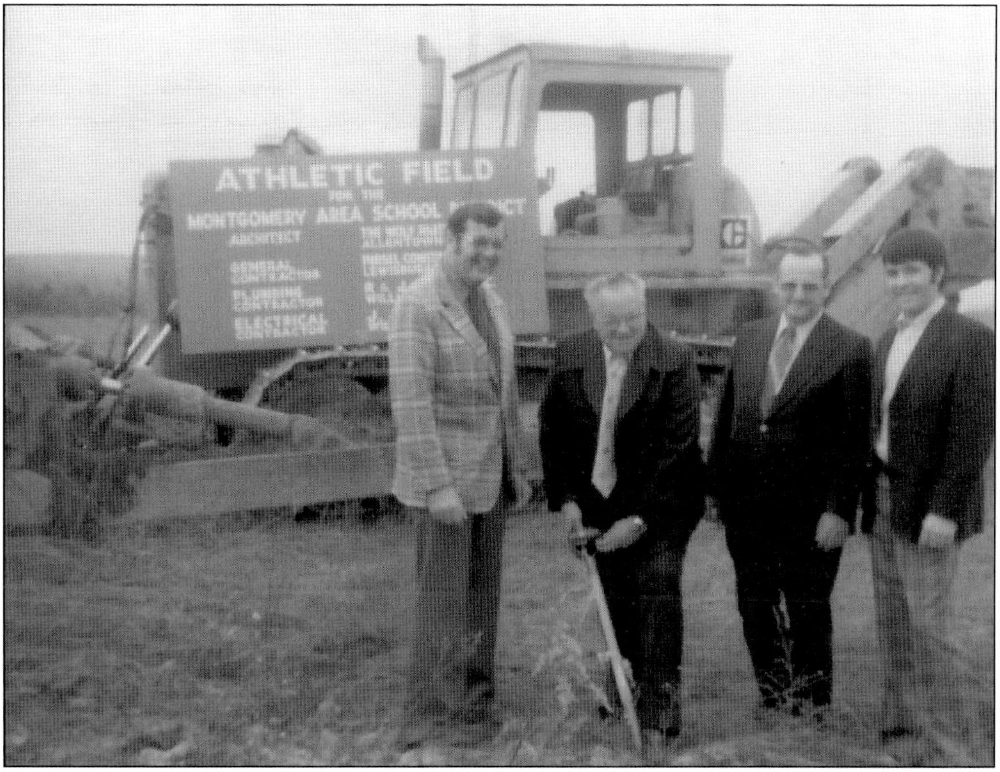

In April 1976, the groundbreaking ceremonies for the Montgomery Area School District athletic complex took place. The seven-acre complex featured a five-and-a-half-acre parking lot, a football field, track and field facilities, five tennis courts, and grandstands with a seating capacity of 2,000. Pictured from left to right are Frank O'Brien, school district superintendent; Raymond R. Taylor, school board president; William Swarthout, school board member, and Charles W. Pursel, representing the project's general contractor. In September, the football field was dedicated to the memory of Michael Guido, who for many years had been a teacher and football coach at the high school. (Both courtesy MAPL.)

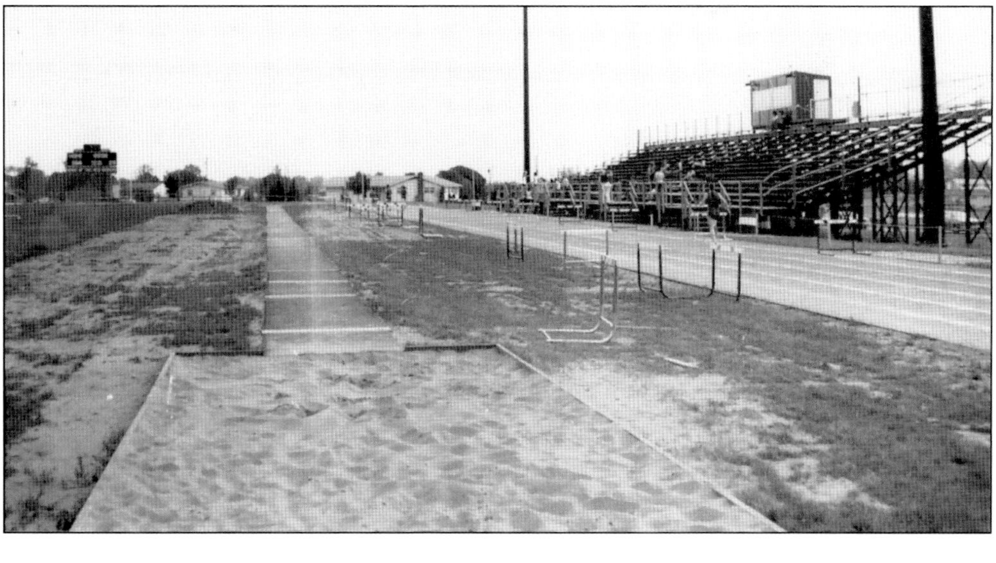

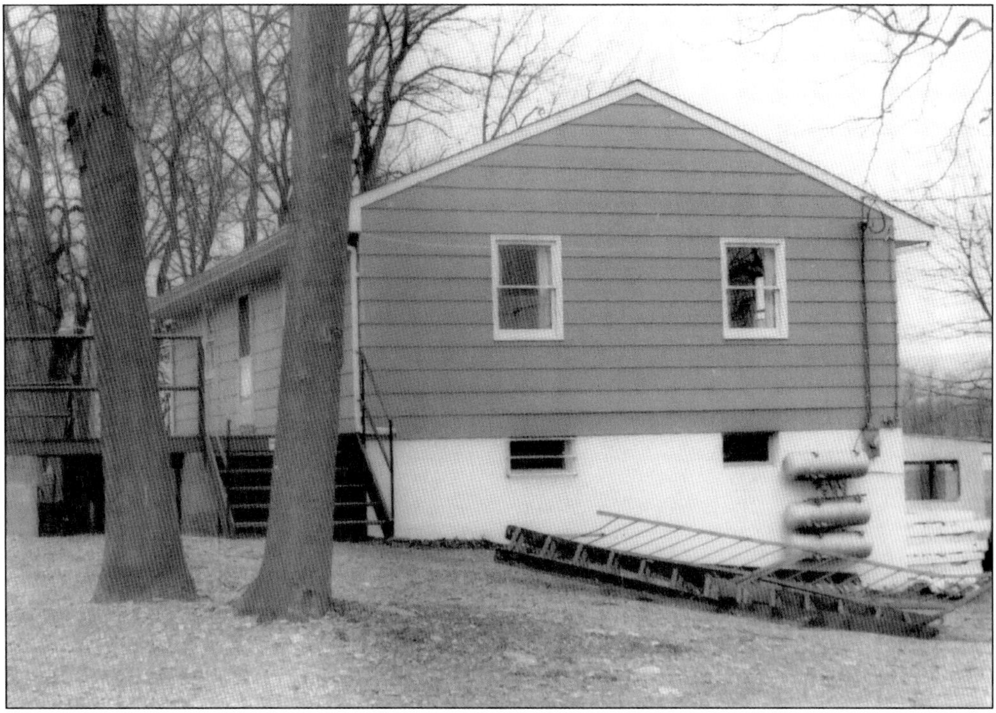

After the original building owned by the Montgomery Boat Club was demolished in the 1972 flood, this structure (above) was built in 1973. Organized in 1950, the boat club accepted land donated by Fred Tebbs upon which they built their first clubhouse. For over 20 years, the Montgomery Boat Club held annual powerboat regattas, during which regatta queens and princesses were crowned. The race competitions involved racing three laps of a one-and-two-thirds-mile course with buoys marking the circuit. Below is a scene of powerboats on the Susquehanna River captured in 1974. (Both courtesy MAPL; below, photographed by William McFadden Jr.)

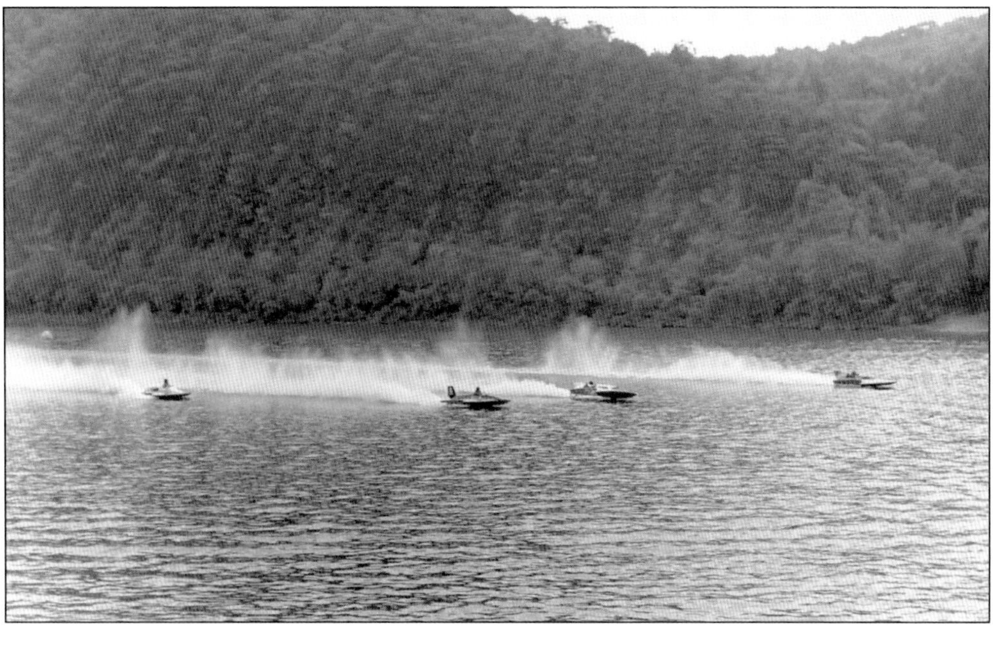

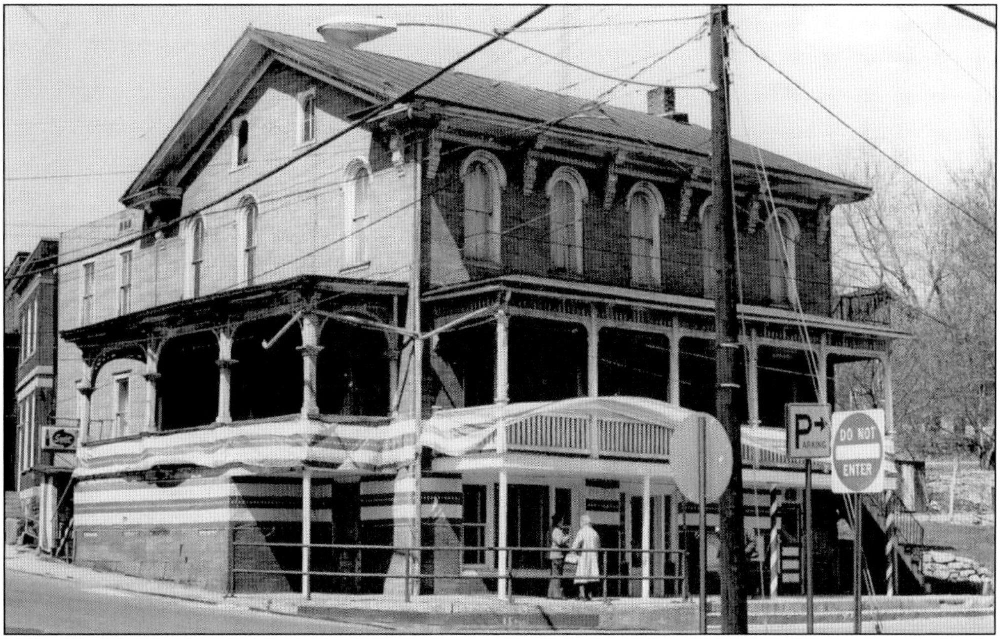

As part of the borough's Main Street Redevelopment Project, the demolition of the Montgomery Hotel was scheduled for the spring of 1976. To honor the history of this 115-year-old building, the borough manager, Max Mull, spearheaded the idea of the Hotel Bash. Mull, with the assistance of Shirley Schneck, Jan O'Brien, Dick Thomas, and George Adams, planned the event, which was held the weekend of April 9–10, 1976. Tours of the hotel were offered as well as a buffet of home-cooked food that featured hams and bean soup prepared over open fires. Over 2,000 attended the Hotel Bash. Pictured are, from left to right, Catherine Blessing Thomas, who was 72 at the time, with Jan O'Brien, and Shirley Schneck. (Both courtesy MAPL.)

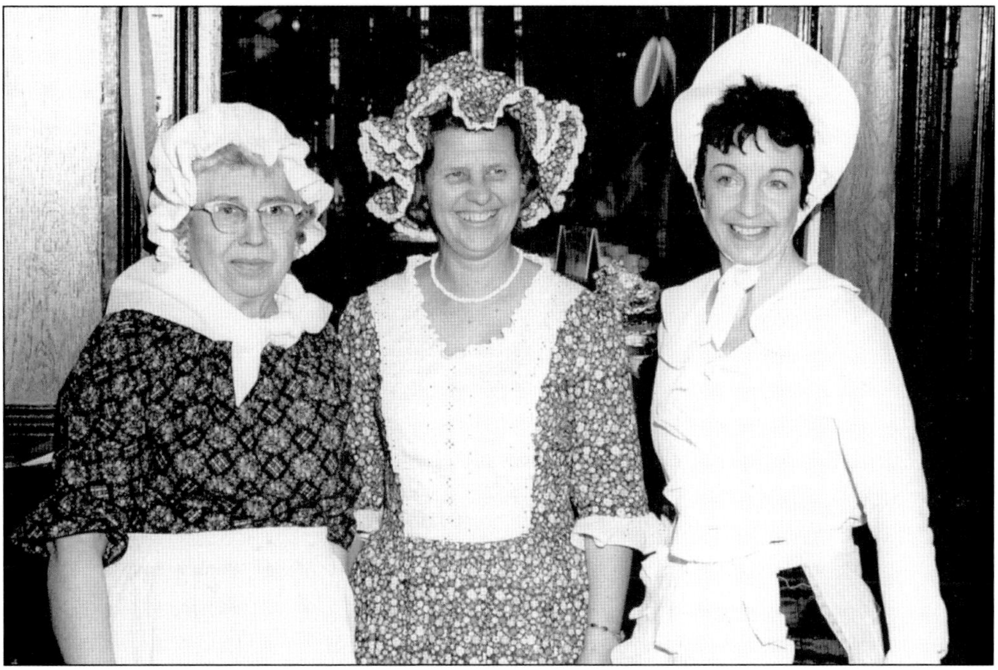

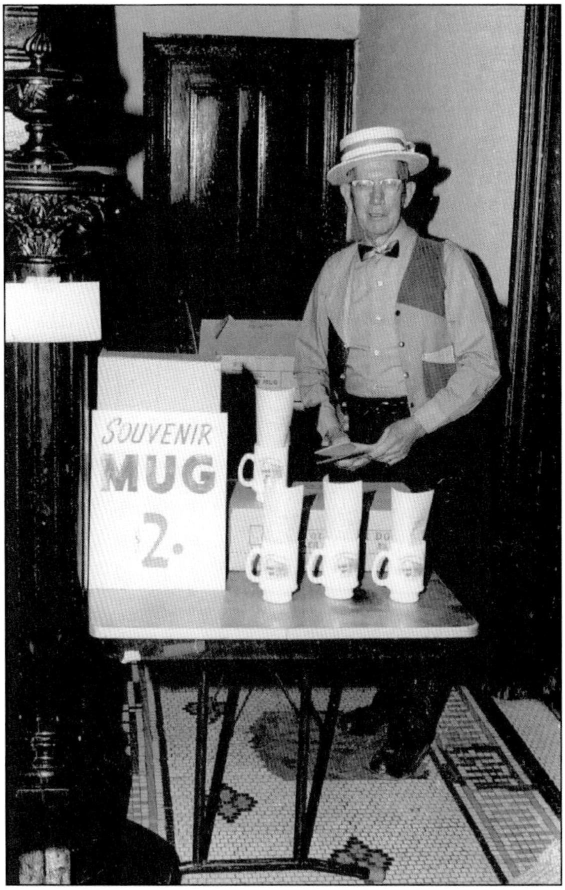

At a table located near the stairs of the historic Montgomery Hotel, Alan Horn supervised the sale of commemorative mugs featuring an image of the building. Representatives of a number of community organizations were responsible for other aspects of the celebration. George Amos Smith and Gary Yocum, members of the borough fire department, served drinks at the hotel tavern. George Page and Jane Wolf cooked hams outdoors over an open fire and made ham and bean soup in butcher kettles. Additional food for the Hotel Bash was prepared across the street in the kitchen of the Lions Hall. Pictured below, from left to right, are Lorraine Harris, Marion McCormick, Jan O'Brien, and Dot Sandmeyer. (Both courtesy MAPL.)

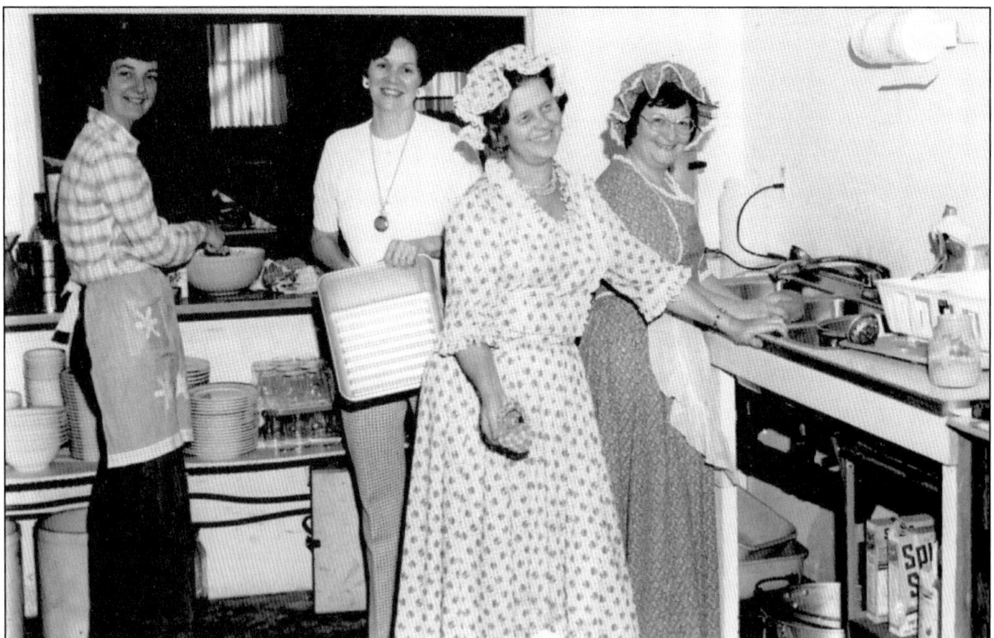

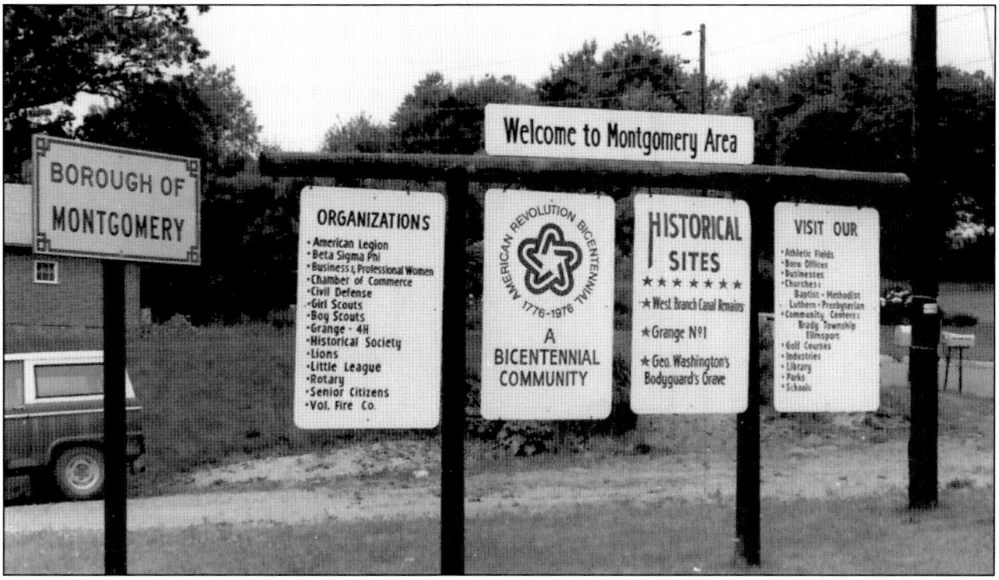

After Montgomery's approval as an official Bicentennial Community for the American Revolution Bicentennial celebration in 1976, these signs were erected to publicize the borough's historic sites. A series of events and activities were planned to commemorate the 200th anniversary of America's independence. The students pictured below were the Bicentennial Dancers who represented Montgomery High School's Junior Historians during the Bicentennial. Their first performance was at the Memorial Day parade and dedication of the renovated park in May 1975. Dressed in colonial costumes made by Jan O'Brien and Shirley West, the group demonstrated square dancing and performed at many of the bicentennial events. Pictured from left to right are (first row) Kelly Orso, Tammy Buck, Shelly Gearhart, Deb Spizziri, Michele Johns, Sharon Pfirman, and Linda Miller; (second row) Paul Shaner, Bill Kahler, Brett McCormick, and Art Bennett. (Both courtesy MAPL.)

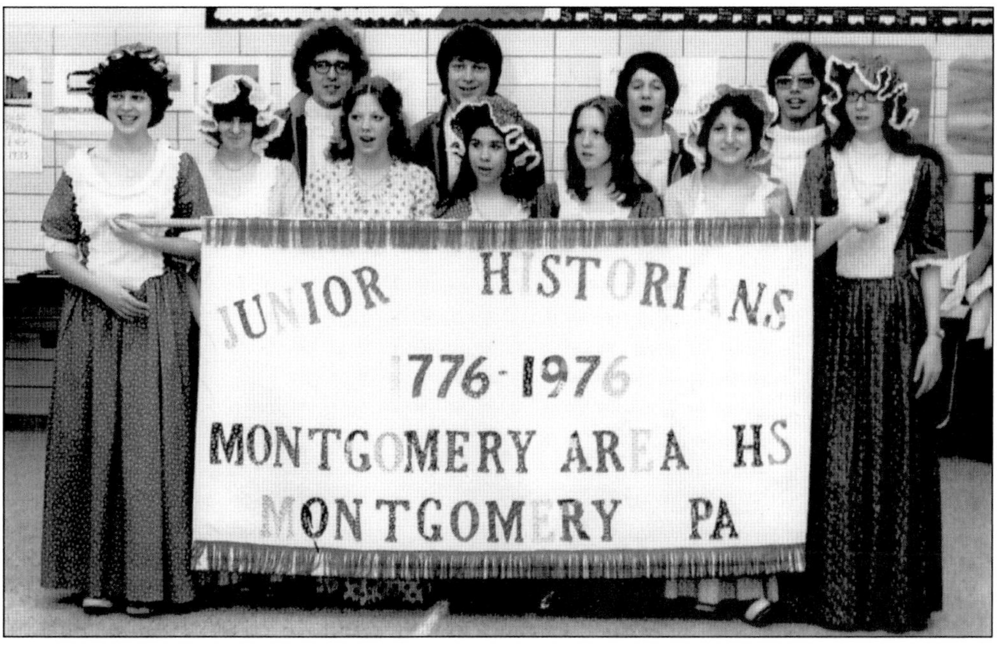

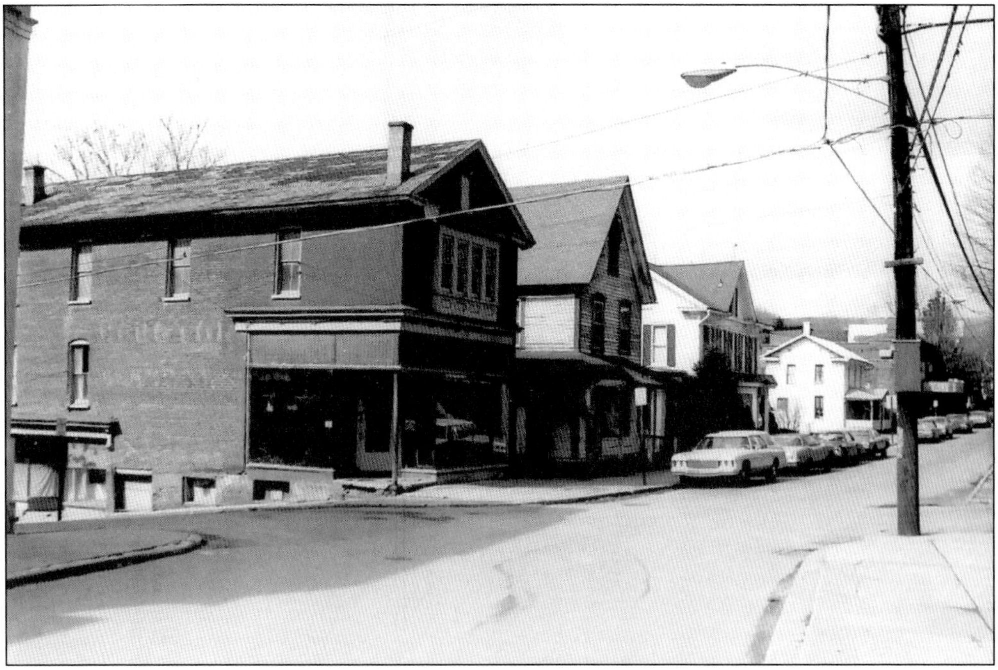

In February 1976, the former hardware store building located at the northwest corner of Main Street and Houston Avenue was demolished. Additionally, the adjacent residence on Main Street that was owned by Dorothy Weaver was also razed to make way for the construction of the Montgomery Municipal parking lot (below) that was utilized by bank customers and shoppers on Main Street. Across the street on the northeast corner, the former Hotel Houston was also torn down, and a small park was landscaped in its place. Other demolitions in the borough included the former Frey Hardware building and the old opera house. (Above, courtesy Peggy and Charles Yohn; below, courtesy MAPL.)

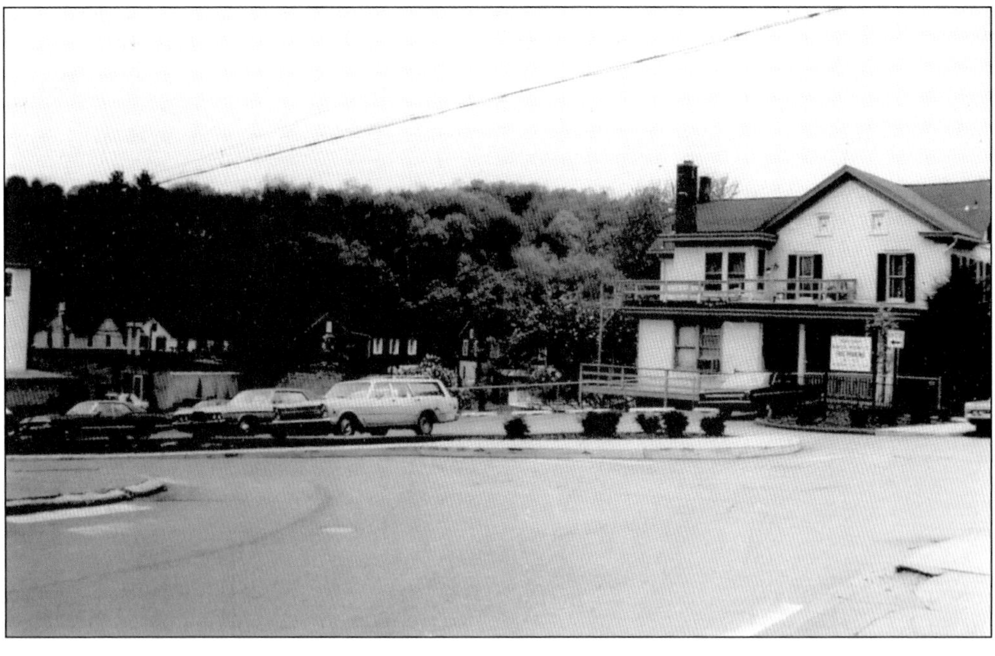

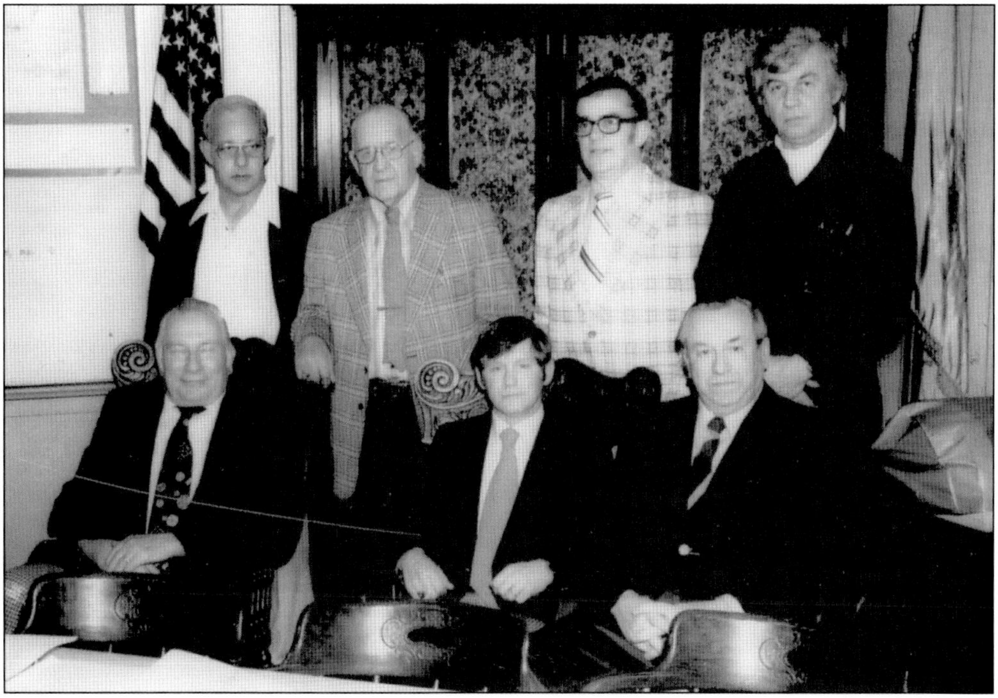

In 1976, the Montgomery borough officials included, from left to right, (first row) mayor Glenn Klobe, council president Charles Yohn Jr., and council member Allen Lupold; (second row) council members Frank Stout and Orville Mase and council vice-president Richard Thomas Sr. Other officials not pictured include borough manager Max Mull, and council members John Everhart and Roberta McClintock, who was the first elected female council member. Below, the manufacturing facilities of Isaac Decker Manufacturing are pictured. This was one of Montgomery's oldest industries, still operating 70 years after it was founded in 1905. The company manufactured upholstered living room and office furniture. (Above, courtesy Montgomery Borough Historical Archives; below, courtesy MAPL.)

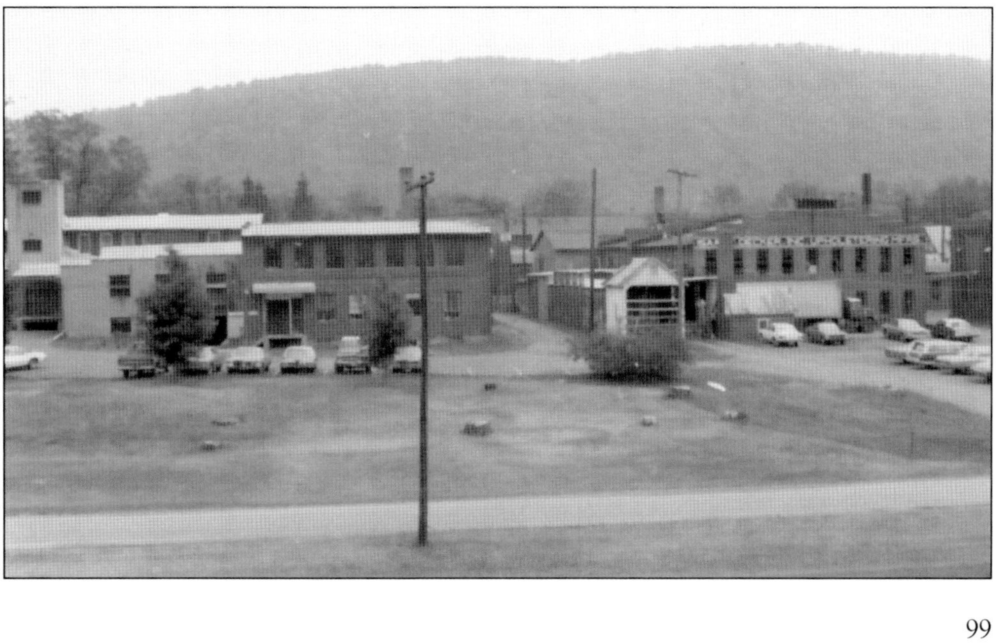

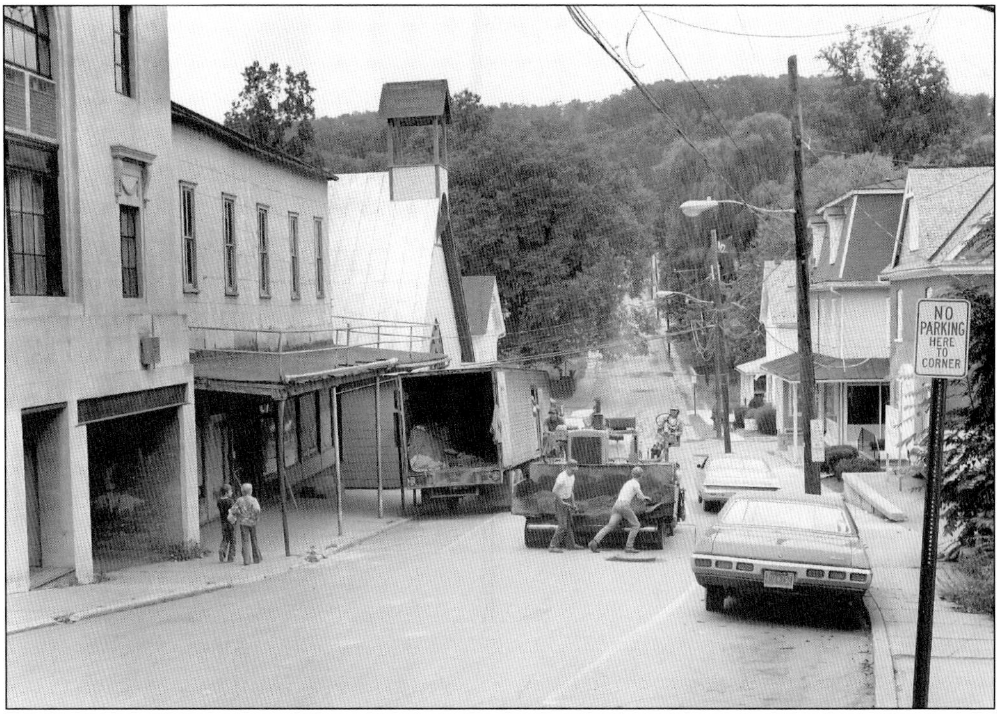

Photographed in the fall of 1974, a borough road crew is fixing a manhole on West Houston Avenue. The Northern Central Bank building is on the left next to the building that had been owned by George Decker. This building was razed in 1975. Next to the Decker building is the former Clinton Baptist Church. (Courtesy MAPL; photographed by William McFadden Jr.)

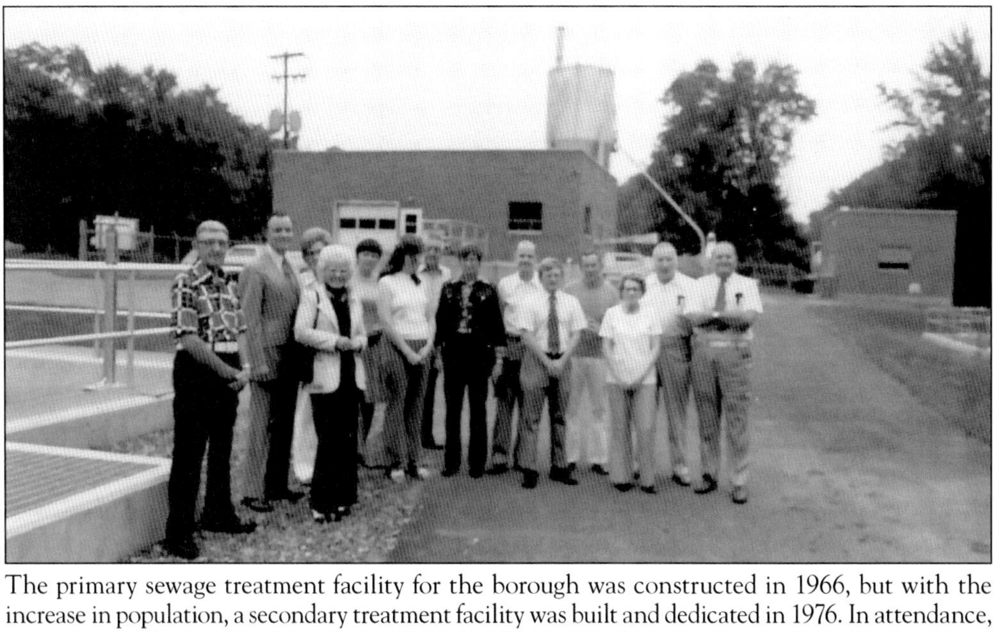

The primary sewage treatment facility for the borough was constructed in 1966, but with the increase in population, a secondary treatment facility was built and dedicated in 1976. In attendance, from left to right, were Karl Bartl, Paul Woodruff, Mrs. Harold Tobias, Jacqueline Mandes, Peggy Yohn, Mrs. Richard Klobe, Kevin Cooper, Harold Tobias, Charles Yohn Jr., Max Mull, Jay Russell, Richard Klobe, Mrs. Glen Klobe, and Glen Klobe. (Courtesy MAPL.)

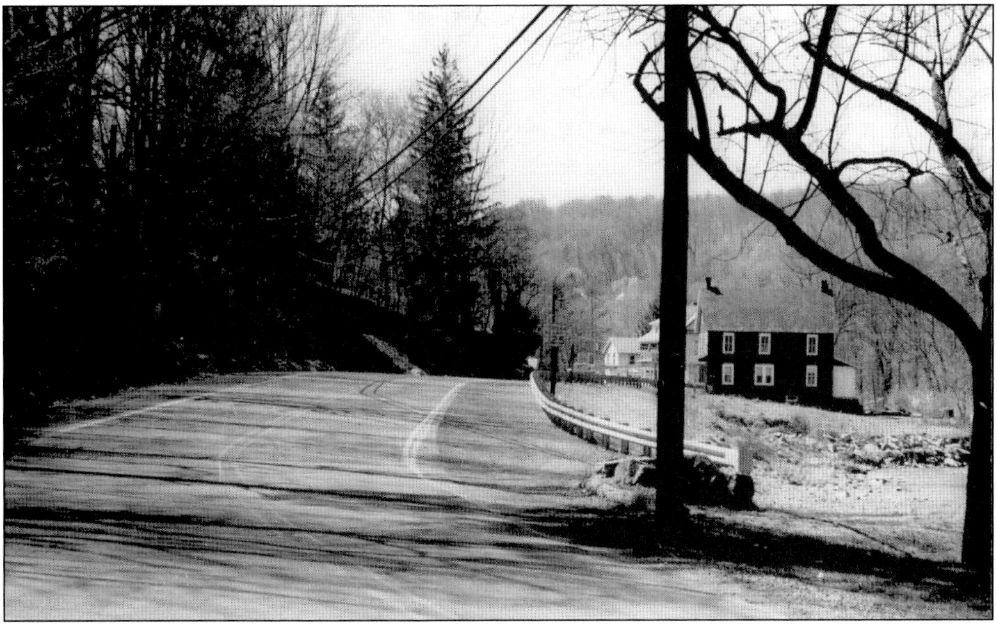

Locally known as the Narrows, this stretch of road located north of the borough was originally a convenient fresh spring water stop for travelers approaching Montgomery. After the 1936 flood washed away the wooden walkway constructed along the road, the Works Progress Administration replaced it with a stone wall. The wall was damaged in the Agnes Flood and removed so the road at the Narrows could be widened. (Courtesy MAPL.)

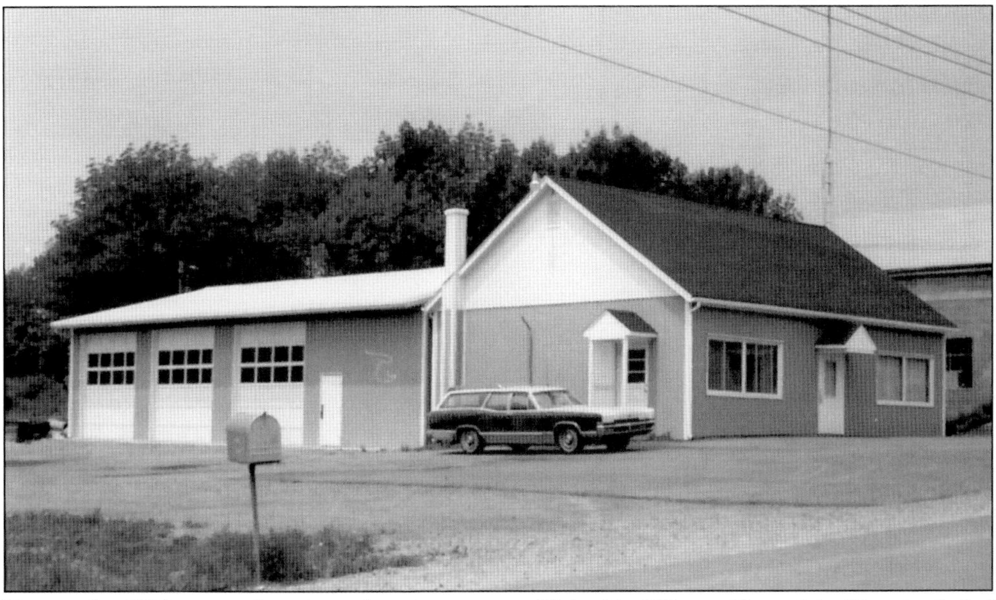

During the 1970s, several major industries were established in Clinton Township. They included Construction Specialties in 1967, the Marathon Carey-McFall Company, Grumman Allied, and Koppers Company in 1972, and the West Company, which was originally established as Plasti-Vac in 1962. For more about Koppers, see pages 83 and 124. Grumman is mentioned on page 118. This photograph shows the Clinton Township Supervisors building, which is located across from the Clinton Township Volunteer Fire Company. (Courtesy MAPL.)

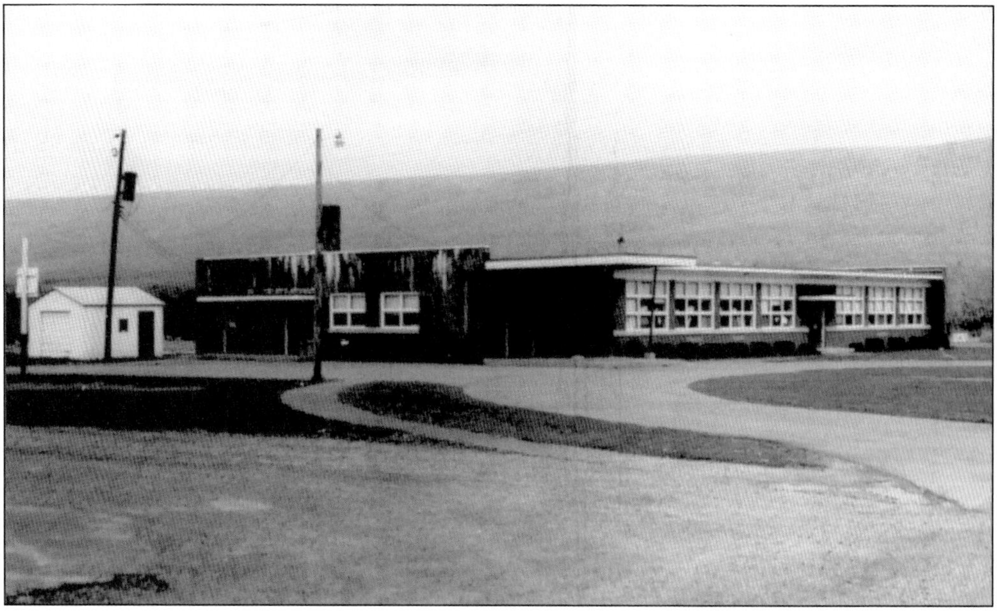

The elementary school in Elimsport was built and opened in October 1957. It had four classrooms with plans to include two additional rooms if necessary. Children in first through sixth grades (initial enrollment was about 120 students) were bussed from throughout Washington Township. The school also featured a modern kitchen that had the capacity to prepare hot lunches daily, and a combination school office and health room. Pictured above is the Elimsport Elementary School in the mid-1970s. Below is a view of Elimsport's Main Street. Two stores, Russell's Market and Starr's General Store, served the Elimsport area in the 1970s. Elimsport also was the home of First Baptist Church of Elimsport, Elimsport United Methodist Church, and St. John's United Methodist Church. (Both courtesy MAPL.)

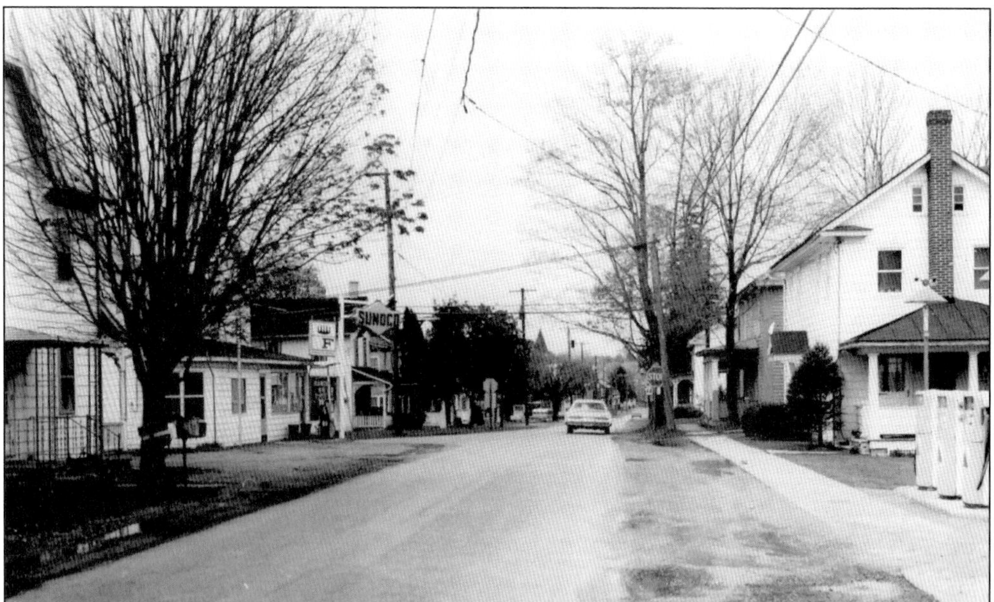

Five

The 1980s

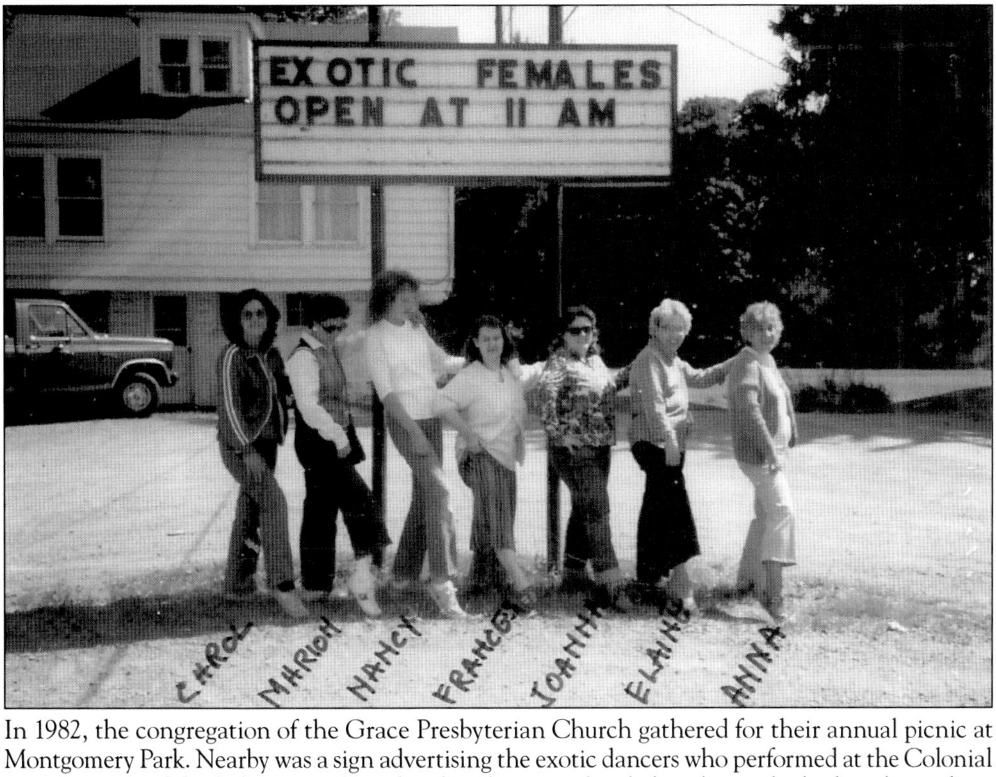

In 1982, the congregation of the Grace Presbyterian Church gathered for their annual picnic at Montgomery Park. Nearby was a sign advertising the exotic dancers who performed at the Colonial House. Some of the ladies attending the church picnic decided to show a little skin themselves. They are, from left to right, Carol Edwards, Marion McCormick, Nancy Engle, Frances Hall, Joanna Miller, Elaine Kobbe, and Anna Taylor. (Courtesy Grace Presbyterian Church.)

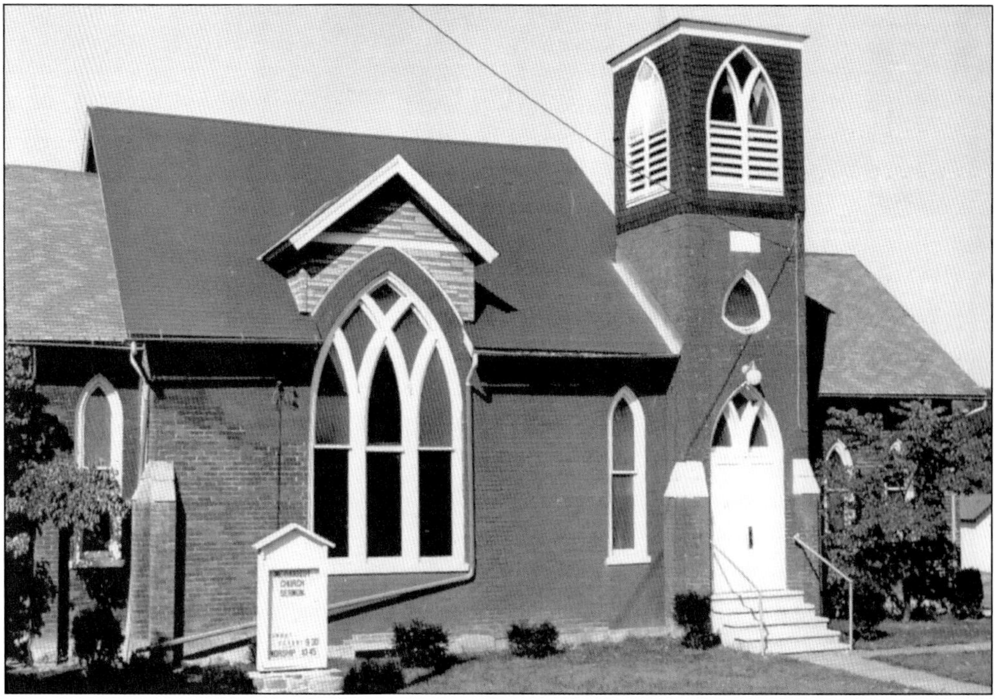

When George Schneider and his family settled in the area now known as Elimsport, he requested a post office be established. In March 1838, Schneider was appointed postmaster of the town, which was named in reference to the biblical oasis of Elam. Schneider was also the first minister of the town's Methodist Church and a store owner. The earliest record of a Methodist church building in Elimsport dates to 1852. In 1885, its replacement was built and dedicated. During an electrical storm on June 29, 1920, however, this building caught fire and was destroyed. Within eight months, a new brick structure (above) was built and dedicated in February 1921. In 1987, an addition (below) was built that included an education and fellowship hall. (Both courtesy Richard and Eleanor Taylor.)

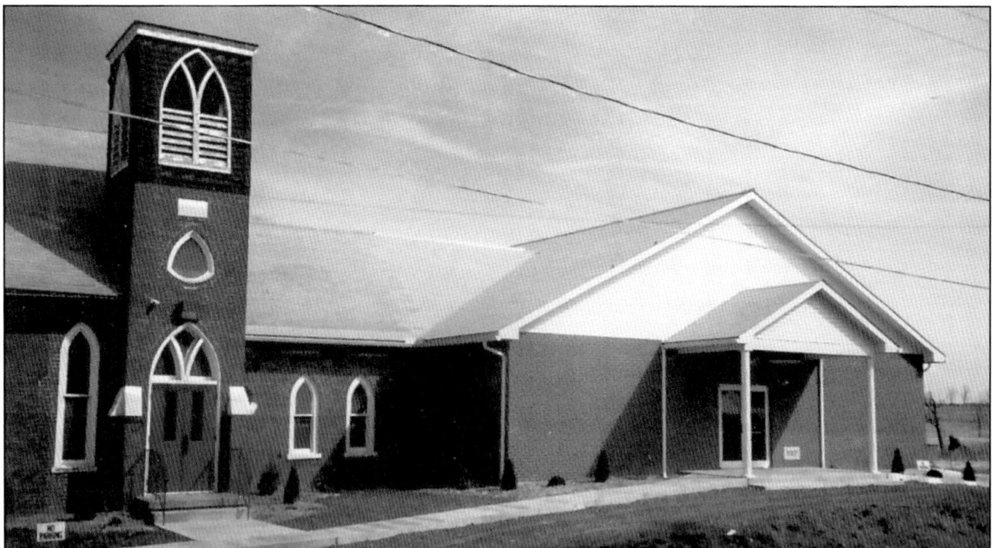

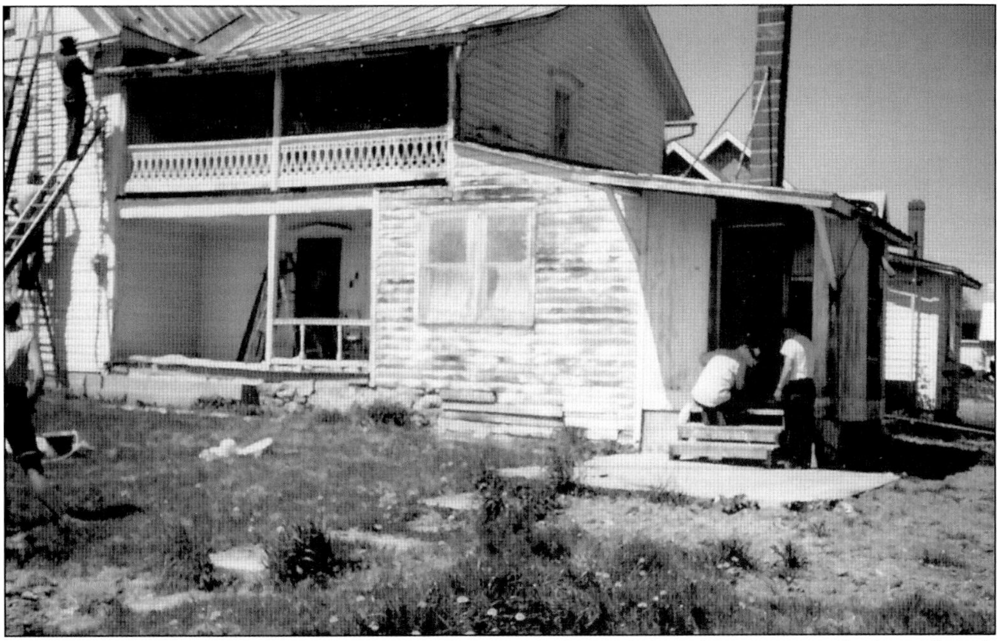

On Saturday, May 15, 1982, approximately 30 members of the Elimsport Methodist Church volunteered to sand, spackle, repair, prime, and paint the building near the church that was used to hold Sunday school classes. This transformation occurred in the course of only one day. Pictured above is Elvin "Stoney" Fry standing in the doorway on the right. Below is the Sunday School house after its facelift. In 1987, the building was torn down to make room for the planned addition to the church building and an adjoining paved parking lot. (Both courtesy Richard and Eleanor Taylor.)

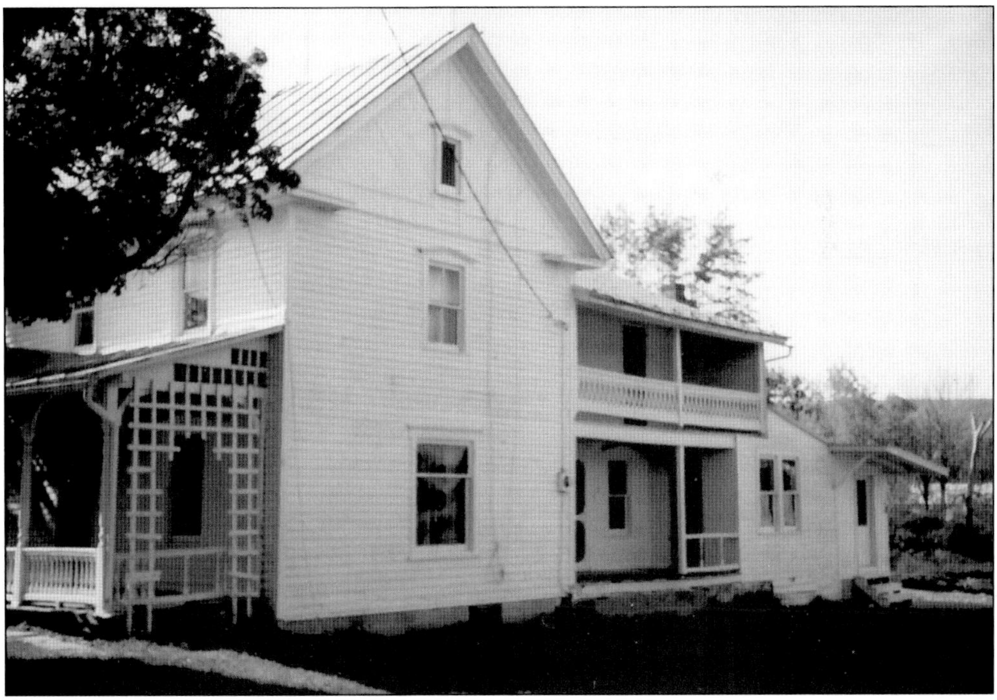

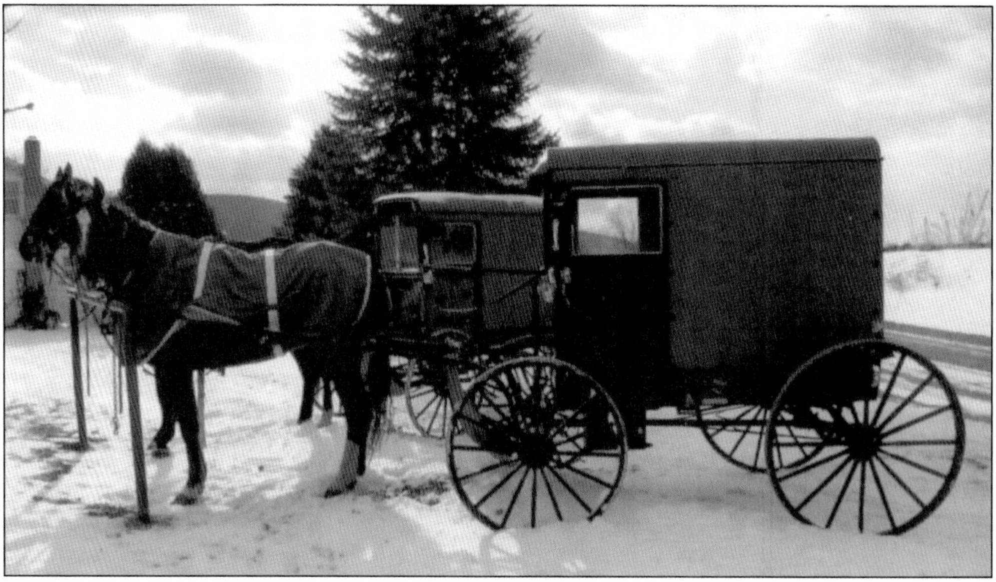

Amish families from Lancaster County began moving into the Elimsport area during the 1970s. These self-sustaining, close-knit groups travel by horse and buggy or wagon, bicycle, scooter, or on foot and are often seen working the fields and tending their gardens. The Amish operate several businesses in Elimsport, including a harness and tack shop and a sawmill; they have also built one-room schools in the area where their children are educated.

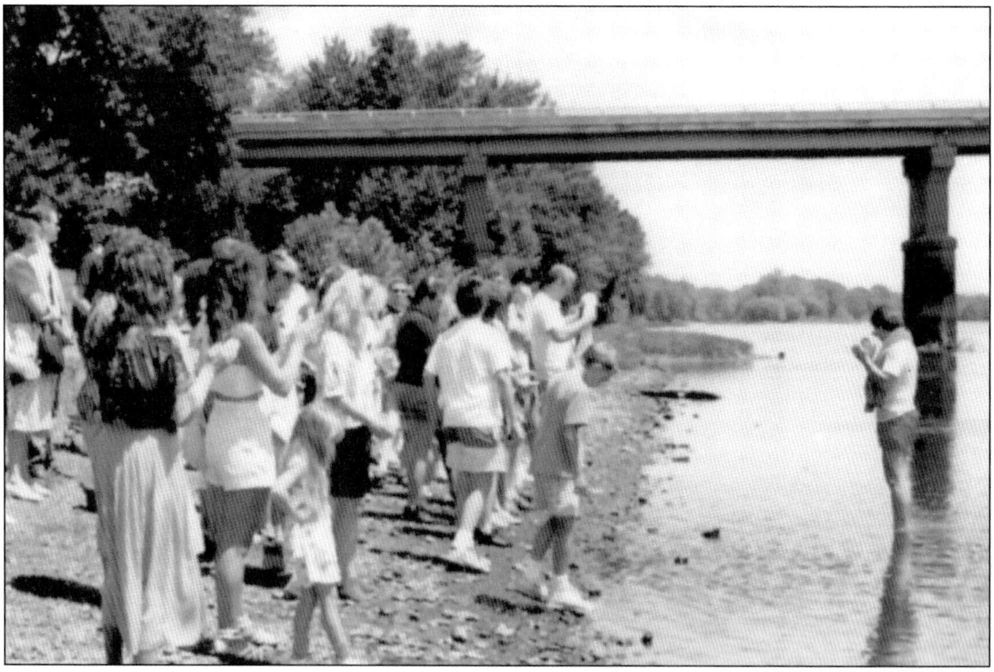

Around the summer of 1984, a small group of adults and children began worshiping in the former Bussler Building on Main Street. James Pentz and his wife, Holly Stover Pentz, graduates of Montgomery High School class of 1971, led the members of the New Covenant Assembly of God. Pictured, Pastor Pentz conducts a baptism at the Susquehanna River. (Courtesy Rev. James and Holly Pentz.)

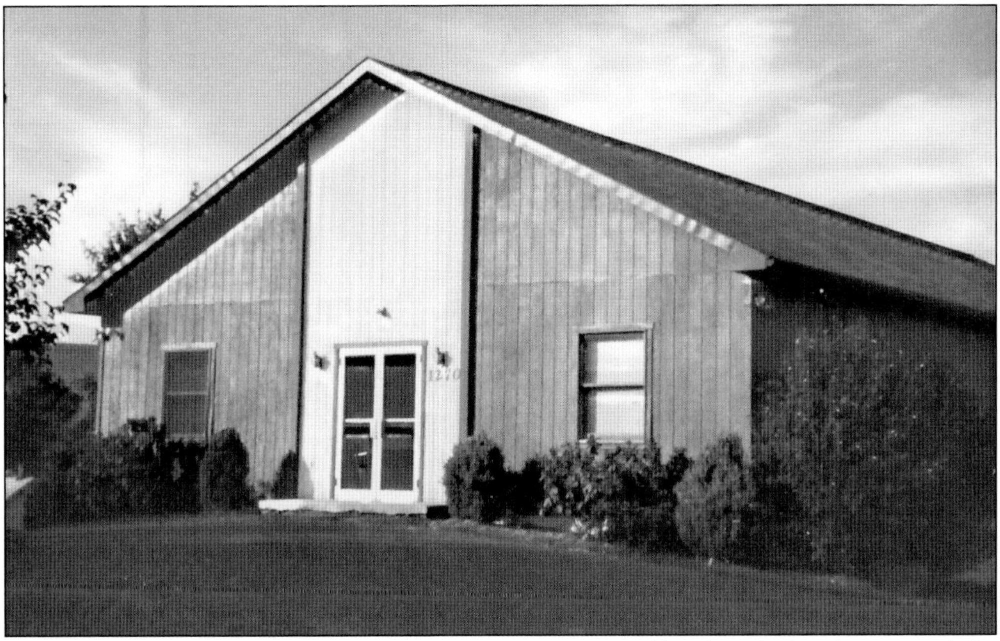

By the late 1980s, membership at the New Covenant Assembly of God Church grew and the decision was made to purchase property east of the borough on Pinchtown Road for a church building. A sanctuary and several classrooms were built, and soon, offices and a gymnasium were added. A Christian education building that featured classrooms, a nursery, and a large activity room was also added. Over the years, New Covenant has offered Latchkey and before and after school care for Montgomery-area children. In addition to a strong community connection, this church is also involved in short-term mission work. (Both courtesy Rev. James and Holly Pentz.)

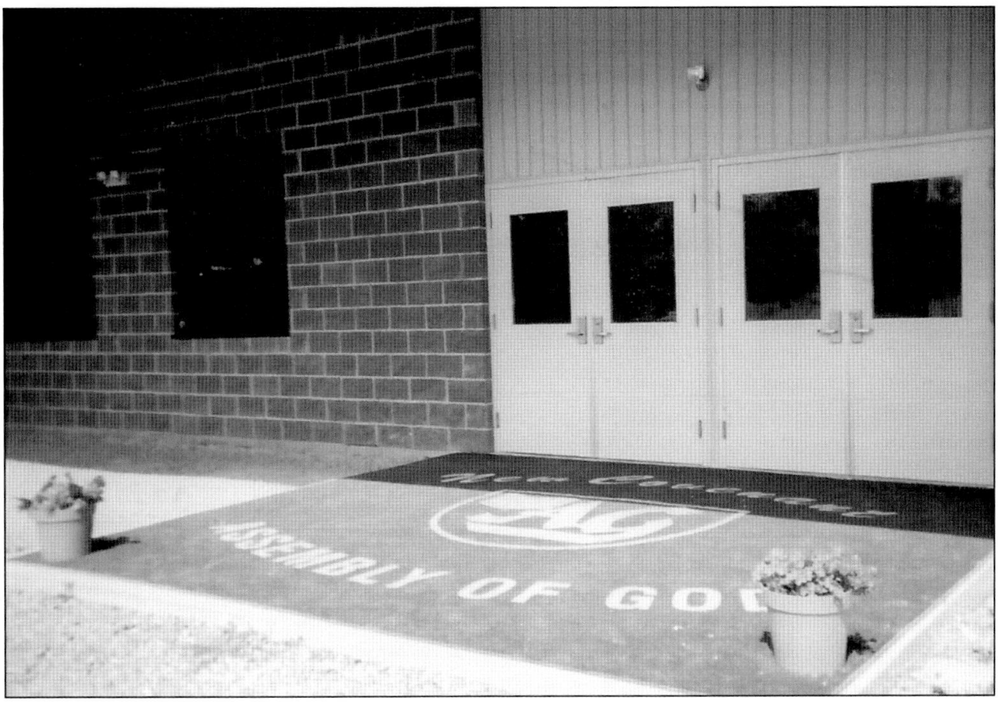

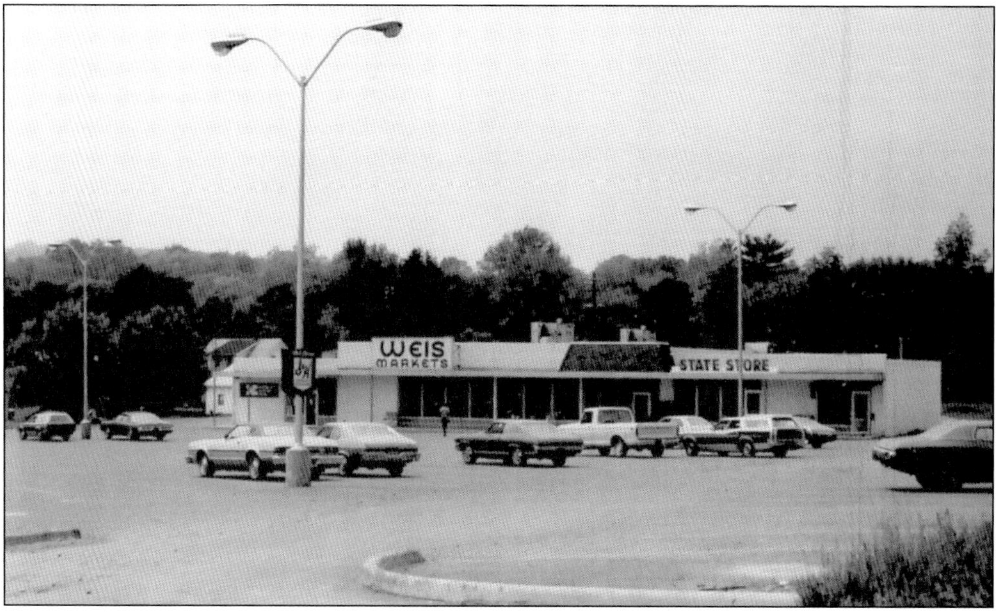

Weis Markets originated in Sunbury, Pennsylvania, when the first Weis Pure Foods was opened by two brothers, Harry and Sigmund Weis, both of whom attended Susquehanna University. By 1933, they were operating 115 self-service stores that were very different from the local grocers who offered personalized service. Established in Montgomery during the 1960s, the Weis Markets at the Clinton Township's Montgomery Plaza north of the borough expanded the size of the store in October 1983 by taking over the area formerly occupied by the Pennsylvania State Liquor Store. In 1986, the building occupied by Northern Central Bank at the corner of Main Street and Houston Avenue (below) was vacated, and all banking operations were moved to the Montgomery Plaza location. (Both courtesy MAPL.)

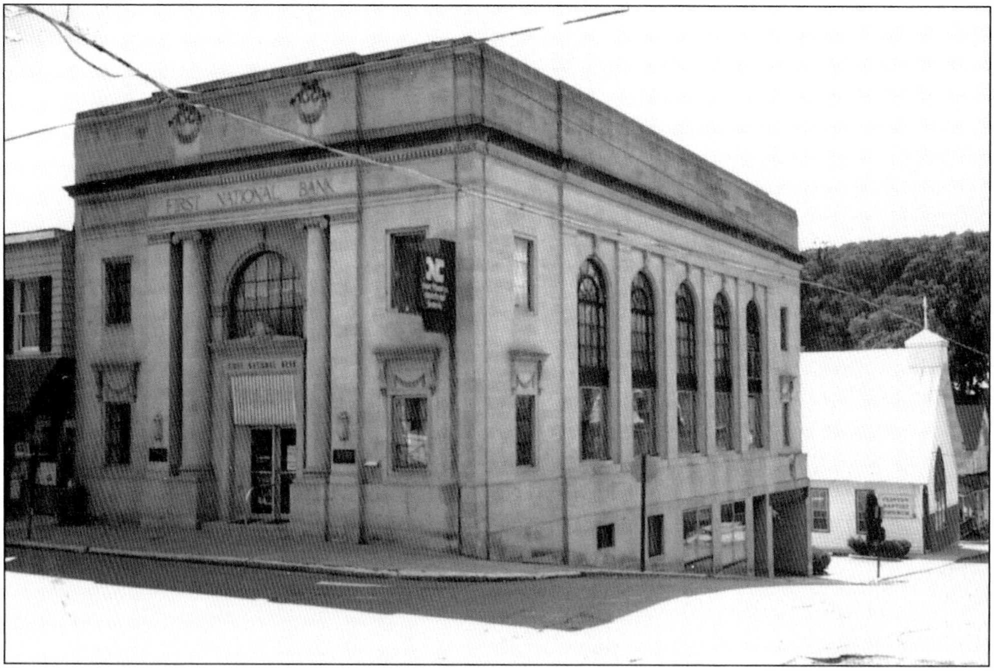

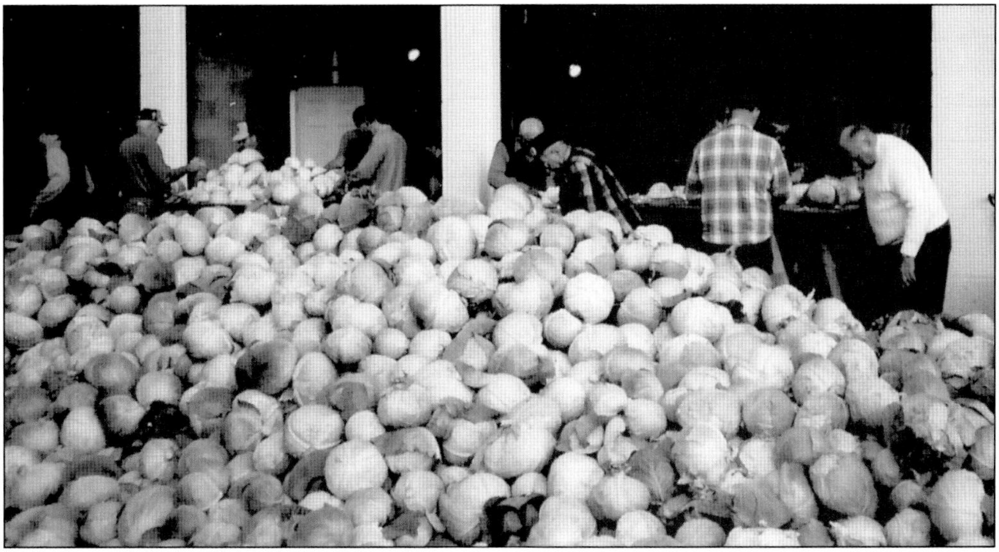

Every fall since 1958, the Montgomery Lions Club has embarked on its annual tradition of sauerkraut-making. Since their first attempt, which resulted in only one barrel of the shredded fermented cabbage, the Lions have gradually increased their output and improved their process. In the early years, the Montgomery Lions worked cooperatively with the Watsontown Lions Club by sharing cabbage cutters at a common location. Over 1,000 heads of cabbage can produce over 8,000 pounds or 17 barrels of sauerkraut. After it is cured, it is sold during the week between Christmas and New Years, just in time for the traditional meal of sauerkraut, pork, and mashed potatoes. Below, from left to right, are Albert Burrows, Paul Bender, Don Hutchinson, and Bill Sandmeyer manning the cabbage cutter. (Both courtesy the Montgomery Lions Club.)

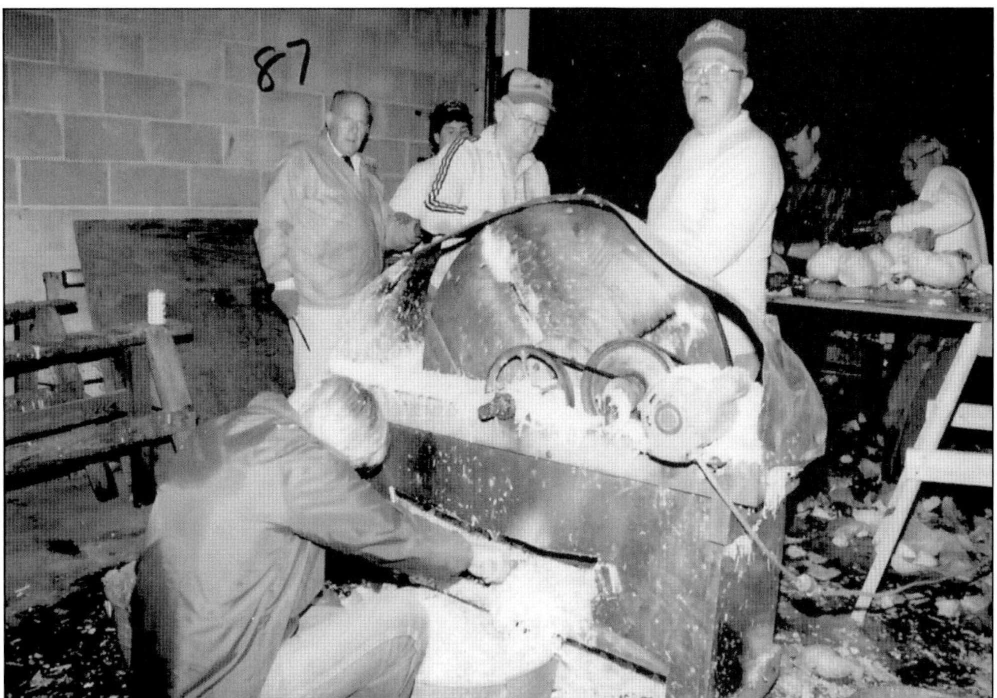

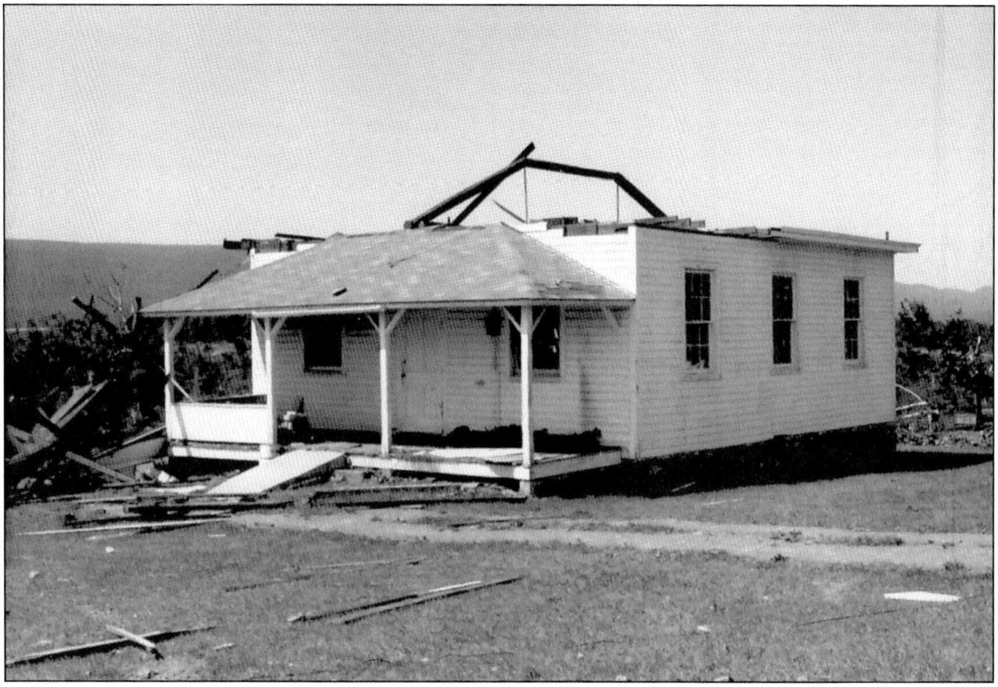

On Friday evening, May 31, 1985, around 9:45 p.m., a tornado tore through the southeast corner of Lycoming County, leaving destruction and death in its path. The storm moved through the Elimsport area where it killed 86-year-old Mae Koser and 69-year-old Thelma Taylor. Both lived in mobile homes about a half mile from each other. There were three additional fatalities in the area: a 12-year-old girl and a 78-year-old woman from nearby Northumberland County and an 11-year-old girl from Union County. On Pikes Peak Road, the historic Pikes Peak one-room school house (above) was being used as a workshop by Richard Taylor. During the tornado, the structure lost its roof and most of its windows. Birch trees nearby were bent and broken in half. (Both courtesy Richard and Eleanor Taylor.)

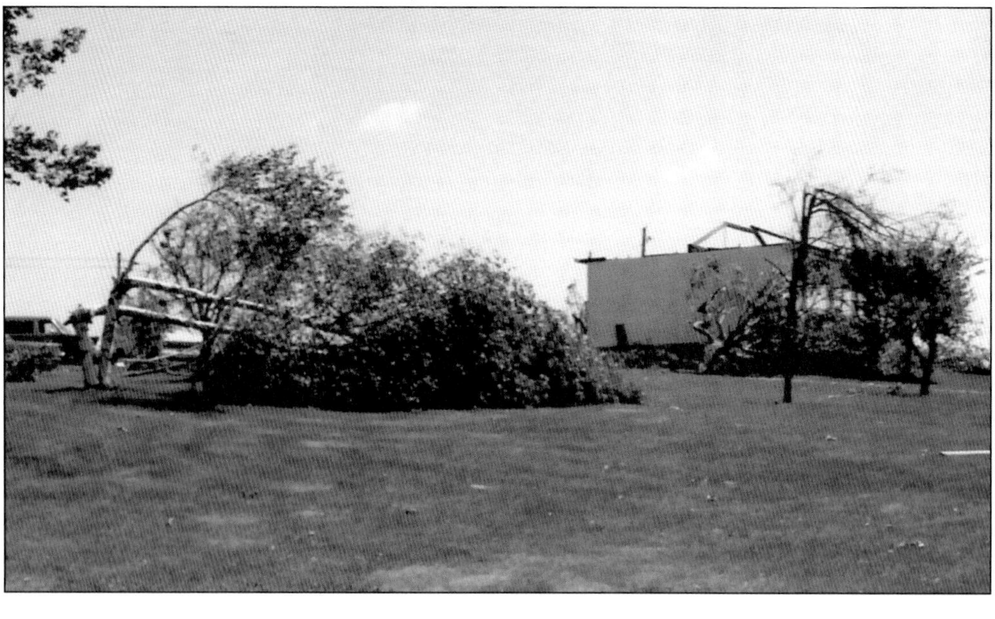

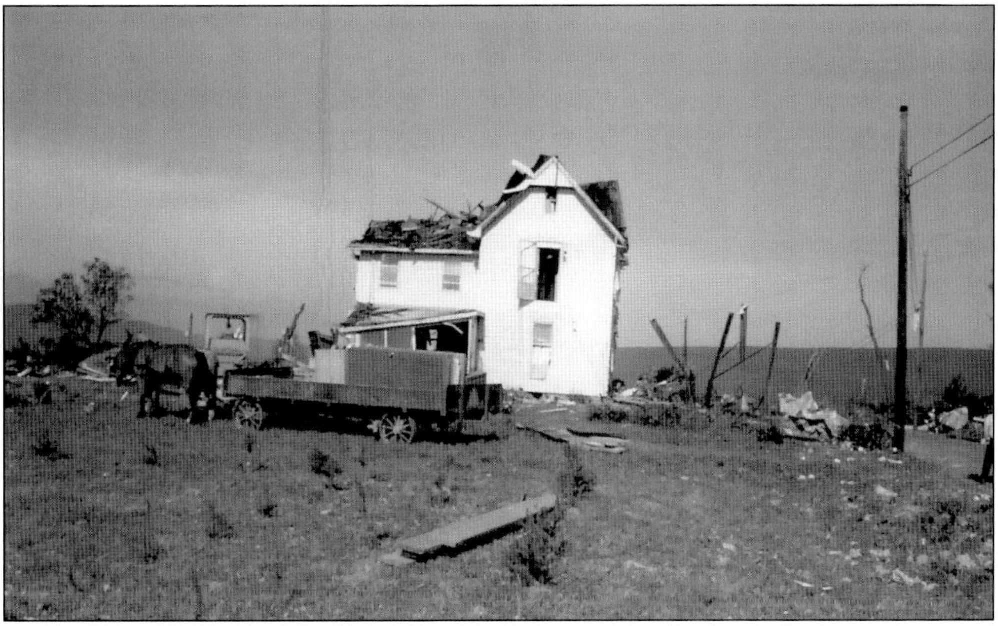

As the storm approached, Taylor's wife, Eleanor, had gone to be with Richard's stepmother, Thelma, who lived nearby in her mobile home. Both Thelma and Eleanor were thrown across the road by the tornado's winds. Although Thelma did not survive, Eleanor recovered after weeks in intensive care. The Taylors owned a house nearby that was used as a rental property. The building was severely damaged and had to be demolished. Amish farmers were invited to salvage any usable materials that they found, including doors and cabinetry. The home of neighbor Tom Weaver (below) was completely blown away—the only thing left was its foundation and the slab that was the house's front porch stoop. The historic White Deer Grange building (see page 82) that was nearby was also destroyed. (Both courtesy Richard and Eleanor Taylor.)

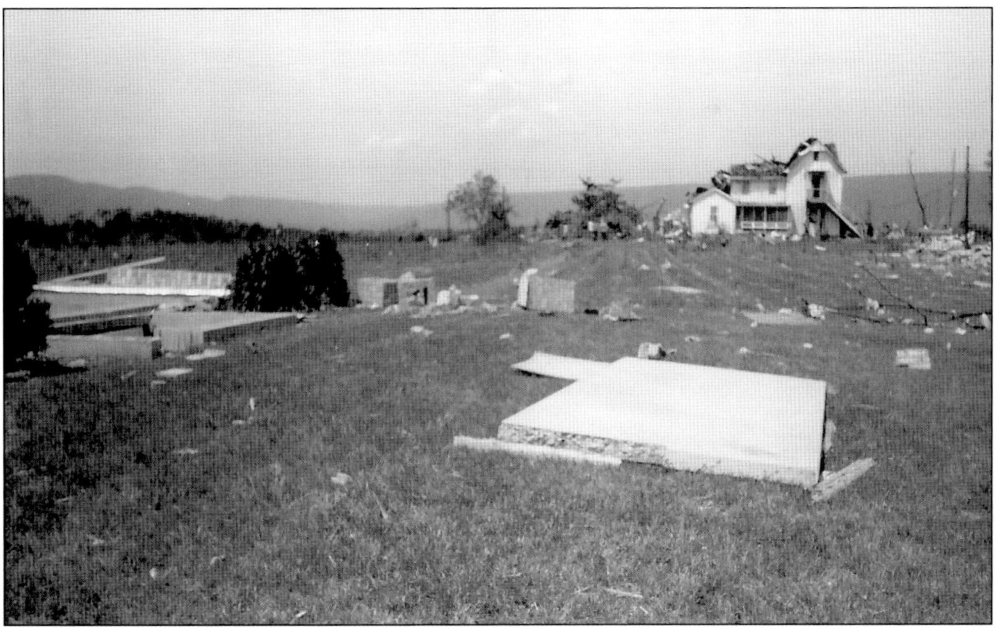

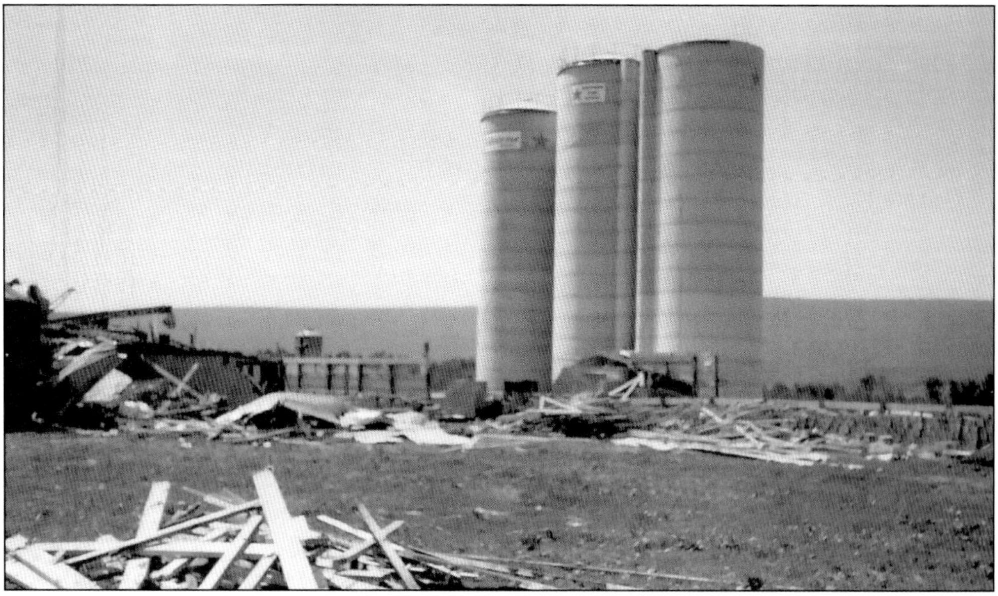

The barn owned by Eleanor Taylor's sister and brother-in-law, Jeannette and Robert Lynch, was flattened by the tornado, as seen in these photographs. Immediately after the storm, over 11,000 Pennsylvania Power & Light (PP&L) customers were left without power but the Williamsport National Guard provided water for residents whose wells did not operate due to the power outage. Police and emergency officials restricted travel on roads leading into the affected areas while PP&L workers untangled miles of wire and replaced transformers and broken and missing poles. Neighbors helped each other by clearing debris and offering assistance in any way that was needed. The county landfill also opened for tornado victims to bring debris and dead animals for disposal free of charge. (Both courtesy Richard and Eleanor Taylor.)

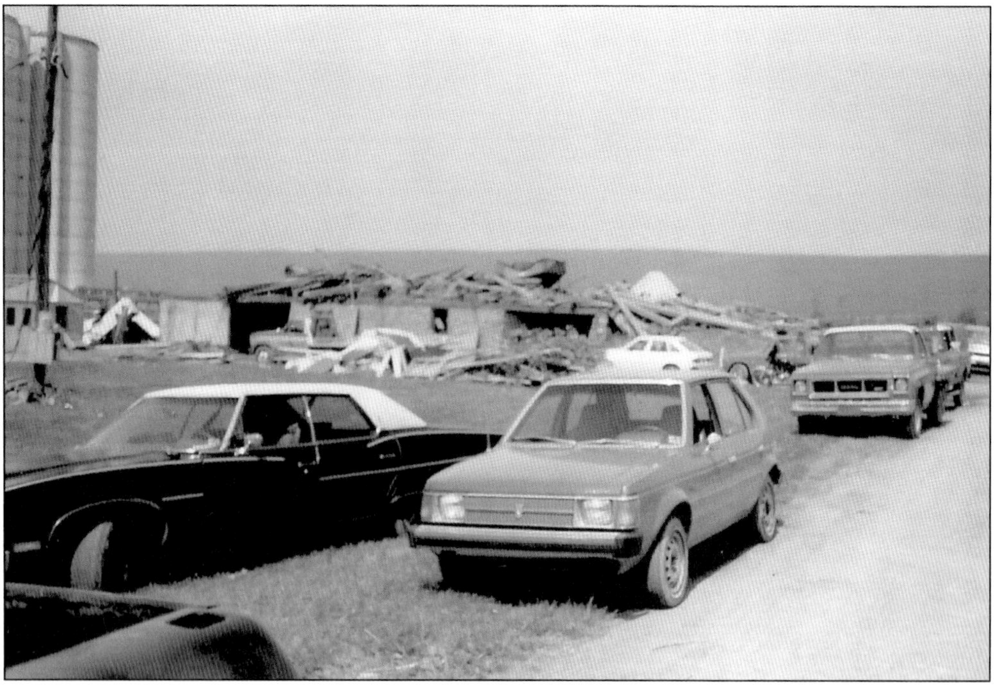

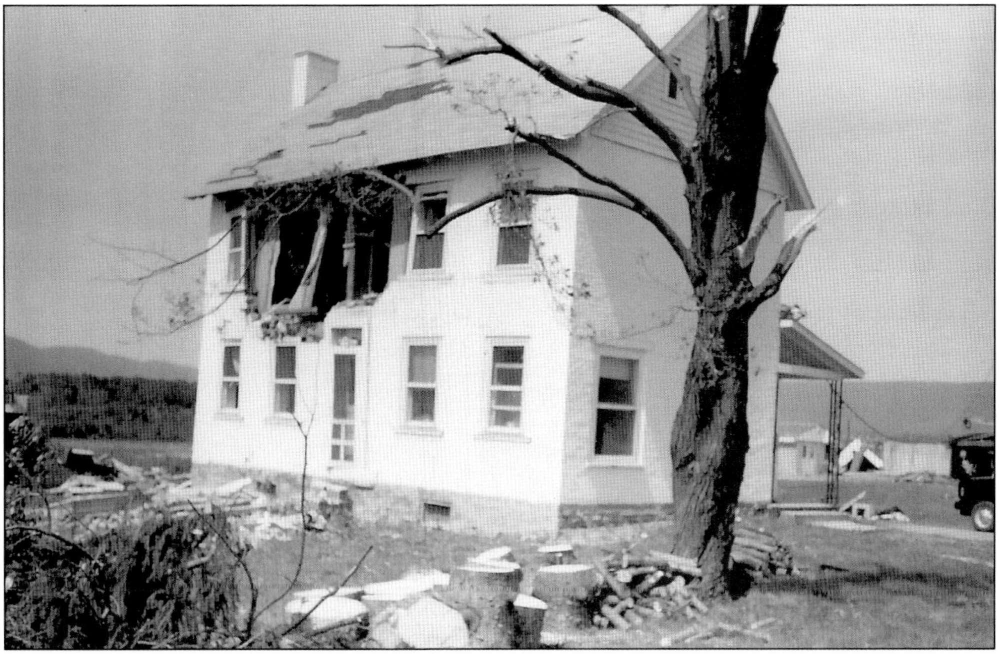

Above, the home of Rodney Lynch suffered major damage, and the barn owned by Eleanor Taylor's sister and brother-in-law, Jeannette and Robert Lynch, was flattened. Some of Lynch's cattle had to be destroyed, and the surviving cows were transported to nearby farms to be milked and fed. Neighbors who helped included Charles Ulrich, whose milking equipment was left intact although part of his barn's roof was blown away. Ulrich cared for a portion of Lynch's herd while nephew Ed Ulrich, Mike Jarrett, and Robert Miller took the rest until Lynch's barn could be rebuilt. (Above, courtesy Richard and Eleanor Taylor; below, courtesy MAPL.)

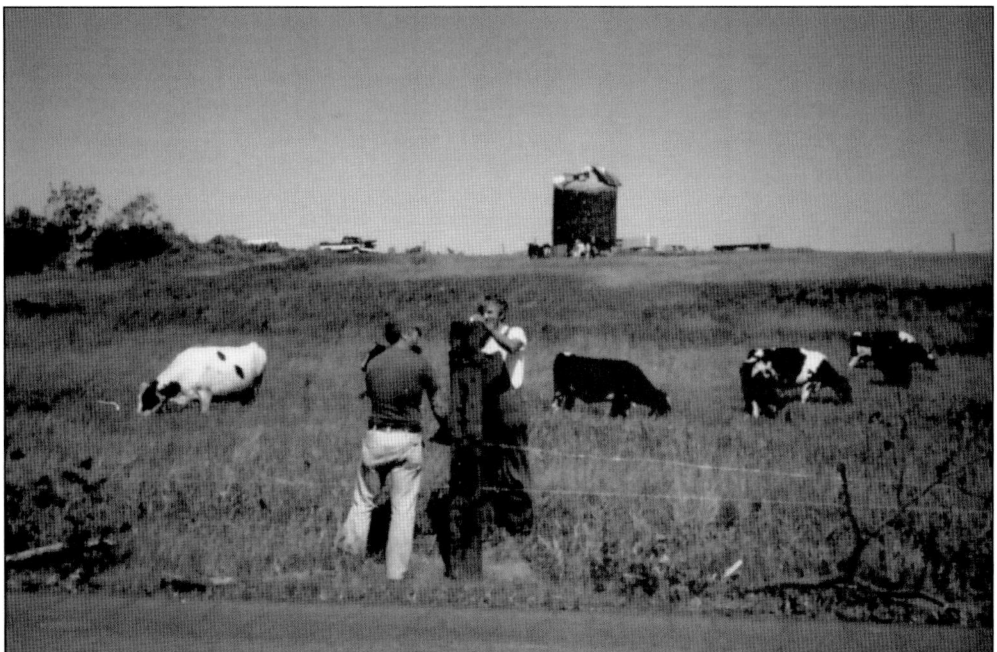

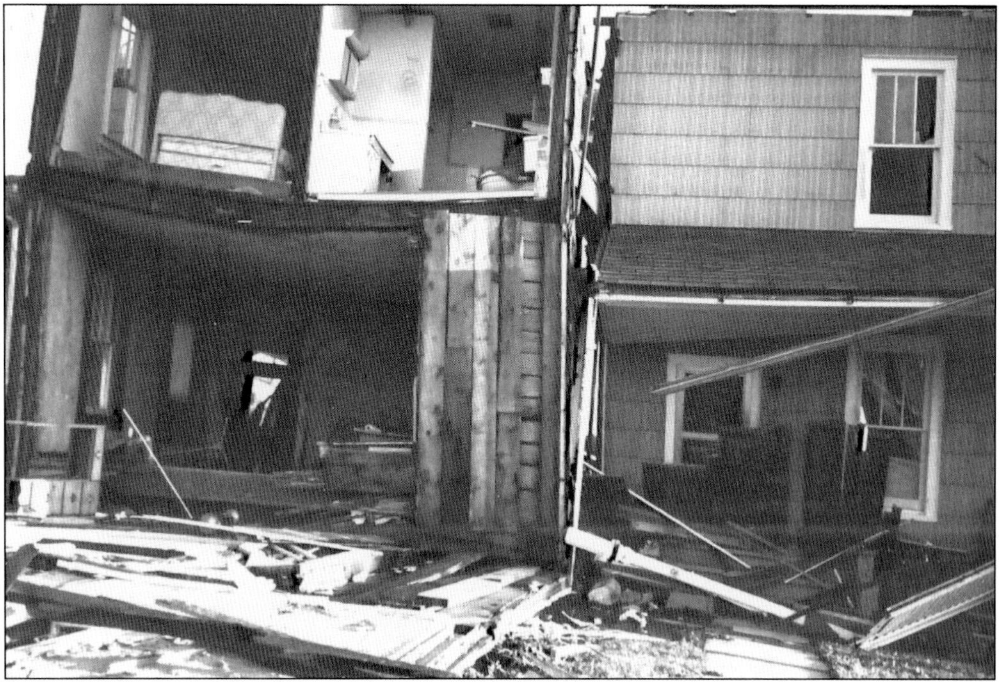

Iva Kennedy was in her historic home when the tornado blew away the wall from the eastern side of the house, exposing the contents of the rooms and giving it the appearance of a dollhouse. According to reports in the *Sunday Patriot News* (Harrisburg), Kennedy said that she heard a "terrible big swishing noise" just before parts of her home were ripped away. She was with daughter Jan Geisler, who described the noise as "incredible" and said she thought the house was going to explode from the pressure. The historic cider press built in the late 1800s on the Kennedy property was also destroyed, as was a car that landed nearby. (Above, courtesy Richard and Eleanor Taylor; below, courtesy MAPL.)

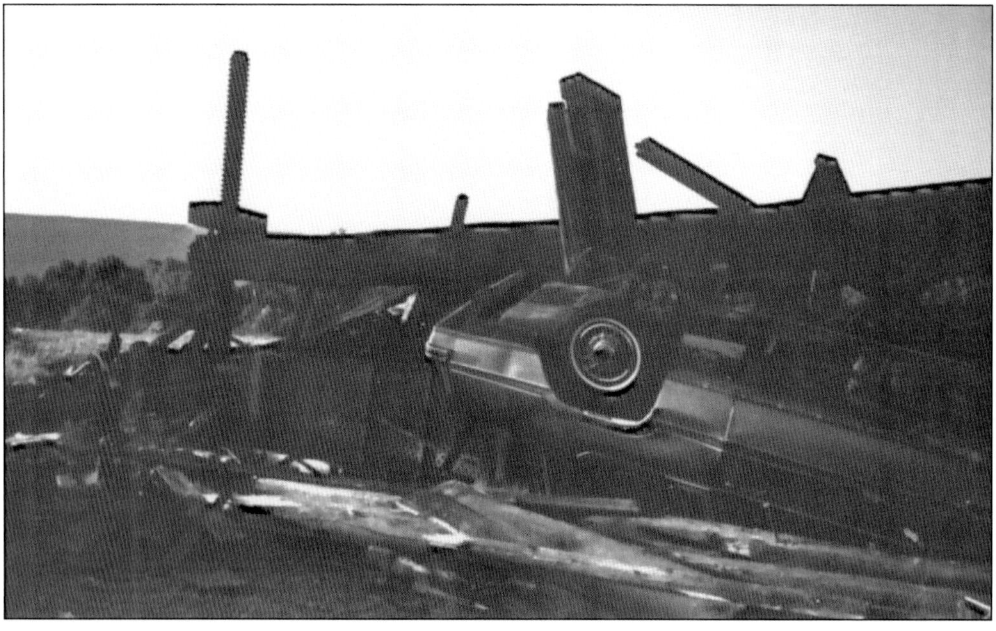

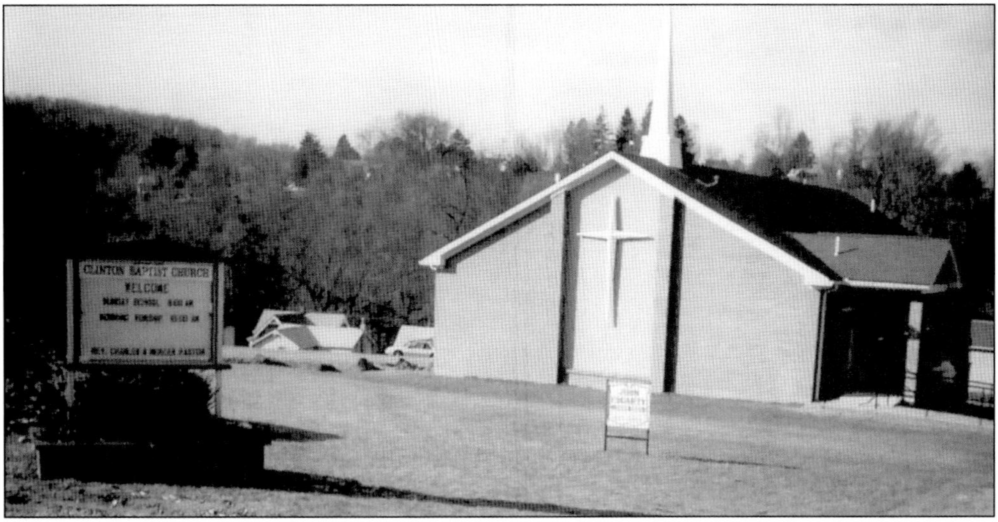

The original Clinton Baptist Church was erected in the 1830s east of the borough in Clinton Township. After the Reading and Pennsylvania Railroads were built directly adjacent to the church building, it was abandoned and another church was built in the borough on West Houston Avenue. In 1986, a new church building, pictured, was constructed at the corner of School and Warren Streets. (Courtesy Clinton Baptist Church.)

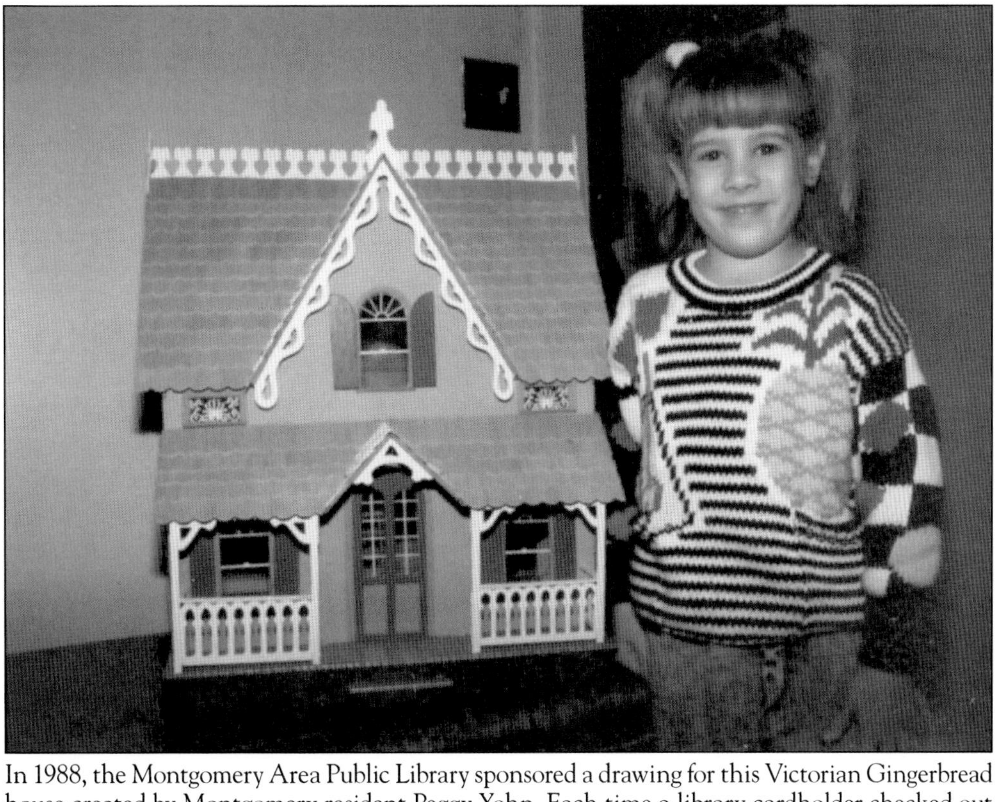

In 1988, the Montgomery Area Public Library sponsored a drawing for this Victorian Gingerbread house created by Montgomery resident Peggy Yohn. Each time a library cardholder checked out a book, he or she was eligible to enter the drawing for the dollhouse. Pictured with the house is the winner, Heather Pick. (Courtesy MAPL.)

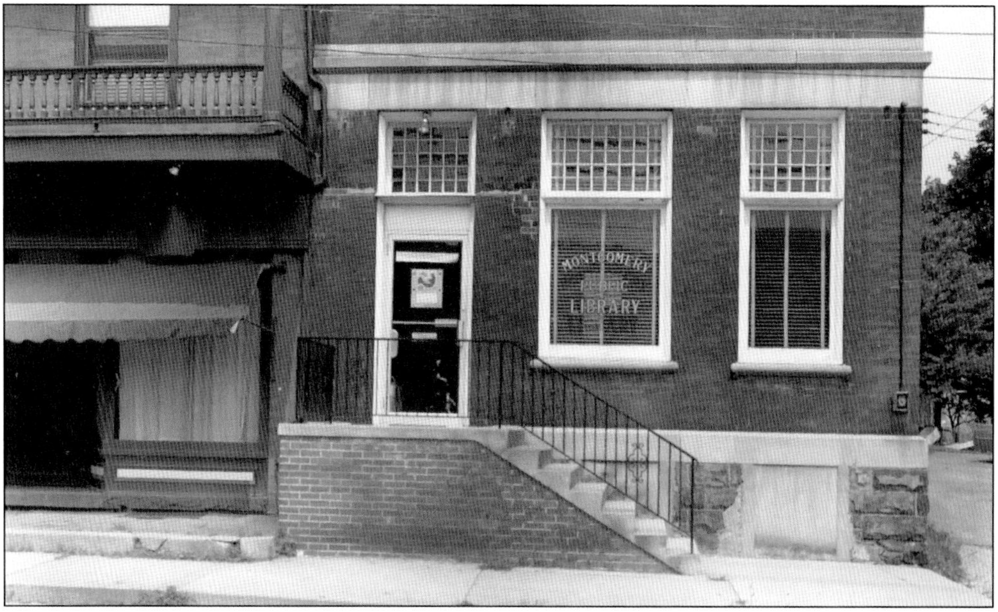

The former First National Bank building (above) was purchased in 1925 and given to the Montgomery Library Association for use as a public library. A fund drive headed by William Decker soon commenced; it resulted in donations totaling over $25,000 to remodel the building, purchase books and furniture, and offset operating costs. In 1974, the Montgomery Public Library became the Montgomery Area Public Library as Clinton Township was added to the library's service area. Also that year, a children's library space was outfitted in the former Bussler building next door. In July 1986, the former Northern Central Bank at the corner of Main Street and Houston Avenue was renovated, and the library was moved into this larger location. Below, helping move books are Michelle Foust (left) and Laurie Thomas. (Both courtesy MAPL.)

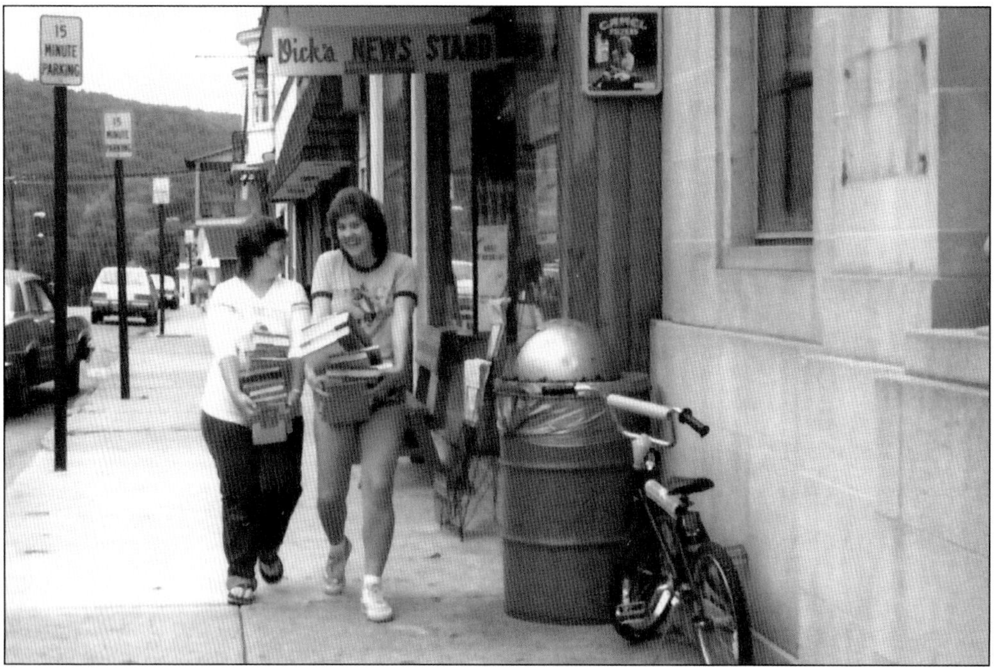

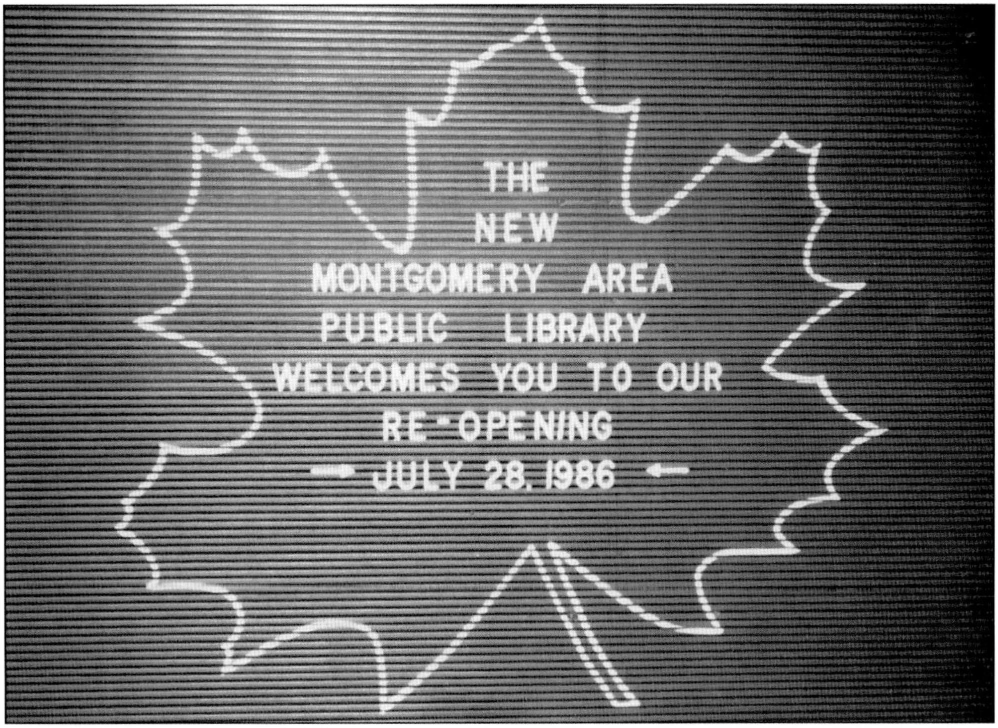

July 28, 1986, was the grand reopening of the Montgomery Area Public Library. Pictured below are Michelle Foust, who was a library aide during the summer of 1987, and Carrie Barnhart, librarian. They are dressed in costume for the celebration of the borough's centennial, which took place in August of that year. The library offered free movies at 7:00 p.m. every Friday evening, ongoing genealogy workshops, and the summer reading program, which attracted children to the downtown library. Barnhart, a dedicated supporter of Montgomery literacy and history, retired as librarian in 1996. (Both courtesy MAPL.)

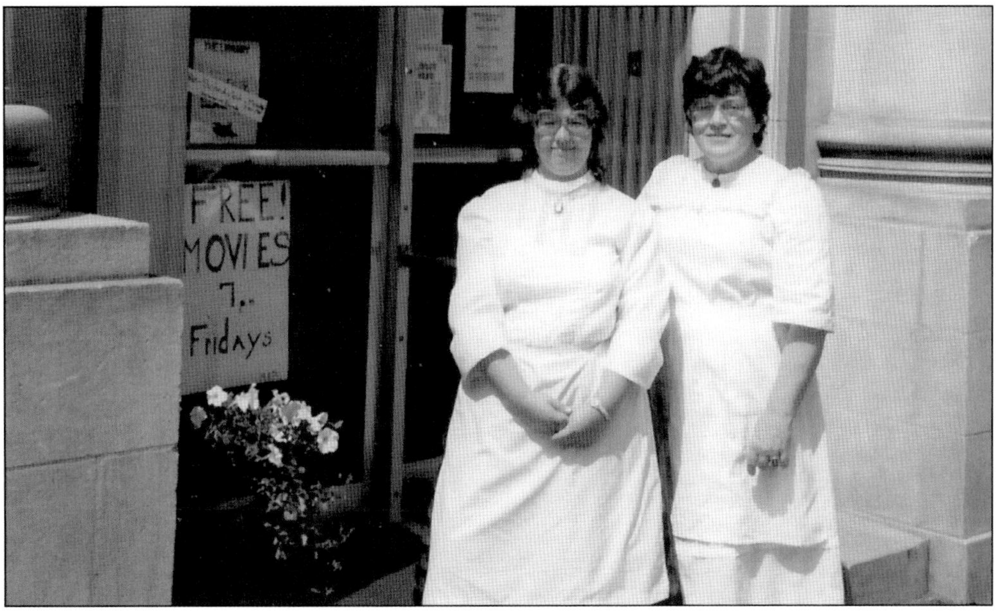

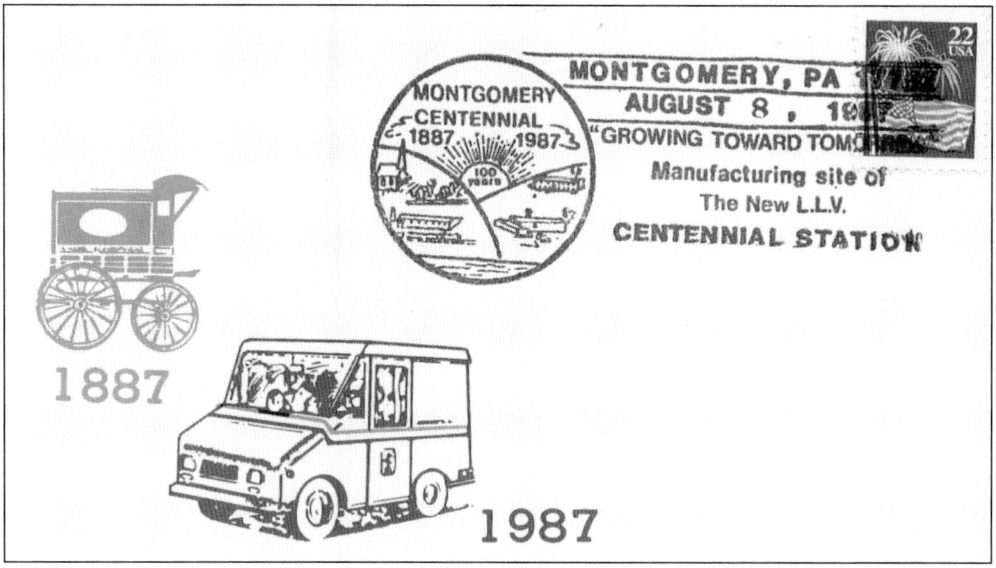

In 1972, Grumman Olson opened a facility in Montgomery to produce modular and motor homes, but slow sales caused the company to change to truck production. In 1982, the US Postal Service wanted to upgrade its fleet of half-ton jeeps and delivery trucks. The billion-dollar contract was awarded to Grumman Allied for its Long-Life Vehicle (LLV) design. It featured a right-hand drive, swivel seat, roll-up rear door, and the durability to withstand a 24,000-mile road test. The Montgomery facility began production of the LLV in 1986 and produced over 50,000 by 1990. (Above, courtesy MAPL; below, courtesy Gale and Cathy Buck.).

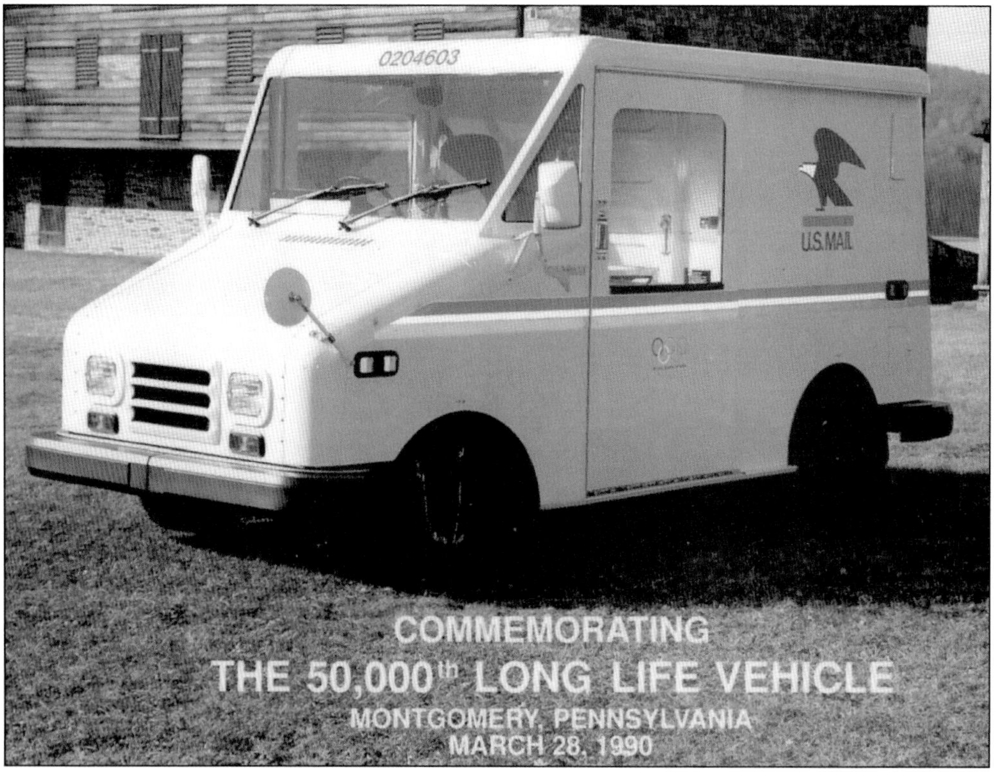

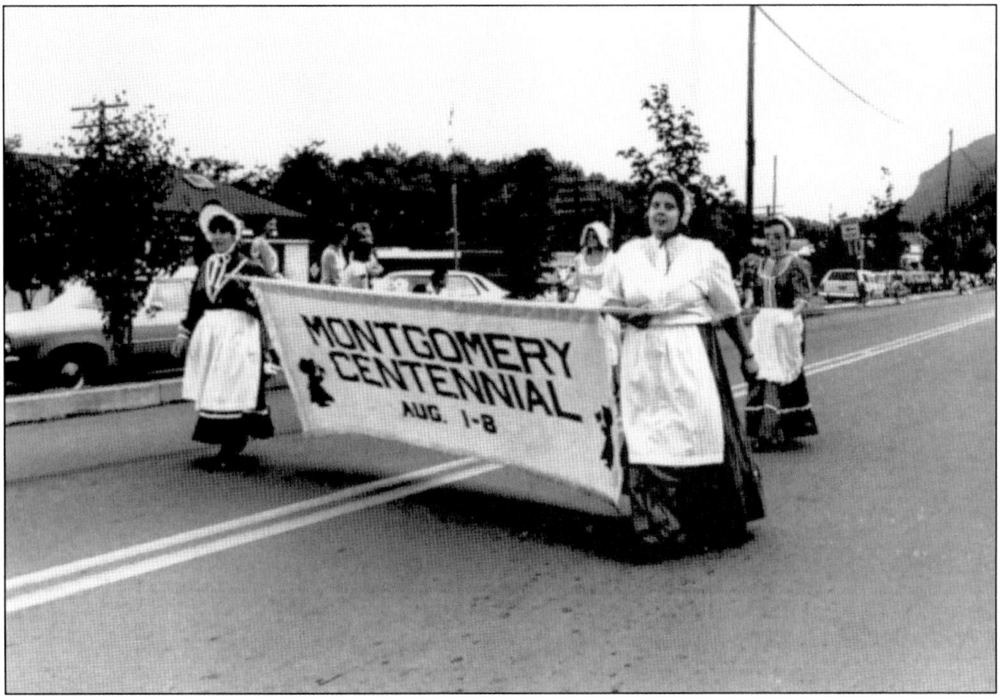

A weeklong celebration of Montgomery's centennial, celebrating the borough's incorporation on March 21, 1887, took place from August 1 through August 8, 1987. Festivities included an antique car show and a parade with marching units, floats, bands, and a clown on a bicycle. The parade capped off a weeklong series of activities featuring a baby contest, old-time Little League games, costume contests, and beard-growing competitions. Some of the winners included Virginia Pfeiffer, prettiest bonnet and apron; Jan Vogelsong, prettiest antique outfit; and Frances Montgomery Gruver and her daughter and granddaughters (descendents of the borough's founder, Robert Montgomery), best mother-daughter outfits. (Both courtesy MAPL.)

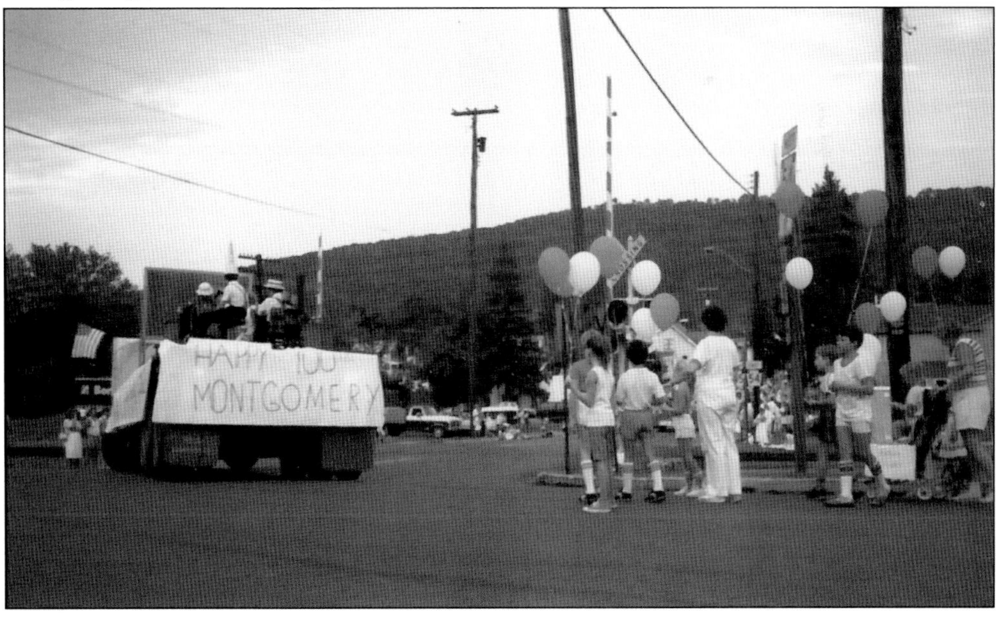

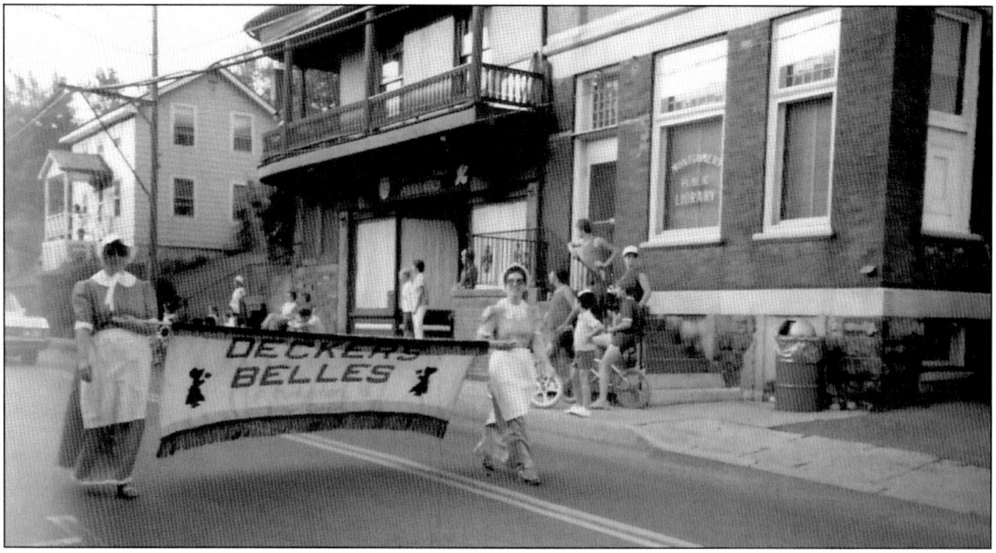

Pictured on this page are two of the local marching units included in the centennial parade held Saturday, August 8. Above, the banner for the Decker's Belles group is carried by two costumed participants. Below, the Junior Belles parade down the west end of Montgomery Street. Float competitions were held: the Grace Presbyterian Church float won the top prize, the J.C. Decker float won second place, and the United Methodist Women's float took third place. The best walking unit was the Precisionnaires of Milton. Grandma's Attic won the award for best period clothing, and the prize for most unique parade entry went to a decorated antique car owned by Richard Boodie of Winfield. (Both courtesy MAPL.)

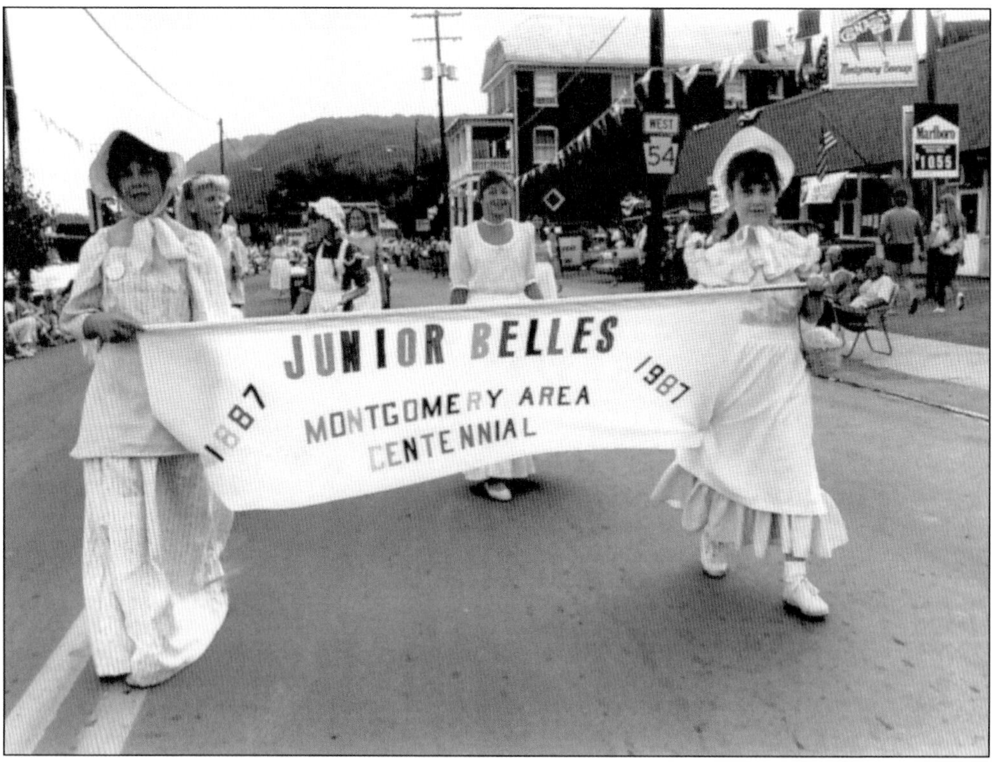

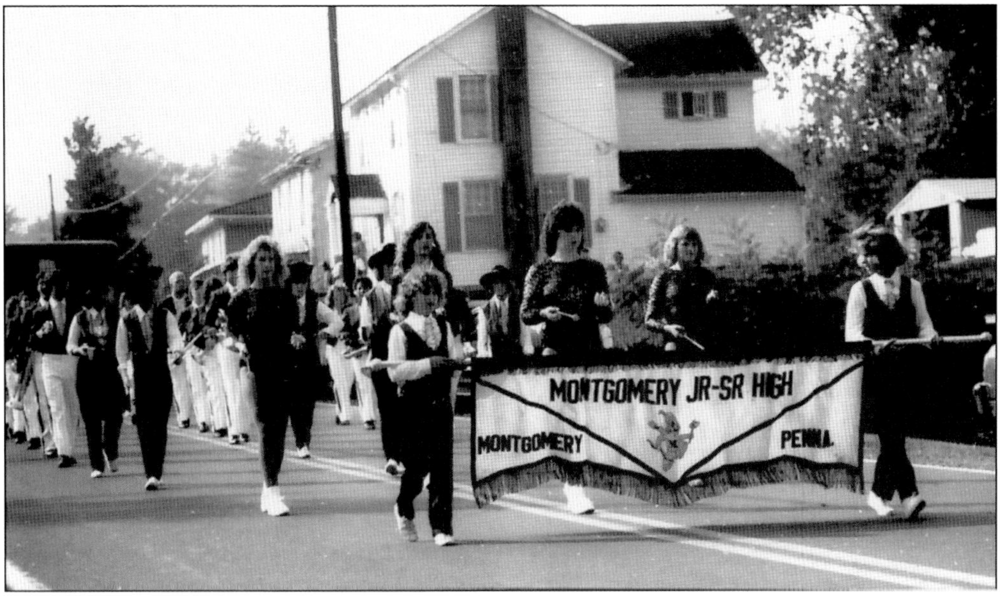

Above, the Montgomery Junior-Senior High School Band is featured in the parade. The Keystone Kops (below) attempted to keep order by making mock arrests and jailing guests. Three jailed individuals, however, issued a proclamation which read: "I, Arthur W. Miller Jr., and Raymond R. Taylor, former mayors, and Wayne S. Miller were arrested at Montgomery Park by Craig Miller, Richard Miller, Wayne Simon, Charles Wright, Bill Wertz, Pete Benfer, Patty Miller, and George Adams. We were sentenced to jail without bail and hosed down with a fire hose by Dr. Howard Weaner. We want it to be known that in the year 2012, the above people in the arresting party will receive their just dues by being jailed and wet down by a fire hose by our grandchildren." (Both courtesy MAPL.)

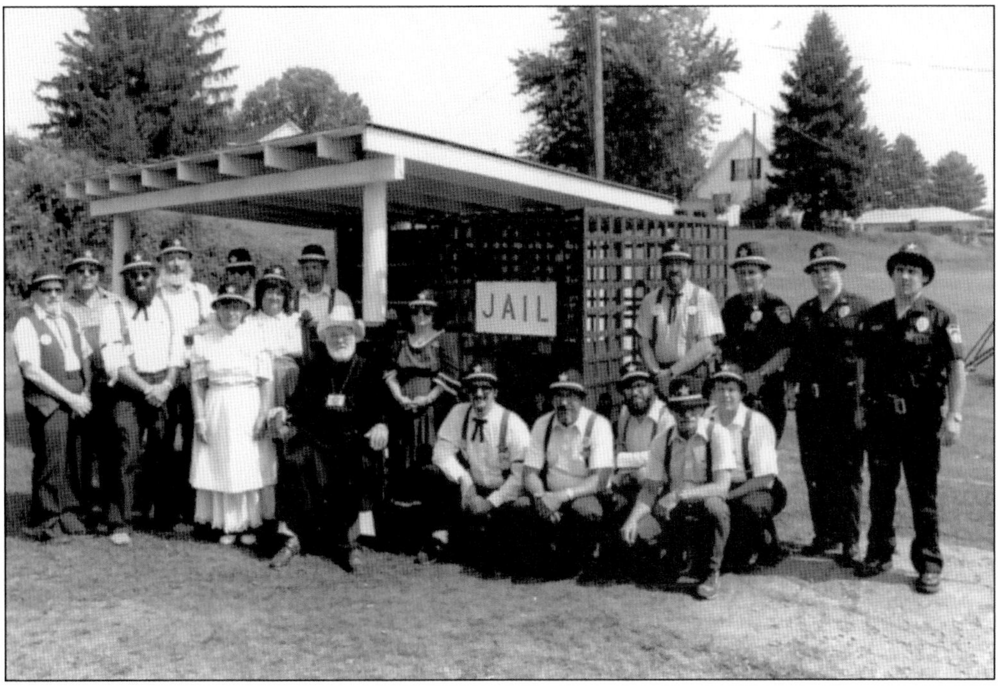

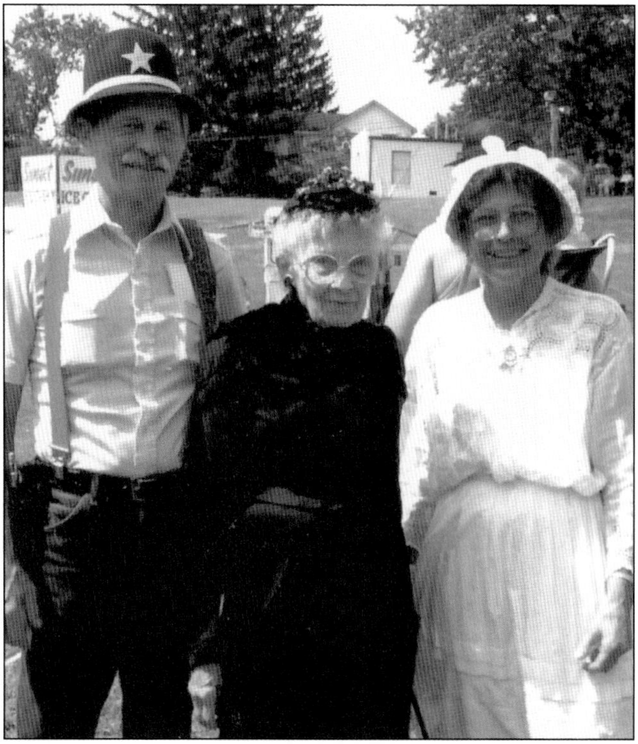

Residents were encouraged to come to the Founder's Day Dance dressed in vintage costumes similar to attire worn 100 years before. At left, George Adams (left), Jessie Waltman (center), and Nancy ? model their centennial attire. Below, on stage, are the Centennial Baby, Scott Bradley Kitner, son of Ken and Carla Kitner, held by his mother; Little Miss Centennial, Megan Frances Wilt, daughter of Mr. and Mrs. Thomas Wilt; and the Centennial Queen, Michelle Wertman, daughter of Shirley Wertman and Paul Wertman. A musical review was also held at the park that featured the Williamsport Consistory Choir, the Cloverleaf Cloggers, and the Lewisburg Barbershop Quartet. (Both courtesy MAPL.)

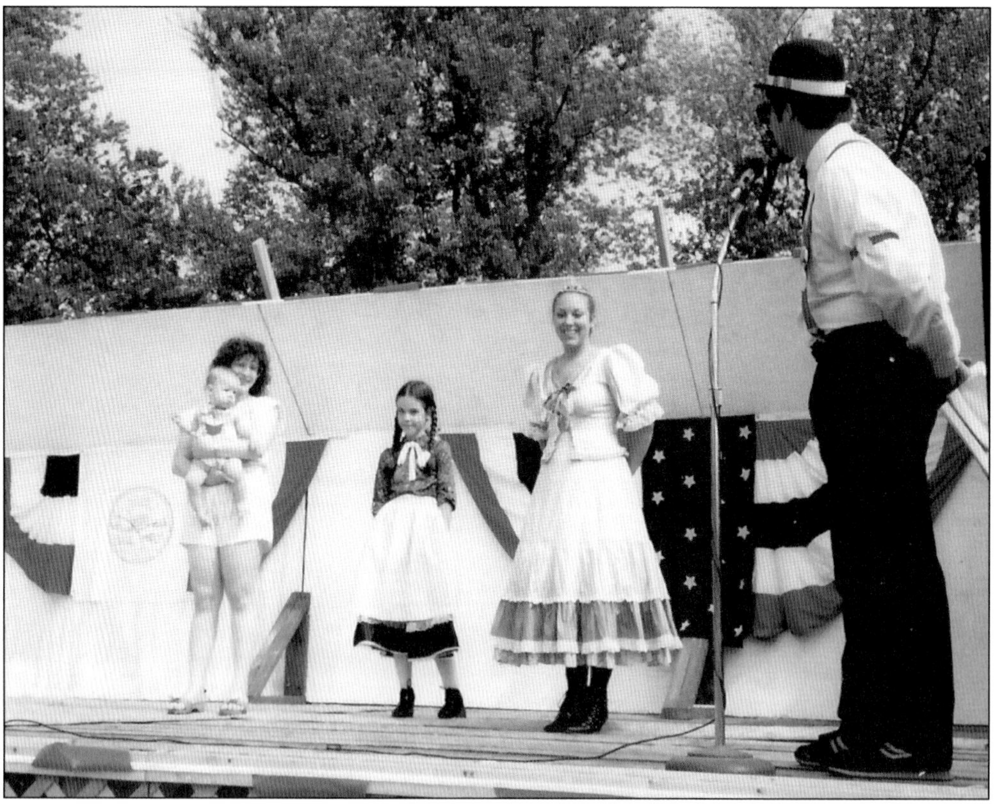

A popular attraction during the centennial celebration was Clyde Peeling's hands-on exhibit of exotic animals. On July 11, 1964, Peeling opened a small zoo on Route 15 between Montgomery and Allenwood. Brother Donald and Bill Ely, who later became a Milton policeman, worked for Peeling during the first year. Considered a local celebrity, Peeling has made three appearances on late-night television shows with Jay Leno and more than a dozen appearances with Conan O'Brien. He also has appeared on the *Live with Regis and Kathy Lee* morning show and *What's My Line* with Gary Moore. In 1986, Reptiland became an Association of Zoos and Aquariums accredited institution. In addition to operating Reptiland, Peeling's family business also produces traveling exhibitions throughout North America and fabricates zoo habitats for other zoos, aquariums, and museums. (Both courtesy MAPL.)

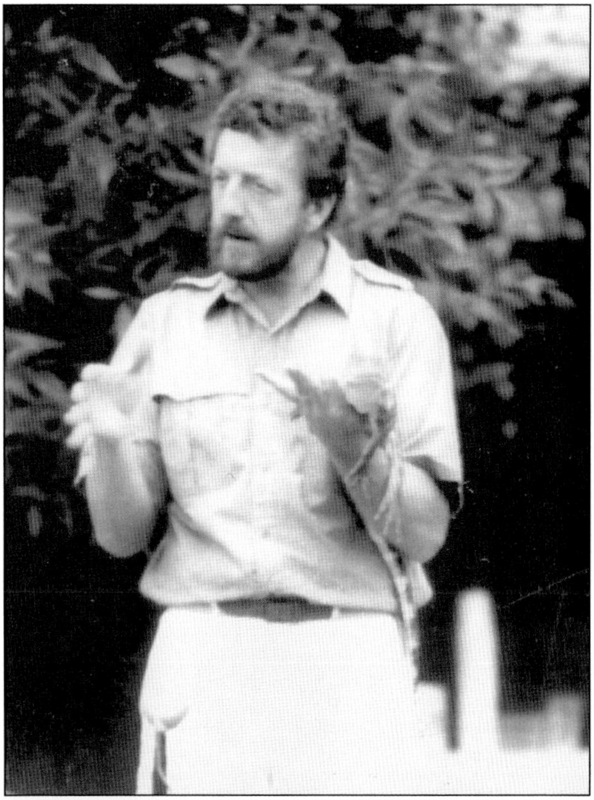

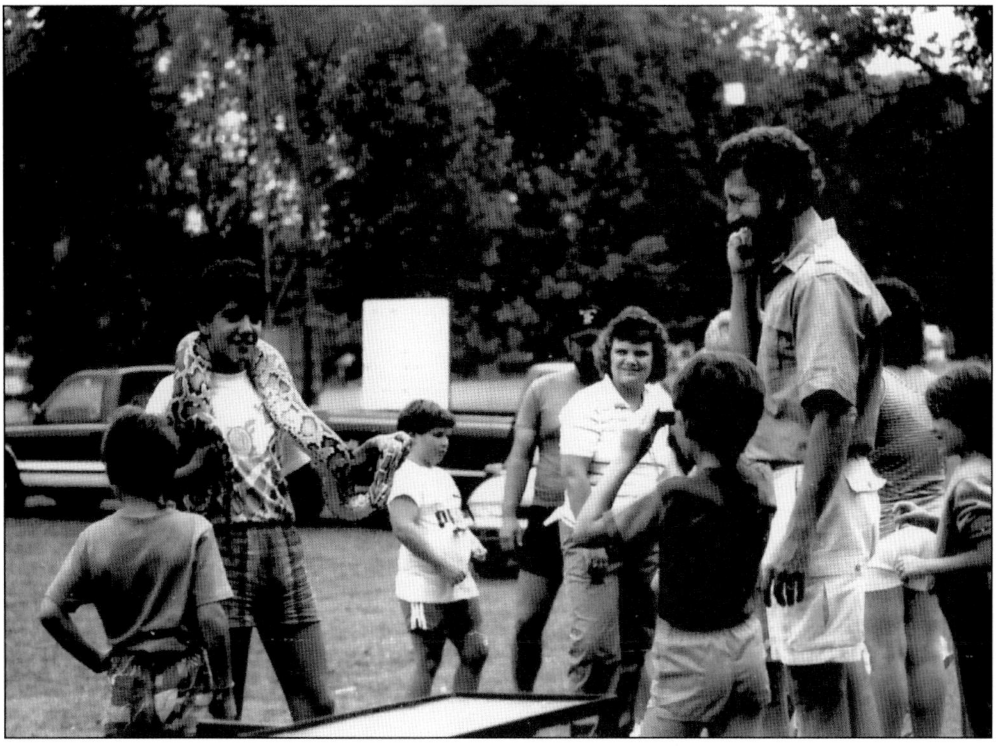

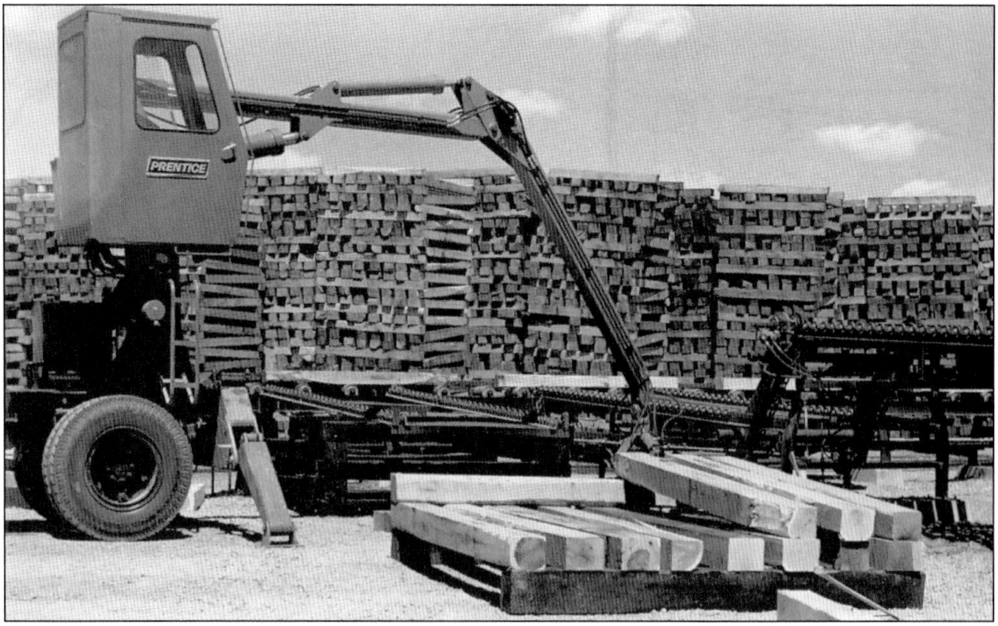

Employees at Koppers' Susquehanna Wood Treating Plant are pictured below in June 1988. From left to right are (first row) Fred Taylor, Terry Force, Tim Duck, Bill Hall, George Budman, Jay LaForme, Roger Schomburg, Paul Zellars, and Butch Stackhouse; (second row) John Rider, George Stromberg, Vince Repaci, Dick Miller, Myron Thompson, Ken Huffman, Jim Edsell, Millard Hagemeyer, Paul McClemons, Judy Yocum, Patty Peterman, Tom Loadman, and Dixie Ranck; (third row) Ron Vanwhy, Dale Harris, Steve Schodt, Steve Peterman, Bill Green Jr., Bob Staggert, Gary Nichols, Paul Ault, Bill Green Sr., Bob Bryson, Bill Munns, Dan Baker, Denny Sites, Larry Andrews, Bob Kiess, and Don Yohn. (Both courtesy Koppers, Inc.)

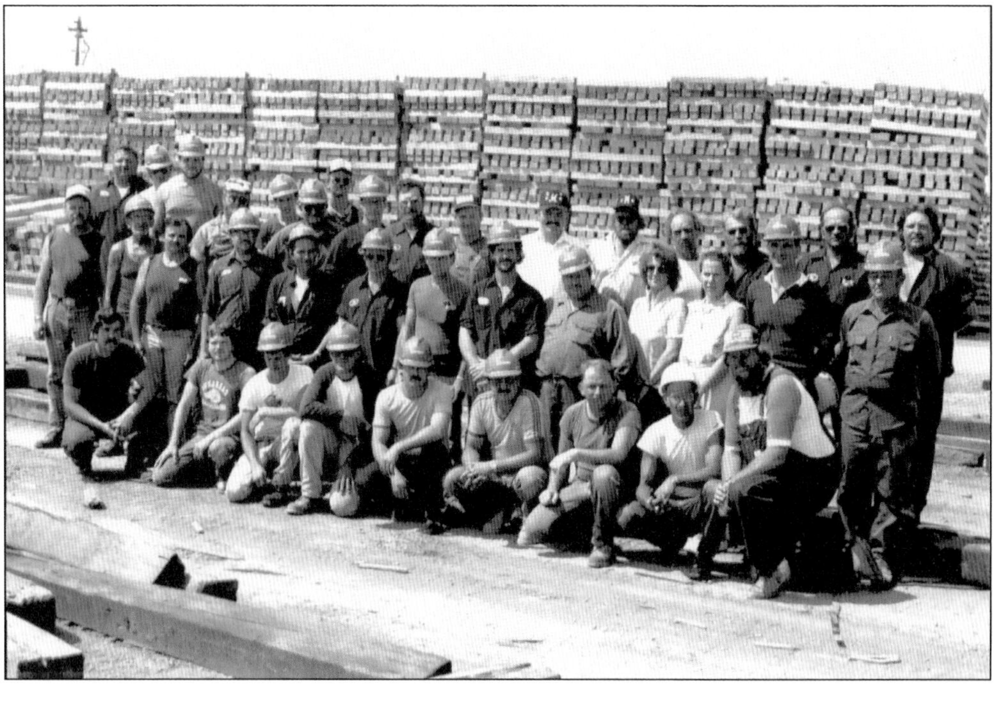

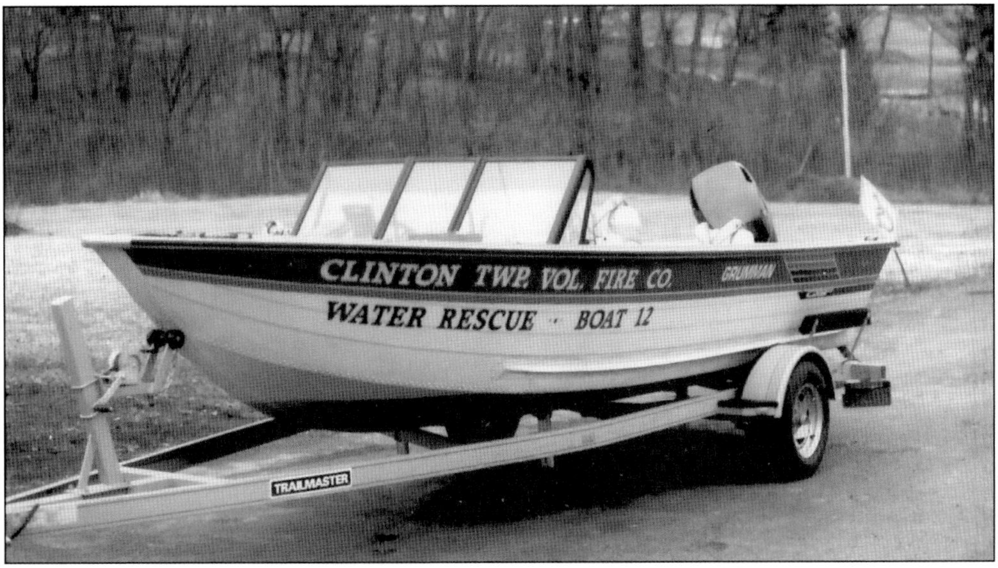

The Clinton Township Volunteer Fire Company established a trained dive team in response to a tragic accident in which two children and their mother perished in a car that became submerged in the Susquehanna River. The team was trained to perform underwater rescues and recoveries in low visibility, cold temperatures, and in depths of 130 feet from this 20-foot Grumman water rescue boat. (Courtesy Clinton Township Volunteer Fire Company.)

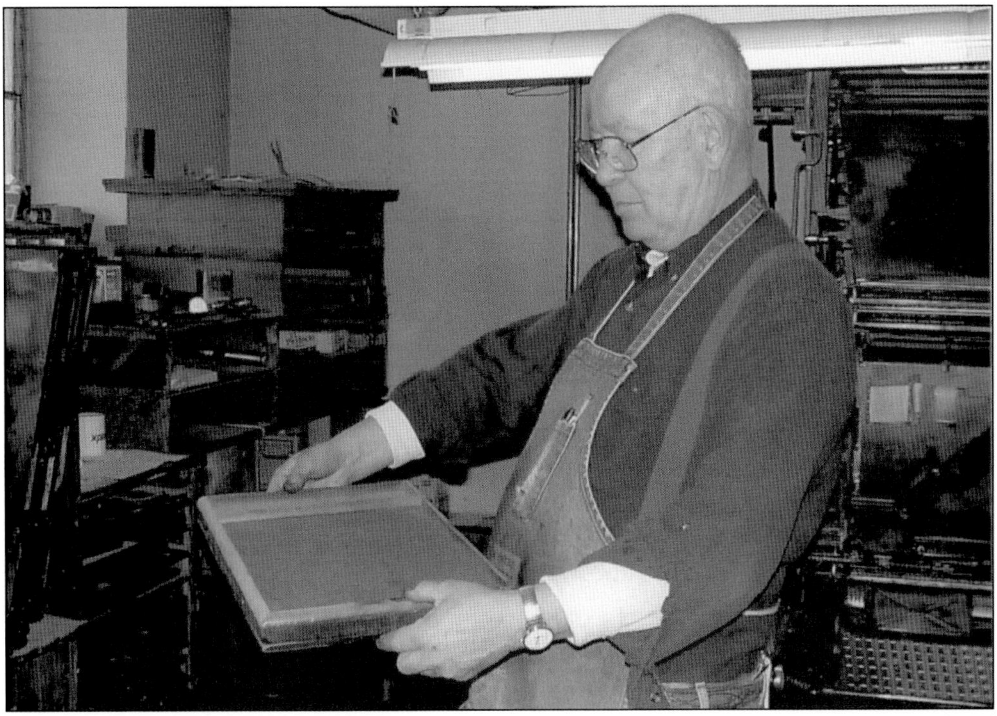

The Adam Print Shop was established on West Houston Avenue in October 1944. Owned and operated by John T. Adam, the Adam Print Shop has been instrumental in providing printing services to the residents of the area for over 60 years. Pictured is son John Adam Jr., who continued in the family business until 2009. (Courtesy Gary Steele.)

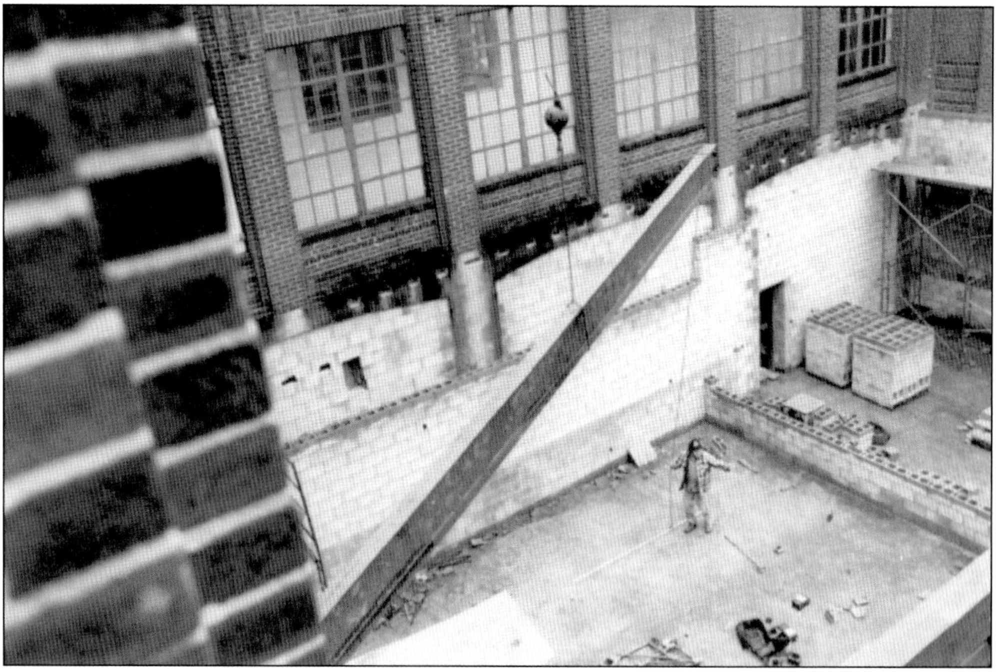

In 1955, the Montgomery-Clinton Joint School merged with the schools of Washington Township and formed an agreement to establish a combined educational district that included students living in Montgomery and the townships of Clinton and Washington. The one-room schools still operating in Washington Township were closed, and an addition was built at the Penn Street school to accommodate the additional students. In 1958, Brady Township merged to become part of the Montgomery Area School District. Within 10 years, the school's classrooms were filled to capacity, and in 1970, several temporary classrooms, pictured below, were purchased to alleviate the overcrowding. Shown above, permanent construction began by 1985. (Both courtesy Montgomery Area School District.)

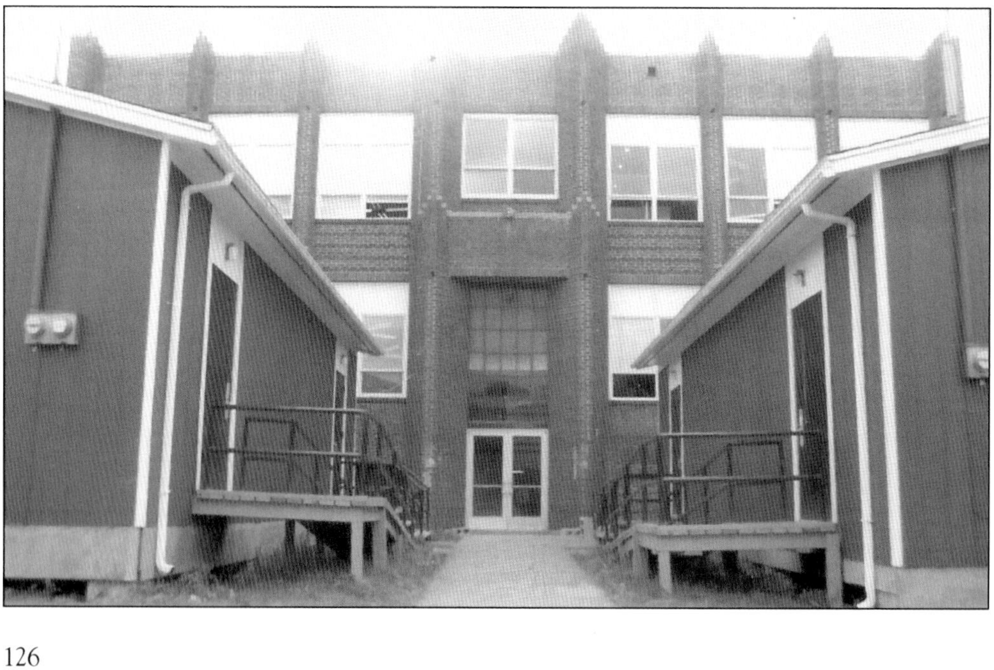

Renovations at the elementary and high school on Penn Street involved constructing an addition to the elementary building that included new classrooms and an all-purpose room, new spaces in the high school for band, art, and computer instruction, and updates in plumbing, electrical, and heating. A private home adjacent to the school was purchased and converted into a building for administrative offices. Energy-efficient windows were installed in all classrooms and a modern library was added to the front of the existing building. The project was completed in 1987. It has been about 25 years since the young graduate pictured below completed her education at Montgomery High School. Every June, alumni are invited back to Montgomery for the annual class reunions. Welcome home! (Both courtesy Montgomery Area School District.)

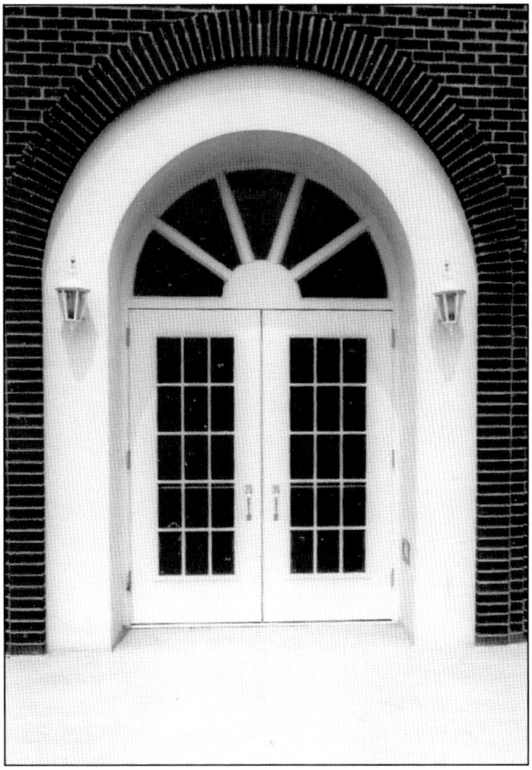

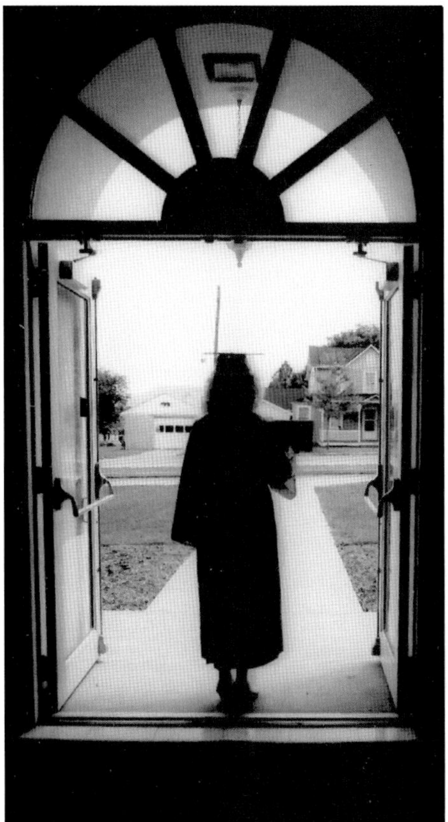